Ultramarathon Training

Wolfgang Olbrich

Ultramarathon Training

Meyer & Meyer Sport

Handbuch Ultralauf
Aachen: Meyer & Meyer 2011
Translated by: Heather Ross

British Library Cataloguing in Publication Data
A catalogue record for this book is available from the British Library

Ultramarathon Training
Maidenhead: Meyer & Meyer Sport (UK) Ltd., 2012
ISBN 978-1-84126-362-5

© 2012 by Meyer & Meyer Sport (UK) Ltd.
Auckland, Beirut, Budapest, Cairo, Cape Town, Dubai, Hägendorf, Indianapolis,
Maidenhead, Singapore, Sydney, Tehran, Wien
Member of the World
Sport Publishers' Association (WSPA)
www.w-s-p-a.org
Printed by: B.O.S.S Druck und Medien GmbH, Germany
ISBN 978-1-84126-362-5
E-Mail: info@m-m-sports.com
www.m-m-sports.com

© Thinkstock/iStockphoto/Fluid Illusion

CONTENTS

Acknowledgements 9
General Comments 10
Author 10
Introduction...11

1   What is an ultramarathon? 12

2   The History of the Ultramarathon...13
    2.1   Six-day Race...15
    2.2   24-hour Race...16
    2.3   100 km 21
    2.4   (Ultra) Trail Running...27
    2.5   Miscellaneous and Outlook 29

3   Associations 31
    3.1   North America 31
          3.1.1   American Ultrarunning Association (AUA) 31
          3.1.2   Association of Canadian Ultramarathoners (ACU)......32
    3.2   International 33
          3.2.1   International Association of Ultrarunners (IAU) 33

4   Ultramarathon stars (past and present)...34
    4.1   Ann Trason, USA 35
    4.2   Dean Karnazes, The North Face Team..................................36
    4.3   Ryoichi Sekiya, Japan...37
    4.4   Scott Jurek, USA 38
    4.5   Robert Wimmer, LAC Quelle Fürth......................................39
    4.6   Yiannis Kouros, Greece..40
    4.7   Rainer Koch, LG Würzburg 41
    4.8   Elizabeth "Lizzy" Hawker, The North Face Team 43

5	**Selected races**	**45**
	5.1 Comrades (56 miles) – South Africa	45
	5.2 Biel/Bienne 100 km - Switzerland	46
	5.3 Badwater Ultramarathon (135 miles) – USA	47
	5.4 Spartathlon (153 miles) – Greece	48
	5.5 Western States 100-Mile Endurance Run – USA	50
	5.6 West Highland Way Race (95 miles) – Scotland, UK	52
	5.7 Gutsmuths Rennsteiglauf – Germany	55
6	**Basic elements of training theory**	**56**
	6.1 What is training for?	56
	6.2 Running training sessions	57
	6.2.1 Long Recovery jogs	57
	6.2.2 Extensive endurance runs	58
	6.2.3 Intensive endurance runs	58
	6.2.4 Fartlek	59
	6.2.5 Interval training	59
	6.2.6 Hill running	60
	6.2.7 Pyramid running	60
	6.2.8 Crescendo runs	60
	6.3 Periodization (training cycles)	61
	6.4 Supercompensation / Training stimuli	62
	6.5 Training session structure	63
7	**Training management methods**	**64**
	7.1 Performance diagnostics and out of competition tests	64
	7.1.1 Lactic acid test / field test	65
	7.1.2 Spiro ergometric test	66
	7.1.3 Conconi test	66
	7.2 Heart rate monitor training	68
	7.2.1 Establishing training zones with performance diagnostics or measuring Heart rate variability (HRV)	68
	7.2.2 Establishing maximal heart rate (HRmax)	68
	7.3 Tempo-oriented training	69
8	**How does training change with the length of the race distance**	**70**
9	**Maintaining flexibility / stretching**	**72**
10	**Complementary training for muscles not used by running (strengthening / stability)**	**77**
	10.1 Strength circuit	85

11 Running drills for ultradistance runners **90**
   11.1 Drills 91

12 Ultramarathon nutrition (Dr. Olaf Hülsmann) **95**
   12.1 Basic nutrition 96
   12.2 Basic nutrition snacks 99
   12.3 Water balance 99
   12.4 Micronutrients 100
   12.5 Carbohydrate loading 102
   12.6 Race nutrition 103
   12.7 Recovery 105

13 Gastro-intestinal disorders during long endurance exercise
   (Dr. Stefan Hinze) **107**
   13.1 Introduction 107
   13.2 Epidemiology 108
   13.3 Heartburn (gastric reflux) 108
   13.4 Stomach function and emptying (gastric motility) 109
   13.5 Exercise-related diarrhea 109
   13.6 Gastro-intestinal bleeding 110
   13.7 Side stitch 111
   13.8 Intestinal blood disturbances (intestinal ischemia) 111
   13.9 Exercising with gastrointestinal disorders 112
   13.10 Summary and recommendations 113

14 Orthopedic strain in ultrarunners (Dr. Dietmar Göbel) **114**
   14.1 Shoulder injuries 115
   14.2 Lower back and hip injuries 116
   14.3 Knee injuries due to ligament overloading 117
      14.3.1 Knee injuries due to overloading 117
      14.3.2 Meniscus overloading and tears 118
      14.3.2 Arthritis 119
   14.4 Fatigue fractures 121
   14.5 Achilles tendon injuries 122
   14.6 Different types of shin splints (periostitis) 124
   14.7 Heel spur, dorsal 124
   14.8 Heel spur, plantar / plantar fasciitis ....
      / overloading of the foot muscles 125
   14.9 Final remarks 126

15 Mental aspects of ultradistance running **127**

16 Basic training **131**

17   Training plans for distances from 50 km to multi-day races....................**135**
   17.1   Miscellaneous...135
   17.2   Training Zones 136
   17.3   Prerequisites 137
   17.4   Your feedback please!...137
   17.5   Training plan for 50 km – entry level...137
   17.6   Training plan for 50 km in/under 5 hours (6:00 min/km) 142
   17.7   Training plan for 50 km in/under 4.3 hours (5:24 min/km) 146
   17.8   Training plan for 50 km in/under 4 hours (4:48 min/km) 151
   17.9   Training plan for 100 km in/under 11 h (6:36 min/km) 156
   17.10 Training plan for 100 km in/under10h (6:00 min/km) 161
   17.11 6 and 12-hour races 165
           17.11.1 Training plan for the 6-hour race 168
           17.11.2 Training plan 12 Hour Run 172
   17.12 Training for the 24-hour run and beyond....................................176
   17.13 Example training plan for a multi-day race 180

18   (Ultra) trail running **185**
   Training plan K 78 Swiss Alpine Marathon......................................188
   Training plan Western States 100 miles...193

19   Equipment **198**

20   Race anecdotes **206**
   20.1   Spartathlon 2009...206
   20.2   Ultra trail Mont Blanc 2004 213
   20.3   1st International Isarlauf 2004, from May 17th – 21th 2004.............217
   20.4   West Highland Way Race 2008 223
   20.5   60 km Monks' Trail (Monnikentocht, Netherlands)...........................
           on September 1st 2007 226
   20.6   Guesting at the Deutschlandlauf (Run Across Germany)..................228
   20.7   Hanau-Rodenbach 100 km, April 29th 2006 230
   20.8   Seven day race in Athens from March 24th to 31st 233

   Useful links **237**

   Bibliography/Sources..**237**

   Credits..**239**

ACKNOWLEDGEMENTS

Equal thanks to several people for helping me to write this book:

Firstly, of course, my equally running-mad partner, Dagmar Liszewitz, and my children Fabienne, Alina, Leon and Daniel, for giving me the time to concentrate on this book.

And special thanks go to those whose technical contributions have enhanced and completed this book. I deliberately chose specialists who are active ultrarunners themselves, and I was lucky enough to gain the services of Dr. Hinze, one of Germany's top ultrarunners (3rd ranked German over 100 km in 2009) and President of the German Ultramarathon Foundation.

Dr. Stefan Hinze, born 1963, is President of the German Ultramarathon Foundation, a medical specialist in internal medicine and gastroenterology, and principal consultant at the Medical Clinic V of the Westpfalz Klinikum GmbH. Dr. Hinze has been an active, elite level runner since 1990. In 2009, he was ranked third in the German 100 km ranking list and, in the same year, he finished in 10th place overall in the Spartathlon nonstop 152-mile race. His "weak point" is also his area of medical specialization, thus giving validity to his writings on the subject of "Disorders of the Gastrointestinal Tract in Endurance Running."

Holder of a PhD Natural Sciences, Olaf Hülsmann is a member of team of experts of the German Ultramarathon Foundation and German Athletics Association and visiting lecturer at the University of Munich on the subject of Sports Nutrition. While he was studying Nutritional Science and Sport, he participated in climbing and kayaking as well as the odd marathon, but he only took up ultrarunning, especially off-road, three years ago. Even before earning his degree in 2001, he was advising athletes. Since then he has dabbled in different sports such as marathon running, triathlon, weight training and ice hockey, and later also advanced training for coaches, physicians and pharmacists. After successfully finishing a 100-mile race in 2011, his next running goal is a 24-hour-race.

source
www.sportonline-foto.de

Dr. Dietmar Göbel, medical specialist in orthopedics and trauma surgery, was an elite youth gymnast and has been running regularly for over 7 years, averaging around 2,500 miles per year. He favors natural trail running and has a marathon best time of 2:55:52 and a 100 km best time of 8:40:28. In 2010 and 2011, he successfully completed the Spartathlon Athens to Sparta nonstop race over 153 miles. He has been a sports physician since 1993 and has also studied neural therapy, chirotherapy, acupuncture and physiotherapy (www.drgoebel-germany.de).

Dr. Dietmar Göbel

AUTHOR

Wolfgang Olbrich

Wolfgang Olbrich was born in 1968 and is himself a passionate ultra distance runner. As of December 2011, he has completed more than 75 ultra distance races since running the Biel 100 km in 2001, as well as successfully finishing more than 50 marathons. These races have ranged from 50 km races, various multi-day races, to the Spartathlon (153 miles with a maximal time limit of 36 hours).

The author is a German Athletics Federation licensed high-performance running coach and looks after diverse ultramarathon running groups ranging from beginners to junior international level. He plans and leads German Ultramarathon Foundation (DUV) Performance Development training camps, to which up to 30 elite ultramarathon specialists are invited. He is also responsible for all sports and high-performance-related issues concerning the German Ultramarathon Foundation Championships in a voluntary capacity. In 2011, he was twice appointed team manager of the German Ultramarathon team at World Championships (World Ultratrail Championships in Ireland and World 100 km Championships in the Netherlands). One of his protégés, Peter Seifert, set a new German record over 50 km in March 2011 (2h52:26) and also won the German Championships over the same distance.

Furthermore, the author is also team manager of the German Ultramarathon Foundation Running team and is responsible for all training issues and organizing the various ultrarunning events (including a five-day multi-stage race, 300 km and 6.500 HM+, a 48-hour track race and the 73-mile nonstop Kölnpfad trail race around the city of Cologne, Germany). He is also Sports and Race Team Manager of the Nordrhein Athletics

Association, Kreis Köln (LVN-Kreis Köln) and administrator of running groups and walking at the Nordrhein Athletics Association.

INTRODUCTION

This book is intended to smooth the way for interested long distance runners to ultra-marathon training. After the success of the first edition, published in Germany in April 2011, the third edition is already due for publication later this year, and I am proud and happy that the English version of this book is now available worldwide.

My intention is to provide information about the sport of ultramarathon running and make it accessible to all. This book has deliberately been written in colloquial language, avoiding the unnecessary use of technical terms and jargon. I hope that this book may inspire readers who have never run an ultramarathon to give one a try. Entry-level races of 50 km and 6 hours are perfectly suited for this, as they give an idea of the atmosphere of an ultramarathon, which is also very strongly influenced by the participating runners, who are quite different from the "typical" marathon runner and are often very friendly.

The book contains a number of training plans and tips for beginners to more ambitious runners. I have deliberately restricted the performance level and not included training advice for elite level runners, as in my opinion it is meaningless to give universal training advice at this level. Instead, a serious discussion between coach and athlete is essential to arrive at an effective training plan. Direct collaboration with an experienced coach is definitely recommended. Unfortunately, ultramarathon coaches are few and far between. You can find the contact details of qualified ultramarathon coaches on the websites of your country's ultramarathon or track and field athletics association. Neither will you find very detailed explanations about the training advice and training forms, as I have assumed that athletes who are interested in ultrarunning already have a few years' experience of running training and have some knowledge of basic training theory. However, some ideas and explanations were necessary for the sake of coherence.

I hope you enjoy the book!
Wolfgang Olbrich

1 WHAT IS AN ULTRAMARATHON?

There are many interpretations, but there is no fixed distance. The most commonly used definition is:

"An ultramarathon is any race that exceeds the length of a marathon (26.2 miles)"

This statement is not universally accepted though, as the marathon distance itself has only been officially ratified since 1921 by the IAAF at 42.195 km (26 miles 385 yards). Prior to this, differing distances were run, e.g., 40 km (24.85 miles) at the 1896 Olympic Games and 42.75 km (26.56 miles) at the 1920 Olympics.

It is often said that only races longer than 50 km can be considered true ultramarathons. Others say, for example, that a challenging mountain marathon, such as the Jungfrau or Zermatt Marathon, should also be classified as an ultramarathon due to its difficulty.

© imago Sportfotodienst

Others still say that only a race without rest breaks can be called an ultramarathon.

I personally judge my own races by the course length. So, if, for example, during a 6-hour race I cover more than the famous 26 miles 385 yards, I consider this to be an ultramarathon, irrespective of how many rest breaks I have had, as these breaks were in accordance with the race rules. It is like everything, there must be a constant value and the only constant and realistically measurable value is the course length.

I therefore agree with the above definition.

2   THE HISTORY OF THE ULTRAMARATHON

The history of ultramarathon running is not so easy to pin down either.

The first "Marathon" was run by Pheidippides in the year 490 BC, who, according to the writings of the historian Herodotus, had to run from Athens to Sparta in two days to seek help in the war against the Persians. Five hundred years later, Plutarch and Lucian of Samosata, with reference to this and to Heraclides Ponticus, formed the legend, according to which after the victory of the Athenians over the Persians on the Plain of Marathon, this same Pheidippides had run from there into the city, where he reportedly said: "We have won!" upon which he then collapsed to the ground and died.

So if we accept the description of Herodotus, the birth of the ultramarathon predates that of the marathon itself. In this case, if we accept the definition of the ultramarathon from the previous chapter, the definition of the marathon should be derived from that of the ultramarathon! But we don't want to be that petty.

So, legend has it that Pheidippides ran from Athens to Sparta in less than two days, then back to the Plain of Marathon and from there to announce the victory of the Athenians over the numerically much stronger Persians then again back to Athens. All things considered, we are therefore talking about a running performance of about 311 miles, assuming that the distance from Athens to Sparta is 153 miles and that from Marathon to Athens, 25 miles.

For more than 25 years (and officially since 1983), an ultramarathon race has been held on the route from Athens to Sparta, which follows the historic route pretty closely. The race is the Spartathlon, of which more details are given later in this book, in the chapter "Selected Races."

There are many reasons for running long distances. In the past, in hunter gatherer times, it was necessary for survival. Long distances had to be covered daily in the search for food or to escape from being eaten by animals.

In armies all over the world, it used to be common practice to use messengers or couriers, who had to run long distances in order to pass on important news or to ask other states for help.

At this point, I would like to try to give a little more historical background of the ultramarathon than can be found in such sources as Wikipedia.

Ultramarathon running can definitely be traced back to the historical military messengers. As well as the "errand" of Pheidippides, several similar messengers can be found in history, especially Greek history, of course, where we read about a certain Euchidas, who in the year 479 BC wanted to run from his home village to Delphi, covering a distance of about 113 miles in the process.

Philonides, a messenger of Alexander the Great, is said to have run from Sicyon to Elis in under a day in the year 325 BC.

Something resembling the first 24-hour races did not appear until the 16th or 17th centuries, although they were not in a competitive form as we know them today. Instead, they were exhibition runners, or professional runners, who wanted to use their running talents to gain fame and fortune. In June 1754, for example, John Cook from England was between £50 that he could run 100 miles in 24-hours. However, after 12 hours and 60 miles, he was forced to give up.

A real race between two people in the context of a 24-hour race took place in October 1806 in London, when Abraham Wood and Robert Barclay raced against each other. Wood had to run 20 miles more in order to win the race and a prize money of 600 guineas. During the event, Barclay had been supplied by another person with an opium-containing drink, after which he fell hopelessly behind. Wood went on to win and to complete a distance of about 154 miles in 24-hours.

Subsequently, more and more running events, or rather exhibition running events, were organized, all of which were money-making ventures and usually with only one participant. The term "gentlemen walkers and runners" was coined at the time to describe these athletes.

The first woman to feature in reports was Mary McMullen in July 1765, who is said to have run from Blencogo to Newcastle (about 72 miles) in a day.

2.1   SIX-DAY RACE

Following the era of the exhibition runner and pedestrianism, there was a renaissance of the 6-day race from September 4th – 9th 1980 in Woodside, CA. The winner, incidentally, was Don Choi, with a distance of 400 miles.

One month later, another 6-day race was held in Pennsauken, NJ, which featured the first-ever official performance by a female runner. Sabins Snow took second place overall with 345 miles, behind the above-mentioned Don Choi (397 miles).

In 1982, four 6-day races were held around the world, including two in Europe, in La Rochelle (France) and Nottingham (England). The best results were achieved in Nottingham, where Tom O'Reilly completed an outstanding 576.45 miles, in front of the second overall finisher and best woman, Margaret Goodwin, with an equally world class 514 miles.

In 1984, the Greek Yiannis Kouros was first to break the 1,000 km (621.37 miles) barrier in New York, with 1,023.54 km (636 miles). He is still holder of the world's best 6-day race performance with a distance of 1,038.83 km (645 miles) set in Colac, Australia on November 22, 2005.

The women's best 6-day race performance is 550 miles, set by New Zealander Sandra Barwick in Campbelltown, New Zealand in 1990.

In 2010, there were a total of eight 6-day races held worldwide, which were often combined with other races in order to finance the now very expensive chip measuring technology. As well as longer races in which 6-day races can be included (e.g., 10 days, 1000 km, 1,000 miles or even 3,100 miles), the shorter distances of 6, 12, 24, 48 and 72 hours are commonly included in the 6-day races. These performances are usually also recognized as split performances and included as such in the respective ranking lists of the IAU and the respective national ranking lists of the country/ies.

2.2   24-HOUR RACE

The first recorded performance over 24-hours was attributed to Edward Weston who covered 112 miles in a time of 23h 44 mins. Billy Howens covered more than 200 km in 24-hours between February 22, and 23, 1878 in London, England.

In 1958, Wally Hayward broke the 250 km barrier, achieving 256.4 km.

Since 1997, Yiannis Kouros of Greece has held the absolute world's best 24-hour performance with 189 miles, set on May 4 – 5, 1997 in Adelaide, Australia.

The absolute world's best women's 24-hour race performance is credited to Mami Kudo of Japan, who ran 158.09 miles December 12 – 13 in Taipei.

In 1979 Germany, Fritz Marquardt who in was the first individual runner to complete what was intended since 1970 to be a 24-hour team relay race. He went to the start saying that he was a "one-man relay."

From then on, individual runners were also allowed to enter relay races and in Germany also, a 24-hour race scene developed. In the neighboring Netherlands, a 24-hour race used to be held in Apeldoorn for individual runners from 1984 until 2007.

Development at the US Championships has been patchy and unfortunately the results list is not available for every single year (see Table 1). However, it is hoped that the development will be positive here. Since such famous trail runners as Jurek and Karnazes have made very successful attempts over this distance, it could definitely be of interest to other runners.

© Thinkstock/iStockphoto/Fluid Illusion

Table 1: Comparison of the development of participant numbers at German and American 24-hour race Championships.

Year	Participants GER	Men	Women	Participants USA	Men	Women
2011	137	104	33	93	67	26
2010	134	101	33	146	101	45
2009	115	91	24	107	83	24
2008	95	77	18	51	35	16
2007	119	90	29	83	59	24
2006	108	89	19	79	55	24
2005	114	95	19	78	59	19
2004	84	67	17	Missing		
2003	75	59	16	Missing		
2002	101	86	15	161	129	32
2001	64	49	15	148	119	29
2000	109	89	20	161	125	36
1999	74	59	15			
1998	71	57	14			
1997	67	62	5			
1996	72	61	11			
1995	58	48	10			
1994	56	46	10			
1993	59	48	11			
1992	53	43	10			
1991	60	59	11			
1990	53	45	8			
1989	57	50	7			

The US record over 24-hours is held by Scott Jurek with 165.7 miles, set in Brive (France) in 2010. The US women's record holder is Connie Garder, who ran 145.26 miles in Grapevine, Texas, in 2007.

On the international scene, 24-hour race championships have been held since 1992, under the aegis of the International Association of Ultrarunners (IAU). It had been staged until 2010 as the World and European Challenge, but since 2011 it is officially called a World Championship. This was officially ratified by the IAAF and the WMA, which can be seen as the official recognition of the distance.

Table 2: World Championships/World Challenge - events

Year	Event	Men	Women	Overall	Kilometer Men	Kilometer women
1990	Milton Keynes/Great Britain	41	12	53	267,543km	237,861km
2001	Verona/Italy	35	19	54	275,828km	235,029km
2003	Uden/The Netherlands	95	44	139	270,087km	237,052km
2004	Brno/Czech Republic	93	48	141	269,085km	237,154km
2005	Wörschach/Austria	119	57	176	268,065km	242,228km
2006	Taipei/Taiwan	75	33	108	272,936km	237,144km
2007	Drummondville/ Canada	90	53	143	263,562km	236,848km
2008	Seoul/South Korea	103	55	161	273,366km	239,685km
2009	Bergamo/Italy	119	62	181	257,046km	243,644km
2010	Brive/France	151	78	229	273,708km	239,797km

Table 3: World Champions

Year	Men's World Champions	Women's World Champions
1990	Donald Ritchie/GBR	Eleanor Adams-Robinson/ GBR
2001	Yiannis Kouros/GRE	Edith Berces/HUN
2003	Paul Beckers/BEL	Irina Reutovich/RUS
2004	Ryoichi Sekiya/JPN	Sumie Inagaki/JPN
2005	Anatoli Krugklikov/RUS	Lyudmila Kalinina/RUS
2006	Ryoichi Sekiya/JPN	Sumie Inagaki/JPN
2007	Ryoichi Sekiya/JPN	Lyudmila Kalinina/RUS
2008	Ryoichi Sekiya/JPN	Anne-Cecile Fontaine/FR
2009	Henrik Olsson/SWE	Anne-Cecile Fontaine/FR
2010	Inoue Shingo/JPN	Anne-Cecile Fontaine/FR

All statistics were obtained from the statistics database of the German Athletics Association at: *http://statistik.d-u-v.org/overview_champions.php*

© Thinkstock/iStockphoto/Fluid Illusion

Table 4: European Championships/European Challenge-Events

Year	Event	Men	Women	Overall	Kilometer Men	Kilometer Women
1992	Apeldoon/ Netherlands	46	11	57	250,698km	231,008km
1993	Basel/Switzerland	103	23	126	259,265km	243,657km
1994	Szeged/Hungary	46	14	60	261,122km	231,482km
1996	Coucon/France				259,922km	231,049km
1997	Basel/Switzerland	65	19	84	249,039km	236,284km
1998	Marquette/France	104	18	122	267,626km	226,457km
1999	Verona/Italy	34	9	43	262,324km	223,763km
2000	Uden/Netherlands	97	28	125	259,273km	225,418km
2001	Apeldoorn/Netherlands	113	23	136	260,559km	226,634km
2002	Gravigny/France	53	22	75	267,294km	232,284km
2003	Uden/Netherlands	83	35	118	270,087km	237,052km
2004	Brno/Czech Republic	80	40	120	259,064km	235,012km
2005	Wörschach/Austria	89	46	135	268,065km	242,228km
2006	Verona/Italy	22	11	33	254,774km	229,452km
2007	Madrid/Spain	39	14	53	257,358km	233,307km
2009	Bergamo/Italy	97	50	147	257,042km	243,644km
2010	Brive/France	125	58	183	263,841km	239,797km

Table 5: European Champions

Year	Men	Women
1992	Helmut Schiecke/GER	Sigrid Lomsky/GER
1993	Helmut Dreyer/GER	Sigrid Lomsky/GER
1994	Janos Bogar/HUN	Sigrid Lomsky/GER
1996	Ferenc Györi/HUN	Marie Bertrand/FR
1997	Vladimir Tivikov/RUS	Irina Reutovich/RUS
1998	Lucien Taelman/BEL	Marie Mayeras-Bertrand/FR
1999	Yiannis Kouros/GRE	Irina Reutovich/RUS
2000	Lubomir Hrmo/SVK	Irina Reutovich/RUS
2001	Paul Beckers/BEL	Irina Reutovich/RUS
2002	Jens Lukas/GER	Edith Berces/HUN
2003	Paul Beckers/BEL	Irina Reutovich/RUS
2004	Lubomir Hrmo/SVK	Galina Eremina/RUS
2005	Anatoli Kruglikov/RUS	Lyudmila Kalinina/RUS
2006	Vladimir Bychkov/RUS	Irina Koval/RUS
2007	Anatoli Kruglikov/RUS	Lyudmila Kalinina/RUS
2009	Olsson, Henrik/SWE	Anne-Cecile Fontaine/FR
2010	Ivan Cudin/ITA	Anne-Cecile Fontaine/FR

All statistics were obtained from the statistics database of the German Athletics Association at: *http://statistik.d-u-v.org/overview_champions.php.* The results list from the year 1996 is incomplete.

© Thinkstock/iStockphoto/Fluid Illusion

© Thinkstock/iStockphoto/Fluid Illusion

2.3 100 KM

The origins of ultrarunning in Europe can definitely be traced to the 100 km, and the Biel 100 km (Switzerland) in particular is the oldest 100 km race. It first took place on November 13, 1959. Although back in 1892 in Geneva (Switzerland), 173 participants started in a 100 km race, of whom 63 managed to finish within 24-hours), this was a one-off event.

The Biel 100 km race was initiated by officers in the Swiss army, led by Colonel Franz Reist, Urs Spörri and Hans Brönnimann. It involved running on a large circuit around the city of Biel. To start with, there was a time limit of 24-hours. Since then, the time limit has been reduced to 21 hours. As before, a military march over the same distance is incorporated into the race, in which soldiers have to march wearing their uniform and kit. Thirty-two runners took part in the inaugural race in 1959, of whom 22 reached the goal. In the heyday of the Biel 100 km, there were more than 3,000 participants. In recent years, apart from the 50th edition in 2008, where 2,348 runners participated, participation levels have tended to range between 1,000 and 1,300. This makes the event the most popular 100 km in Europe, and possibly even in the world. In the meantime, other ultrarunning events have sprung up that are more popular in terms of numbers (Comrades, Two Oceans Marathon or the Ultra Trail Tour Mont Blanc).

The first USA national championships were held in New York on February 27, 1993, with 35 athletes participating (25 men and 10 women). The 100 km road course was unremarkable both in terms of the number of runners and the level of performance.

In fact, not until the last US Championships were very good results of under 7 hours produced. This was brought home quite clearly to the US team at the World Championships in Winschoten, Netherlands, in 2011.

Table 1: Development in participant numbers at German and US Championships in 100 km road races

Year	Participants GER	Men	Women	Participants USA	Men	Women
2011	48	40	8	23	18	5
2010	N/A			22	12	10
2009	94	69	25	no NC		
2008	134	104	30	21	15	6
2007	107	86	21	30	19	11
2006	231	191	40	no NC		
2005	166	137	29	no NC		
2004	114	89	25	partial		
2003	80	63	17	no NC		
2002	102	79	23	no NC		
2001	97	64	33	33	25	8
2000	111	88	23	35	25	10
1999	157	128	29	no NC		
1998	99	79	20	partial		
1997	118	97	21	43	36	7
1996	196	161	35	no NC		
1995	100	85	15	no NC		
1994	171	139	32	no NC		
1993	151	127	24	80	67	13
1992	176	149	27			
1991	157	128	29			
1990	217	184	33			
1989	198	170	28			
1988	157	135	22			
1987	293	256	37			

Table 2: IAU World Championships since 1992 [1987]

Year	Event	Men	Women	Overall	Winning Time -M	Winning Time- W
1987	Torhout/Belgium	75	8	83	6:19:35h	8:01:31h
1988	Santander/Spain	156	15	171	06:34:41h	7:30:49h
1989	Paris/France				6:47:06h	8:07:41h
1990	Duluth/USA	98	27	125	6:34:02h	7:55:08h
1991	Firenze/Italy	1073	74	1147	6:35:39h	7:52:15h
1992	Palamos/Spain				6:23:35h	7:44:37h
1993	Torhout/Belgium	169	46	215	6:26:26h	7:27:19h
1994	Yubetsu/Japan				6:22:43h	7:34:58h
1995	Winschoten/Netherlands	171	51	222	6:18:09h	7:00:47h
1996	Moscow/Russia				6:32:41h	7:33:10h
1997	Winschoten/Netherlands	105	48	153	6:25:25h	7:30:37h
1998	Nakamura/Japan				6:30:06h	8:16:07h
1999	Chavagnes en Paillers/ France	95	47	142	6:24:05h	7:33:02h
2000	Winschoten/Netherlands	153	41	194	6:23:15h	7:25:21h
2001	Cléder/France	94	52	146	6:33:28h	7:31:12h
2002	Torhout/Belgium	138	40	178	6:34:23h	7:37:06h
2003	Taipei/Taiwan	102	47	149	7:04:57h	8:04:47h
2004	Winschoten/Netherlands	141	61	202	6:18:24h	7:10:32h
2005	Yubetsu/Japan	71	27	98	6:24:15h	7:53:41h
2006	Seoul/South Korea	69	47	116	6:38:27h	7:28:56h
2007	Winschoten/Netherlands	76	47	123	6:23:21h	7:00:27h
2008	Tuscany/Italy	103	56	159	6:37:41h	7:23:33h
2009	Torhout/Belgium	79	47	126	6:40:44h	7:37:24h
2010	Gibraltar/GBR	92	46	138	6:43:44h	7:29:05h
2011	Winschoten/Netherlands	96	50	146	6:27:32h	7:27:19h

Table 3: World Champions since 1987

Year	World Champion – Men	World Champion - Women
1987	Domingo Catalan Lera/ESP	Agnes Eberle/SWI
1988	Domingo Catalan Lera/ESP	Ann Trason/USA
1989	Bruno Scelsi/FR	Katharina Janicke/GER
1990	Roland Vuillemenot/FR	Eleanor Adams-Robinson/GBR
1991	Valmir Nunes/BRA	Eleanor Adams-Robinson/GBR
1992	Kontantin Santalov/RUS	Nursia Baghmanova/RUS
1993	Kontantin Santalov/RUS	Carolyn Hunter-Rowe/GBR
1994	Aleksey Volgin/RUS	Valentina Shatyaeva/RUS
1995	Valmir Nunes/BRA	Ann Trason/USA
1996	Kontantin Santalov/RUS	Valentina Shatyaeva/RUS
1997	Sergey Yanenko/UKR	Valentina Shatyaeva/RUS
1998	Grigory Murzin/RUS	Carolyn Hunter-Rowe/GBR
1999	Simon Pride/GBR	Anna Balosakova/SVK
2000	Pascal Fetizon/FR	Edith Berces/HUN
2001	Ayasufumi Mikami/JPN	Elvira Kolpakova/RUS
2002	Mario Fattore/ITA	Tatyana Zhirkova/RUS
2003	Mario Fattore/ITA	Monica Casiraghi/ITA
2004	Mario Ardemagni/ITA	Tatyana Zhirkova/RUS
2005	Grigory Murzin/RUS	Hiroko Syou/JPN
2006	Yannick Djouadi/FR	Elisabeth Hawker/GBR
2007	Shinichi Watanabe/JPN	Norimi Sakurai/JPN
2008	Giorgio Calcaterra/ITA	Tatyana Zhirkova/RUS
2009	Yasukazu Miyazato/JPN	Kami Semick/USA
2010	Shinji Nakadei/JPN	Ellie Greenwood/GBR
2011	Giorgio Calcaterra/ITA	Marina Bychkova/RUS

From years 1997 and 2004, only the overall lists for the open race and the European Championships are available. These figures are therefore incomplete or falsified (participant numbers). All data was obtained from the statistics database of the German Athletics Association at: *http://statistik.d-u-v.org/overview_champions.php.*

Table 4: European Championships / European Challenge Events

Year	Event	Men	Women	Total	Men's winning time	Women's winning time
1992	Winschoten/ Netherlands	89	12	101	6:16:41h	7:55:12h
1993	Winschoten/ Netherlands	92	22	114	6:25:52h	7:43:06h
1994	Winschoten/ Netherlands	107	30	137	6:33:43h	7:36:39h
1997	Florence/Italy	986	80	1066	6:47:35h	8:13:49h
1998	Torhout/Bel- gium	63	20	83	6:23:29h	7:45:43h
1999	Winschoten/ Netherlands	57	18	75	6:39:16h	7:33:39h
2000	Belves/France	47	16	63	6:33:36h	7:53:12h
2001	Winschoten/ Netherlands	67	20	87	6:45:43h	7:31:55h
2002	Winschoten/ Netherlands	74	26	100	6:34:16h	7:24:52h
2003	Chernogolovka/ Russia	59	26	85	6:29:41h	7:19:51h
2004	Florence/Italy	1050	125	1175	6:31:44h	8:03:03h
2005	Winschoten/ Netherlands	90	27	117	6:30:31h	7:53:25h
2006	Torhout/Bel- gium	103	25	128	6:23:44h	7:58:44h
2007	Winschoten/ Netherlands	53	30	83	6:30:22h	7:26:44h
2008	Tuscany/Italy	67	34	101	6:37:41h	7:23:33h
2009	Torhout/Bel- gium	60	33	93	6:41:50h	7:46:26h
2010	Gibraltar/GBR	69	33	102	6:47:40h	7:29:05h
2011	Winschoten/ Netherlands	73	33	106	6:27:32h	7:27:19h

Table 5: European Champions

Year	Winner – Men	Winner – Women
1992	Jean-Paul Praet/BEL	Hilary Walker/GBR
1993	Konstantin Santalov/RUS	Marta Vass/HUN
1994	Jaroslaw Janicki/POL	Valentina Lyachova/RUS
1997	Aleksey Kononov/RUS	Olga Lapina/RUS
1998	Grigory Murzin/RUS	Svetlana Savoskina/RUS
1999	Pascal Fetizon/FR	Elvira Kolpakova/RUS
2000	Farit Ganiev/RUS	Edith Berces/HUN
2001	Netreba Vladimir/RUS	Ricarda Botzon/GER
2002	Pascal Fetizon/FR	Elvira Kolpakova/RUS
2003	Grigory Murzin/RUS	Tatyana Zhorkova/RUS
2004	Mario Ardemagni/ITA	Monica Casiraghi/ITA
2005	Oleg Kharitonov/RUS	Monica Casiraghi/ITA
2006	Jose Maria Gonzales Munoz/ESP	Birgit Schönherr-Hölscher/GER
2007	Oleg Kharitonov/RUS	Laurence Fricotteaux-Klein/FR
2008	Giorgio Calcaterra/ITA	Tatyana Zhirkova/RUS
2009	Jonas Buud/SWE	Irina Vishnevskaya/RUS
2010	Jonas Buud/SWE	Ellie Greenwood/GBR
2011	Giorgio Calcaterra/ITA	Marina Bychkova/RUS

Table 6: Asian Championships

Year	Event	Men	Women	Overall	Men's Winning Time	Women's Winning Time
2010	Jeju/South Korea	10	9	19	7:23:20h	8:01:32h
2011	Jeju/South Korea	5	4	9	6:52:07h	8:28:10h

Table 7: Asian Champions

Year	Winner – Men	Winner - Women
2010	Dong-Mun Lee/KOR	Mai Fujisawa/JPN
2011	Hara Yoshikazu/JPN	Mai Fujisawa/JPN

All data was obtained from the statistics database of the German Athletics Association at: *http://statistik.d-u-v.org/overview_champions.php.*

2.4   (ULTRA)TRAIL RUNNING

Trail running is as old as running itself, as in the beginning, there were no roads to run on. As trail running involves running on natural footpaths, it has no special historical background. A chapter of this book is devoted to trail running, which includes training plans.

Trail running itself has boomed in recent years like no other ultramarathon event. Running off-road is a trend. For many trailrunners, the paths can never be difficult nor steep enough, and in terms of course length also, the sky's the limit.

The trail running countries par excellence are France, USA, Belgium and Great Britain. The sport has also undergone something of a boom in Germany in recent years, unfortunately at the expense of the 100 km distance.

Table 1: Development of participant numbers in the US Championships in trail running over 50 miles

Year	Participants	Men	Women
2011	35	30	5
2010	194	140	54
2009	166	129	37
2008	202	155	47
2007	144	108	36
2006	124	99	25
2005	115	84	31
2004	104	78	26
2003	132	107	25
2002	106	87	19
2001	128	99	29
2000	306	269	37
1999	no NC		
1998	83	58	25
1997	95	70	25

© Thinkstock/iStockphoto/Fluid Illusion

On an international level, the IAU has also recognized the trend, and 2007 saw the running of the inaugural World Championships, then still a World Challenge, which is now held biennially.

Table 2: Ultratrail World Championships

Year	Event	Men	Women	Overall	Course Length	Winning Time – Men	Winning Time – Women
2007	Huntsville/USA	128	44	172	50mi	6:07:45h	6:34:57h
2009	Sierre Chevalier/France	32	14	46	68km	6:38:18h	7:53:18h
2011	Connemara/Ireland	68	30	98	71,5km	6:39:07h	7:41:31h

Table 3: Ultratrail World Champions

Year	Champion – Men	Champion - Women
2007	Jaroslaw Janicki/POL	Norimi Sakurai/JPN
2009	Thomas Lorblanchet/FR	Mora Cecilia/ITA
2011	Erik Clavery/FR	Maud Gobert/FR

All data was obtained from the statistics database of the German Athletics Association at: *http://statistik.d-u-v.org/overview_champions.php.*

2.5   MISCELLANEOUS AND OUTLOOK

Trail running is currently very popular, and races attract thousands of participants. Also growing in popularity are the so-called time runs, which are growing both in terms of the number of races organized and the number of participants. The classic 100 km road races are now struggling, with participant numbers dwindling.

The table below clearly reflects the growth in popularity of ultrarunning worldwide. Since 2005, statistics are complete from almost all of Europe and also the USA in the statistics database of the German Athletics Association, and the trend is obvious. The growth in the number of participants is particularly striking in the case of trailrunning, as is the number of races organized. Unfortunately, this has been at the expense of the classic ultradistances 100 km road race and 24-hour race. It is up to the national governing bodies to address this decline.

Table 1: Development of ultrarunning in the USA (Source: German Athletics Association statistics database as of 02.10.2012)

Performances of Runners with US nationality

| Year | Men | | | Women | | | Totals M+W | | |
	Races	Runners	Races/ Runners	Races	Runners	Races/ Runners	Ratio M/W	Races	Runners
2012	1693	1586	1.07	608	571	1.06	74:26	2301	2157
2011	23713	14762	1.61	8967	5802	1.55	72:28	32680	20564
2010	19387	12256	1.58	7132	4560	1.56	73:27	26519	16816
2009	14547	9459	1.54	5269	3382	1.56	74:26	19816	12841
2008	10685	7044	1.52	3854	2531	1.52	74:26	14539	9575
2007	9341	6151	1.52	3320	2206	1.50	74:26	12661	8357
2006	7727	5233	1.48	2709	1903	1.42	73:27	10436	7136
2005	6194	4286	1.45	2031	1378	1.47	76:24	8225	5664
2004	5069	3526	1.44	1680	1164	1.44	75:25	6749	4690
2003	4993	3457	1.44	1573	1084	1.45	76:24	6566	4541
2002	4251	3040	1.40	1272	912	1.39	77:23	5523	3952
2001	3962	2854	1.39	1121	819	1.37	78:22	5083	3673
2000	3732	2660	140	935	660	1.42	80:20	4667	3320

There are therefore currently 14,762 active ultrarunners in the USA (2012), and here too a clear trend is visible. The figures in the German Athletics Association's database can also be seen as representative, as since 2009 (nearly) all ultra performances have been recorded. The figures should actually be considered to be on the high rather than the low side.

Table 2: Development of ultrarunning worldwide (Source: DUV statistics database as of 01.26.2012)

Year	Men			Women			Total M+W		
	Races	Run-ners	Races/ Run-ners	Races	Run-ners	Races/ Run-ners	Ratio M/W	Races	Run-ners
2012	1323	1298	1.02	415	410	1.01	76:24	1738	1708
2011	117349	76966	1.52	25379	16611	1.53	82:18	142728	93577
2010	95316	64290	1.48	20424	13518	1.51	83:17	115740	77808
2009	79828	54190	1.47	16157	10750	1.50	83:17	95985	64940
2008	59474	41645	1.43	11885	8058	1.47	84:16	71359	49703
2007	48745	33743	1.44	9980	6786	1.47	83:17	58725	40529
2006	36406	25975	1.40	7572	5314	1.42	83:17	43978	31289
2005	30040	21790	1.38	6075	4189	1.45	84:16	36115	25979
2004	22878	16373	1.40	4639	3157	1.47	84:16	27517	19530
2003	20290	15093	1.34	4010	2804	1.43	84:16:00	24300	17897
2002	17219	12817	1.34	3248	2338	1.39	85:15:00	20467	15155
2001	15914	11819	1.35	3009	2111	1.43	85:15:00	18923	13930
2000	13733	10232	1.34	2440	1710	1.43	86:14:00	16173	11942

According to the DUV database, as of Jan. 26, 2012, there had been a total of 833,866 races worldwide run by 256,635 people, of which 215,911 were men and 43,111 women, which corresponds to a ratio of about 83:17. According to this analysis, France is the world's top ultrarunning nation, followed by the USA and Germany.

However, the analysis is incomplete when it comes to Asian statistics. For Europe and North America, however, it is almost completely representative as all major races have been included. So at the present time, there are more than 76,966 ultrarunners throughout the world!

© Damiano Levati

3   ASSOCIATIONS

The sport of ultrarunning is a rather unusual one. Although it is certainly considered a track and field athletics discipline, in many countries, it is not integrated into the national track and field athletics associations. And if it is, usually only one, or at the most two, distances are ratified as race distances by the national association. These are usually the 100 km road race and the 24-hour race. Compared with the myriad Olympic sprints, middle and long distance events, this is definitely unfair.

3.1   NORTH AMERICA

3.1.1   AMERICAN ULTRARUNNING ASSOCIATION (AUA)

The AUA is a non-profit organization under US law. It is accepted as a member of the IAU (International Association of Ultrarunners) and is therefore a point of contact for the IAU for the nomination of national teams and authorized representative at the general assemblies of the IAU, held every 4 years.

On a national level, the AUA is a member of the national body USA Track and Field (USATF), which is responsible for all national running-related issues. The AUA has an official seat and voice there and is the only organization there that has responsibility for all ultramarathon issues, i.e., all distances longer than the famous 26.2 miles. It is also responsible for the national US team that contests the following disciplines:

- 24-hour race
- 50-mile ultratrail

- 100-km road race
- 100-mile road race

The executive leadership of the AUA consists of president, vice president and treasurer. The current president is Roy Pirrung from Kohler, Wisconsin, who can boast a best performance of more than 248 km over 24-hours (set in 1990) and who is still an active ultra distance runner.

All of the AUA's work is voluntary, and it sees its focus as being the promotion of ultra distance running. It is financially dependent upon sponsors and donations.

The AUA website, www.americanultra.org, contains a great variety of information about the US ultrarunning scene. Unfortunately, it is not regularly updated and links on the website are not always valid.

3.1.2   ASSOCIATION OF CANADIAN ULTRAMARATHONERS / ASSOCIATION CANADIENNE DES ULTRAMARATHONIENS (ACU)

The ACU was founded on March 14, 1992, in Burlington, Ontario. The founding members were Jo Wells, Michael Careau, Laurie Dexter, Ed Alexander, Cor Potma and David Blaikie from Maotick, Ontario, who was also the first ACU President.

Two years later, the ACU started its work as a structured organization with a plenary meeting, selected representatives of the individual provinces and territories, and a constitution determined according to democratic principles.

The ACU holds national championships in these events:

- 50 km ultratrail
- 50-mile ultratrail
- 100-mile ultratrail
- 24-hour race and
- 100 km road race

Occasionally, championships are also held for the 48-hour race, 6-hour trail runs and 12-hour trail runs.

The current president is Armand Leblanc, from Angus, Ontario. In his day job, after 24 years as a member of the Canadian Air Force, he is now regional coordinator for youth recruitment for the Canadian Army, and he is also an entrepreneur in the furniture industry.

As an ultrarunner, he can still be found racing all recognized distances on or off-road. The vice president is radiologist Nadeem Khan, who is also Director of Communications for the IAU.

The IAU website, www.acu100k.com, contains a great deal of information about the ACU and its goals.

3.2.1 INTERNATIONAL ASSOCIATION OF ULTRARUNNERS (IAU)

The IAU oversees the interests of ultrarunners throughout the world. It also holds international championships, including World and European Championships over 100 km and 24-hour races, as well as World Trailrunning Championships (ultradistance).

The IAU was founded in 1984. Since 1988, the IAU has had quasi-legal status since being ratified by and becoming a member of the IAAF, and since then has been the contact for the national track and field athletics association and the national ultramarathon associations, if the national body has no ultramarathon provision. The IAU is responsible for maintaining international ranking lists and the ratification of best performances and records in all ultramarathon events. The executive council of the IAU is composed of 11 members from nine different countries, chaired by Belgian Dirk Strumane.

In order to deal with the tasks of an international association, the IAU has formed three committees, membership of which is constitutionally limited to 12 members.

The IAU Technical Committee mainly deals with the interpretation of the rules and the quality of equipment used in races. It is currently composed of three people and is chaired by Lisbeth Jansen of the Netherlands.

The IAU Records Committee deals with the ratification of international records and best performances, as well as the definition of the corresponding rules. It currently consists of nine people and is chaired by Norman Wilson of Great Britain.

Last but not least is the IAU Medical Committee, which deals with all medical issues, particularly concerning sports medicine and doping. This committee is currently composed of five members and is chaired by Canadian Nadeem Khan.

The term of office of the governing body is four years, and elections are held in an assembly of the members. The last elections were held in Soregno, Italy, in April 2012.

4   ULTRAMARATHON STARS (PAST AND PRESENT)

In this chapter, I'd like to introduce you to some of the best-known and most successful ultramarathon runners, based on their responses to a questionnaire I sent them.

I have reproduced the answers of those athletes who responded "un cut," and would like to thank these athletes again for their kind collaboration, as this kind of personal note is much more meaningful than a third person's interpretation.

Please note that the space available in this book is limited and the nature of my selection is inevitably subjective. I do not claim to have compiled an exhaustive nor objective list.

Ann Trason lives in Kensington, California, and can definitely be considered an American ultrarunning legend.

When in college, she was already a very talented runner but was unfortunately unable to fulfil her potential due to knee injuries.

Although her achievements include being two-time World Champion over 100 km (1988 and 1995) with 7:00:47 (1995 in Winschoten/Netherlands), the second-best time ever run by a woman over this distance, her first love is long distance trail running. She has won the Western States 100 miles 14 times and holds the course record at 17:37:51. She is also a two-time winner of the biggest ultramarathon in the world in terms of number of participants, the Comrades Marathon in Cape Town, South Africa, in 1996 and 1997, after winning the Western States 12 days previously.

Below is a brief list of her still valid US records (as of 02.07.2012)

Event	Time/performance	Place/Year
100km road	7:00:48 h	Winschoten/NETH 1995
50 Miles road	5:40:18 h	Houston/TX 1991
100 Miles road	13:47:42 h	Queens/NY 1994
12 Hours road	144,840 km	Queens/NY 1991
50km track	3:20:23 h	Santa Rosa/CA 1995
50 Miles road	6:09:27 h	Nantes/FRA
100 km track	7:50:08 h	Hayward/CA
100 Miles track	14:29:44 h	Santa Rosa/CA 1989
12 hours track	147,600 km	Hayward/CA

After a serious injury to and operation on a leg, Ann never returned to competitive running.

I first met Dean Karnazes briefly at the Ultratrail Mont Blanc (UTMB) when I catered for him as a substitute in La Fouly. It was at about km 100 of the race and things were not going quite as Dean would have liked. Unfortunately, he had to drop out completely at Champex Lac (km 117).

Dean was a latecomer to running. A former marketing director, he at some point turned his passion for ultrarunning into his profession and marketed himself brilliantly via books and lectures. On his website, www.ultramarathonman.com, you can find out everything you need to know about Dean.

1. **How do you practice?**
   125km to 300+km/week base running, mountain-biking, surfing, climbing, windsurfing, gym cross-training 4-5 days/week.

2. **How did you get into ultramarathon?**
   Ran 50km on 30th birthday without training. Started training and racing afterward.

3. **What is your greatest sporting success?**
   Winning the 4 Deserts Championship. Why? Running multiday endurance events in such extreme conditions (Atacama desert in South America, Gobi desert in Central Asia, Sahara desert in Africa and Antarctica) was incredibly challenging, and I had to prepare and condition for each unique event differently. Not only was I able to win the overall championship, I was the first person ever to run all four of the competitions in a single calendar year.

4. **What are your next running goals?**
   My dream is to run a marathon in every country of the world (all 204) in a single year. This will happen next year.

5. **What do you do in your spare time?**
   I enjoy writing and have written several books, two of which have become *NY Times* bestsellers.

Name: .... Dean	
Surname: ....Karnazes	
Year of birth: 1969	
Nationality:.. US	
Discipline (Ultramarathon route):.......................	
.... Ultramarathon & Extreme Endurance	

Best times:...
162 km mountain trail run:................. 16:21:35h
Other noteable achievements:...........................
...................Badwater Ultramarathon Champion
.......50 Marathons, 50 States, 50 Days 5.600km
....Run Across America
Training sessions/week: .... 4-5 Cross-training
.... sessions per week

Ryoichi Sekiya is the Japanese 24-hour record holder and four-time 24-hour race World Champion! Here in Europe we know him very well as he is a frequent competitor over 24-hours and 48 hours. In an invitation race over 48 hours in Surgères, France, he won in a personal record time and also in 2009, Ryoichi was first to reach the statue of King Leonidas in the Spartathlon.

1. **How do you train? (Emphasis and weekly mileage in basic and competition-specific training)**
   I usually run about 100 km per week. About 2 months before a race, I increase the weekly mileage to about 200-250 km per week, with a tempo of between 5-6 min/km.

2. **How did you get into ultramarathon running? (previous sporting background)**
   At some point, I found I was just more interested in running long distances than working on my speed.

3. **What is your greatest sporting success and why?**
   Being four-time World 24-hour Champion. I was especially proud of this because it also made me world number 1.

4. **What are you doing now?**
   Right now I am training for the 24-hour race in Soochow (Taiwan) in December 2010.

5. **What are your next running goals?**
   I would really like to improve my 24-hour and 48-hour best times.

6. **What do you do in your "free time"? (hobbies outside of running)**
   I like reading, listening to music and going shopping with my family.

7. **Can you tell us something about the ultramarathon scene in Japan?**
   Japan is currently undergoing an ultramarathon boom and many people are interested in running long distances, such as ultramarathons. That's why I'm sure that the Japanese National Ultramarathon Team will be able to maintain its current high level in the future.

Name:...................................... Ryoichi	Six Hours:... 75.4 km
Surname:................................... Sekiya	12 Hours:.. 146.29 km
Birth year/Age:...................................... 1967/43	24 Hours:.. 274.884 km
Nationality:............................... Japanese	...any other distances:..... 48 hours: 407.966 km
Event (Ultramarathon): .... 24-Hour race	National Records: .... Japanese Record,
	.... 24-Hour race
Best times:..	International Records: .... N/A
10 km:.................................... 36:05 min	Club: .... 24-Hour Team Japan
HM:.. 1:18:02 h	Residence:.. Japan
Marathon: .... 2:35:16 h	Height: .... 183 cm
50 km:.. 3:40:00 h	Race weight:... 67 kg
100 km:.. 7:25:07 h	Training sessions/Week:............About 15 hours

I first met Scott Jurek at the 2006 Spartathlon in Greece. The first thing that struck me about him was his eating habits. He sat in the breakfast room of the hotel surrounded by packets of various powders, cereals and fruit. At the time, I thought, what on earth is he eating, you can't run 153 miles from Athens to Sparta on that.

How wrong I was: the vegetarian Scott won the race, and I had to drop out after 40 miles!

What I absolutely didn't know at that point was that Scott was already an ultrarunning legend in the USA. Between 1999 and 2005, he won the Western States 100-mile Endurance Run 7 times in a row. In 2005 and 2006, he also won the Badwater Ultramarathon. He also won the Spartathlon three times in succession and has the second fastest course time after Yiannis Kouros (Kouros has set the four fastest times ever run there).

Since then, Scott has also been an outstandingly successful member of the US team. He was able to set a new US record in the 2010 24-hours World Championships in Brive, France, of 266.677 km, while winning a silver medal in the process.

His best times[1] make impressive reading:

Name: .... Scott	50m: 5:50h
Surname: .... Jurek	100km: 7:28h
Year of birth: 1973	50-miles Trail: 6:21h
Nationality: .... US	100-miles Trail 15:36h
Discipline (Ultramarathon route):	24-Hour race: .... 266,677km (US-record)
.... 24-Hour race, Trail	...any other distances: ....
	.... three time winner Spartathlon
Best times:	..... seven time winner Western States 100-miles
Marathon: 2:38h	.... two time winner Badwater Ultramarathon

At the age of 39 (as of February 2012), Scott is one of the younger ultrarunners, so we are bound to be hearing and seeing more of him.

[1] source: www.scottjurek.com

Robert Wimmer is something of an all-rounder among the top athletes in Germany. His sporting highlight was surely winning the TransEurope Footrace from Lisbon, Portugal across Europe to Moscow, Russia, when he also made ultrarunning history. His performance despite very tough conditions in the Eastern part of the race from Poland onward was exceptional. But Robert is also at home over the standard ultradistances, such as 50 km, 6 hours or 100 km, and can expect top performances, as demonstrated by his list of best times.

Name:	Robert
Surname:	Wimmer
Year of birth/Age:	1965/45
Nationality:	German
Event (ultramarathon distance):	
	50 KM to continental races
10 km:	39:50 min
HM:	1:15:50 h
Marathon:	2:39:56 h
50 km:	3:20:20 h
100 km:	7:22:56 h
6 hours:	85.260 km
12 hours:	145.2 km
...any other distances:	Spreelauf 2002;
	Isarlauf 2004;
	Deutschlandlauf 2008;
	2 x Transeuropalauf
National records:	Six hours team 241 km
	(F. Raumer, R. Wimmer, A. Heukemes)
International records:	treadmill 100 km
	with 7:28 h;
	treadmill 12 h with 145,2 km
Club:	LAC Quelle Fürth
Residence:	Nürnberg
Height:	180 cm
Race weight:	76 kg
Training sessions / Week:	
	12, with 150-300 km

He also finds time for many other activities, such as his tireless work as a fundraiser for children with Down Syndrome. I can give a snapshot of his personal side from when I was at the stopover of Vettweiss, Germany, during the 2003 TransEurope Footrace:

Robert was the first to arrive there and, after running across Portugal, Spain and France, his legs were feeling the pain. However, his family was there too, and his little boy ran up to him with a soccer ball and wanted to play. This was not a problem for Robert, and he immediately took his son out onto the fields and played soccer with him for almost an hour, although you could see from his face that his legs were suffering. So this was Robert Wimmer the family man, and since that day, I have had great respect for him. So now back to his running abilities, which is the reason for this article:

1. **How do you train? (Emphasis and weekly mileage in basic and competition training periods)**
   150 km / week in basic training period 1, and 30 km/ week in basic training period 2, with intervals and hill training and tempo endurance runs = 2 – 3 tempo sessions per week.

2. **How did you get into ultramarathon running? (previous sporting background)**
   I started running to get rid of my pot belly, then ran a marathon in Berlin, followed by a 100 km in Rodenbach, Germany.

3. **What is your greatest sporting achievement and why?**
   TransEurope Footrace in 2003 – unique event – to MOSCOW!!!

5. **What are your next running goals?**
   24-hour treadmill world record, podium finish over 24-hours and at the Spartathlon.

6. **What do you do in your free time? (hobbies outside of running)**
   Spend time with my family (two kids). Otherwise nothing.

Yiannis Kouros is definitely the superstar of the world ultramarathon scene! He was born in Greece in 1956 and since emigrating to Australia in 1990, he has set more than 100 world records over all ultramarathon distances, many of them breaking the previous record by a considerable margin.

Alongside his passion for ultramarathon running, he also finds time to be an author, composer, singer and lyricist. He also has a BA in Greek History[2].

Kouros won each of his four attempts at the Spartathlon, and he holds four of the race's best performances. The interesting thing about Kouros' sporting background is that he is also good at the shorter distances, such as the marathon and 100 km, but his performances are not outstanding. Although he was a proficient marathoner, his PR is "only" 2:25 over the classic distance. Over 100 km, however, Kouros's PR of 6:25hr, set in Torhout, Belgium, in 1995, is a great time, but one that many runners are capable of. However, from 24-hours and beyond, Kouros' special qualities start to show. The longer the distance, the greater his dominance, as the impressive figures below testify.

Despite his stellar performance record, Kouros is also a somewhat controversial figure on the ultramarathon scene.

Here are the hard figures:

Event	Time/Performance	When and Where
100 km	6:25:00 h	Torhout/Belgium 1995
100 Miles	11:46:37 h	NY/USA 1985 (Split)
1000 km	5 days, 02:27:00 h	Sydney-Melbourne 1985
1000 Miles	10 days, 10:30:35 h	NY/USA 1988
24-hours	303,506 km	Adelaide/AUS 1997
48 hours	473,979 km	Sugères/France 1996
6 days (144 days)	1038,850 km	Colac/AUS 2005

2 http://www.yianniskouros.com/biography.html

The Badwater Ultramarathon is a 135-mile ultradistance race. In 1977, the American Al Arnold first attempted to run from Badwater to Mount Whitney and reached the finish (the summit) after 84 hours. The first official Badwater Ultramarathon did not take place until 10 years later, with 5 participants who all reached the finish. In those days, the course was 146 miles long.

The course length was changed to its current distance in 1989, and the finish was changed to Mount Whitney Portal.

What is special about this race? First, the starting point. Badwater, in Death Valley, is the lowest point in the United States at -282 feet below sea level. The finish is situated at a height of 14,505 ft above sea level.

But it is not just these facts alone that make the event special. The great challenge of this event is mastering the extreme heat at the time of year the event is held. It takes place in July, i.e., the middle of summer and the course goes through Death Valley, where the average daytime temperature is 120°F!

Every runner must be looked after by a support crew consisting of at least two people and a vehicle. There are no aid stations, etc., on the course like there are at other events such as the Spartathlon. The entry fee, currently $995, only ensures participation. The runner must bear all other costs (accommodation, crew, flights, etc.). The total cost of participation in the Badwater Ultramarathon can therefore quickly exceed $10,000.

Anyone who reaches the finish at Mount Whitney Portal within 48 hours also receives a belt buckle to show their official Badwater finisher status. Those runners who finish in between 48 and 60 hours are also designated official finishers but they do not receive the belt buckle.

Runners who need an infusion due to dehydration are disqualified.

Much more information about the race can be found at www.badwater.com

5.4   SPARTATHLON (153 MILES) – GREECE

The Spartathlon is a 153-mile non-stop race from Athens to Sparta, in Greece.

The race is based on a traditional legend from the year 490 BC. Prior to the battle on the Plain of Marathon, Miltiades, the King of Athens, sent his military courier Pheidippides to Leonidas, the King of Sparta, to ask for his support in the fight against the Persian invaders.

According to the legend, Pheidippides reached Sparta at the end of the next day. The events are said to have taken place in the last weekend of September, hence the timing of the modern-day race.

In 1982, Major John Foden of the Royal Air Force (RAF) had the idea of testing himself over this legendary course. Historians had doubted that it was possible to run the course in this time.

Together with two other members of the RAF, John Scholtens and John McCarthy, he set off on October 8, 1982, supported by friends in the British Army who provided

Starting point in front of the Roman theatre of the Acropolis. From this point, there are 246 km to go.

refreshments for the runners, and they all reached Sparta the following day. John Foden took 37 hours and 37 minutes, his colleague John Scholtens only took 34:30 hrs to reach the statue of Leonidas in Sparta. John McCarthy arrived in Sparta after 39 hours. These runners were unable to benefit from the excellent refreshment provision at 75 aid stations, and at times went for hours without a drink, until their support crew could get supplies to them.

An idea was born and already the following year, an organized race was held from Athens to Sparta, contested by 45 ultrarunners from 11 different countries. A club was formed: the International Spartathlon Association (ISA), which runs the event to this day. The president of this club is former bank manager Panagiotis Tsiakiris.

The time limit for completion of the Spartathlon is 36 hours. The course itself follows the legendary route, leading from the Acropolis in Athens, via the Corinthian Strait, Nemea, Lyrkia, through the 3,937 foot high Sangas Pass, which must be crossed in the middle of the night, then on to Nestani and Tegea and finally to Sparta. During the day, the athletes have to deal with extreme heat and during the night in the mountainous regions, temperatures can drop below freezing. The strict cut-off times are particularly feared, and they are imposed even at the start of the race. Anyone who cannot keep up with the pace is disqualified.

The finish is reached when runners touch the left foot of the statue of King Leonidas in the center of Sparta.

Just to have your race entry accepted, you must meet stringent qualification standards (as of 2011: have run 100 km in less than 10:30hr, or have competed in a 200 km / 120 -mile race and finished the event, irrespective of the time). Even so, only 35-50% of starters actually reach the statue of Leonidas in Sparta.

The standout Greek ultramarathon runner and living ultrarunning legend Yiannis Kouros holds the course record with an unbelievable 20:25hr. He has run the race 4 times and won all 4 races. He also currently holds all 4 best times for the race.

As for the women, Sumie Inagaki of Japan set a new course record of 27:39:49 in 2009.

Every year, the world's best 24-hour racers meet there, and victory is as hotly contested as at the World 24-hour Championships. There are no prizes; the only reward at the end of the 153 mile course from Athens to Sparta is a laurel wreath and a souvenir gift.

A lot of information on the race itself can be found at *www.spartathlon.gr*.

5.5   WESTERN STATES 100-MILE ENDURANCE RUN – USA

The Western States is definitely one of the most famous 100 mile trail runs in the USA.

The run starts in Squaw Valley at a height of about 6,200 feet above sea level and climbs steeply up to the Emigrant Pass at 8,750 feet above sea level, which represents a climb of 2,550 feet in the first 4.5 miles. The course then follows the original train that the gold and silver miners took in 1850 during the Gold Rush and ends after a climb of another 15,540 feet and descending 22,970 feet before reaching Auburn, California.

The run takes place on the last full weekend in June and starts on the Saturday morning at 5am. Runners must reach the finish line no later than 11 am the following day in order to be eligible for an award. Those who complete the demanding trail in less than 24-hours receive the famous handmade belt buckle made of solid silver. Those who finish in a time between 24 and 30 hours receive one made of bronze. Anyone who does not finish within 30 hours does not appear on the results list.

There are 25 checkpoints to run past on the way to Auburn, each of which has an absolute cut-off time that must be adhered to. Anyone arriving too late will be pulled from the run.

© Thinkstock/iStockphoto/Fluid Illusion

If you want to enter the Western States, you should apply well in advance as for a long time now it has booked up very quickly. Qualification standards for participation are:

- 50 miles in less than 11 hours or
- 100 km in less than 14 hours or
- Completing a 100-mile run.

Runners must be able to prove that they have achieved the above in the 12 months prior to the race, which takes place on the first Saturday in December.

The first to run the Western States course was Grody Ainsleigh, in 1974, in a time of 23 hours and 42 minutes, thus proving that it was possible to complete the horse trail in less than 24-hours, even without a horse.

The first official race was held in 1977, with 14 runners, of whom only 3 reached the finish. The then 22-year-old Andy Gonzales entered history as the first winner in just 22 hours and 57 minutes.

The record winner of the Western States is Scott Jurek, who was first to cross the finish line seven times in a row, while Ann Trason has won the ladies' race 14 times.

The course record is held by Geoff Roes, who finished in 15 hours, 7 minutes and 4 seconds in 2010. The ladies course record was set by Ann Trason in 1994 when she covered the course in 17 hours, 37 minutes and 51 seconds.

Further information on the event can be found at *http://ws100.com/*.

5.6　WEST HIGHLAND WAY RACE (95 MILES) – SCOTLAND, UK

The West Highland Way (WHW) is Scotland's best known long distance footpath and officially opened on October 6, 1980.

On June 22, 1985, the WHW was first run in one go by two ultrarunners Duncan Watson and Bobby Shields. At that time, the course was slightly different than it is now, because it included some long road sections that are no longer part of the race. They ran the whole course together and finished after 17 hours and 48 minutes.

The race was born! In 1986, race director Duncan Watson opened it up for a few running friends. In that year, it was run from North to South and in the following year, in the opposite direction. In 1987, 7 out of 11 starters reached the finish.

In 1989, David Wallace ran the whole course in a time of 15 hours and 26 minutes that is still the course record today. Only 6 minutes later, Mike Hartley crossed the finish line. The official course record for the current course is held by Jezz Bragg, who ran the new course in 15:44:50 hrs in 2006. Holder of the women's course record is Luc Colquhoun, who ran a time of 17:16:20 in 2007.

In the '90s, the race became an annual event, firstly under the leadership of Peter While and of Jim Stewart from 1991. The race was only advertized by word of mouth.

From 2000, the popularity of the race grew significantly thanks to promotional work by Dario Melaragni and Stan Mile. Dario went on to organize the race for 9 more years until 2009. Today, the race director is Ian Beattie. In 2011, there were 150 entries of whom 123 actually started the race and 113 managed to finish within the time limit of 35 hours (93 men and 20 women).

The starting point is the railway station at Milngavie (7 miles north of Glasgow) and the finish is 95 miles away in Fort William's leisure centre. There are 6 checkpoints along the course that must be reached within a set cut-off time. Participation is conditional on having a motorized support crew of at least 2 people, of whom one must be able to run alongside the competitor on the last sections of the race or to find him if he needs help (on foot). There are also certain items of equipment that must be brought along. There is an entry limit of 200 people.

Please see the race website, *www.westhighlandwayrace.org,* for further information about the event.

5.7 GUTSMUTHS RENNSTEIGLAUF, GERMANY

The Rennsteig Footrace is the most popular ultrarunning event in Germany. The official first running of the race was in 1975, and already had 903 entries. Originally it was a mixed running and walking race in which it was possible to race over shorter distances. In 1976, the number of entries had already reached 1,350.

Since 2003, the length of the ultra course has been fixed at 72.7 km (45.17 miles); prior to this the length had varied each year.

The number of entries on the ultra course alone is always well over 1,000. The course runs from Eisenach to Schmiedefeld, still along the Rennsteig footpath that traverses the Thüringer Wald in Germany.

Please see www.rennsteiglauf.

6   BASIC ELEMENTS OF
      TRAINING THEORY

6.1   WHAT IS TRAINING FOR?

The purpose of training is to improve performance, i.e., to enable you to run faster, farther or for longer. If at any point an improvement in performance is no longer possible (e.g., you are getting older or have just exhausted your potential) then the primary training goal should be to maintain your current performance level as long as possible or to minimize any drop in performance as much as possible.

Runners who move up to ultramarathon distances often do so because no matter how hard or well they train for the shorter distances, they have been unable to improve their performance or have been unable to place better in races despite training very hard. Let us consider the example of an athlete with a marathon performance potential of about 2hr 30mins.

He couldn't make the German national team with this time, but with very good basic speed he could, at least in theory, be capable of running 100km in under 7 hours, which would put him in contention for a German Championships title and a place on the national team. This is purely theoretical; a lot of work is needed to get to this stage.

Running training should be appropriate and performance-related in order to attain maximal performance increase, and this can be achieved by analyzing previous training and competition performances.

It is a good idea to get the advice of an objective/neutral individual who has experience with planning endurance running training (e.g., a qualified coach or sports scientist). If you have been working for some time with a coach and your performance has not improved or even plateaued, this may indicate that your analysis should be carried out by someone who has not previously been involved in your training, and ideally a coach who has experience of coaching ultramarathon runners.

It only makes sense to draw up a training plan once you have established your current state of fitness.

6.2   RUNNING TRAINING SESSIONS

6.2.1   LONG RECOVERY RUNS

Long recovery runs are performed within a range of effort of 65-70% HRmax, and target those muscles solicited in shorter runs. Long endurance runs performed at this tempo are also known as long jogs.

This type of endurance running specifically trains the fat metabolism, and is usually the race pace for 24-hour and multi-day races.

Example: 3 miles at 70% heart rate max

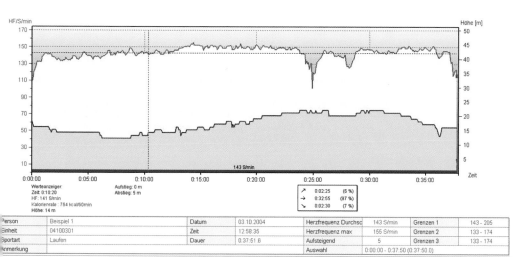

6.2.2 EXTENSIVE ENDURANCE RUNS

Extensive endurance runs are performed at 75-80% of maximal effort and are usually used for medium to long endurance workouts. In a workout for the 100 km distance, this training zone is used for long endurance runs and is also the race pace for the 100 km.

Example: 15km extensive endurance run slightly undulating terrain

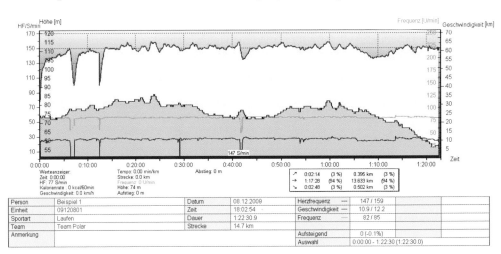

6.2.3 INTENSIVE ENDURANCE RUNS

Intensive endurance runs are performed at 80-85% of maximal effort and are used to increase basic speed. In ultra distance training, they are usually performed just once a week.

Example: 10km intensive endurance run (tempo run)

6.2.4 FARTLEK

Fartlek means "speed play" in Swedish, and it involves varying the running tempo. It is a good idea is to perform it on hilly terrain, in which case the pace remains as even as possible, so that running uphill means increased effort and running downhill is a recovery phase. The combination of the flat and hilly parts of the course means that the training load is constantly changing. This type of tempo training is particularly enjoyed by trail runners and those who do not enjoy what they consider to be boring track running. The range of effort in Fartlek training is 65-90% HRmax.

Example: Fartlek on hilly terrain

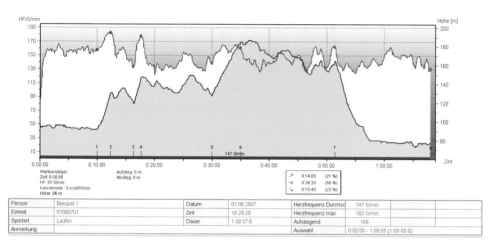

Person	Beispiel 1		Datum	07.08.2007	Herzfrequenz Durchsc	147 S/min	
Einheit	07080701		Zeit	18:29:29	Herzfrequenz max	183 S/min	
Sportart	Laufen		Dauer	1:08:07.6	Aufsteigend	189	
Anmerkung					Auswahl	0:00:00 - 1:08:05 (1:08:05.0)	

6.2.5 INTERVAL TRAINING

Classic interval training involves running intervals of different lengths interspersed with jog breaks. It is very intensive tempo training, usually performed above the anaerobic threshold, i.e., at 90% of maximal effort or higher. Depending on the training

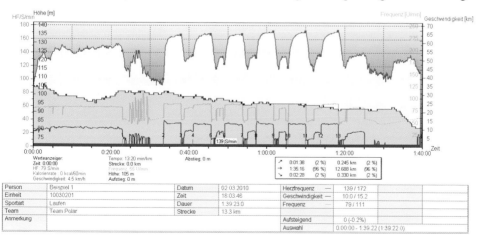

Person	Beispiel 1		Datum	02.03.2010	Herzfrequenz	—	139 / 172	
Einheit	10030201		Zeit	18:03.46	Geschwindigkeit	—	10.0 / 15.2	
Sportart	Laufen		Dauer	1:39:23.0	Frequenz		79 / 111	
Team	Team Polar		Strecke	13.3 km				
Anmerkung					Aufsteigend		0 (-0.2%)	
					Auswahl		0:00:00 - 1:39:22 (1:39:22.0)	

goal, interval lengths can vary between 200 m and 5 km. The jog recovery can vary from 50% to 100% of the interval distance. Elite 100 km runners may, for example, run 20 x 1 km with a 200 m jogging break, and splits of 3.30 min/km and quicker!

Example: interval training with jog recovery, with jogs to warm-up and warm-down

6.2.6   HILL RUNNING

Hill running involves running uphill over the training distance as fast as possible. Usually these are short runs performed with a very high pulse rate. Ideally the course should be entirely uphill. In training, this can be varied by running a hilly to mountainous course in which the uphill sections (ideally at least 500m long) are run at maximal speed.

6.2.7   PYRAMID RUNNING

Pyramid running starts with a jog, followed by sections such as 3 minutes fast, 2 minutes jog, 5 minutes fast, 2 minutes jog, 7 minutes fast, 2 minutes jog and then back down the pyramid again.

6.2.8   CRESCENDO RUNNING

In crescendo training, the tempo of certain sections is constantly increased, and the sections are longer than in a "normal" run at different intensities in which the speed is constantly increased up to a sprint. The tempo is usually increased every 10-15 minutes until 10km race pace has been reached in the final phase. The starting speed should resemble that of a long recovery run. The length of the run will depend on your training condition. After the final fast phase, jog for at least 2km.

Example: Crescendo

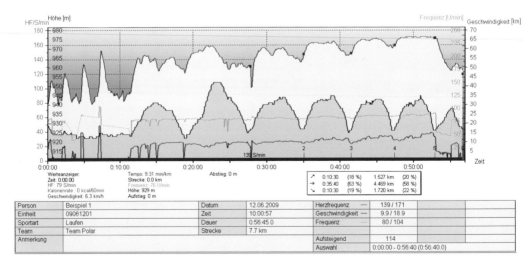

6.3 PERIODIZATION (TRAINING CYCLES)

As the ultra distance runner cannot run at peak levels year-round, training must be periodized. There are many different periodization models.

Elite ultra distance runners usually plan to peak two or three times per year, when their best performances are to be produced, irrespective of whether they run 100km, 24-hours or even longer distances. In marathon training, a 10km and a half-marathon are usually part of the race preparation, and for the ultrarunner, these preparation races can be even longer in order to test their form. For example, a 100km runner could run a marathon, a 24-hour runner could run a 100 km or 12 hour race and a multiday racer could run a 24-hour race or a stage race. In marathon training, the shorter distances are run as test races as fast as possible, but in ultra distance training, this is not the case. The longer the competition race, the slower the test race tempo. Usually, a 100 km runner completes a marathon at 85% HRmax; the 24-hour runner runs his 100 km test race at 75-80% HRmax and the multiday racer runs a test 24-hour race at 65% HRmax.

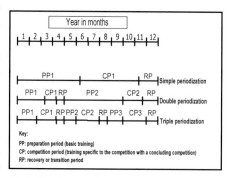

Periodization model (example)

Each training period is divided into three phases. First comes the preparation period, which focuses on basic endurance and is the period when the foundations for further improvement in fitness are also laid. Training is initially very slow-paced, with a slow and continual increase in training content. In the later stages of this phase, some training is done to improve basic speed. This is a definite departure from traditional running training plans, in which very little work is done on basic speed in the preparation period. However ultra distance running is just the opposite, for it is in the preparation phase that tempo work is carried out over the shorter distances (e.g., 10km and half-marathon), in order to increase basic speed before embarking on the very long training distances.

In an annual training plan with three peaks, it lasts about four weeks; in a plan with two peaks, it lasts up to three months.

The next phase is the competition period. In ultra distance running, as opposed to traditional running training plans, special preparation is included in this phase because it is fundamentally different from the training in the preparation phase. For the "infra" marathon distances, the aim during the competition phase is to run several maximal performances within a certain timeframe (particularly in the case of middle and long distances on the track). However, in ultrarunning, 6-8 weeks of special training are similar to the training recommendations in this book. The competition period always culminates in the actual race.

The big race is always followed by the recovery or transition period. Depending on the athlete, this lasts from two to four weeks. Recovery does not just mean doing nothing at all, instead the idea is to do other completely different forms of exercise, such as cycling, swimming, etc., even easy jogging. No activity should be performed at more than 70% HRmax though.

6.4   SUPERCOMPENSATION / TRAINING STIMULI

The concept of supercompensation is now a key component of training theory and is applicable to all sports.

Performance improvement is attained by means of targeted training stimuli (training sessions). This is the correct definition of supercompensation. However, finding the right combination is the art of good training planning. Unfortunately, there are many elements of training management for which generalizations cannot be made. There are great differences between the various track and field events and therefore the proportions of technical and physical parameters. In running training, the improvement of technique by perfecting the economy of the running style and the targeted strengthening of the supporting muscle groups becomes more important the greater the athlete's ability, in order to gain precious seconds, minutes or even a few miles (in the case of very long races).

Figure 1: Ideal supercompensation = linear performance improvement

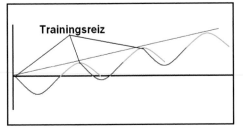

If the training stimuli are set at the right time and at the right intensity, they should lead to regular performance improvement over the training phase. (see Figure 1).

If the training stimuli are too close together or performed at the wrong (usually too high) intensity, then the result will be a drop in performance instead of the desired improvement. This is referred to in training theory as overtraining (see figure 2).

Neither will performance improve if the training stimuli are too far apart (see Figure 3). If the gap between the training stimuli is even greater, performance will decline. In running training, training stimuli should be no more than four days apart. This means that training should be carried out at least twice per week in order to maintain a minimum level of performance. Performance can only

Figure 2: Typical overtraining, premature or excessive training stimuli.

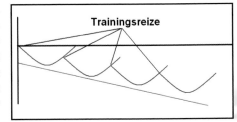

be improved by training three times a week. There are, of course, exceptions.

Someone who is new to running or has not done any training for a long while will improve even with two weekly workouts, but this will be very shortlived. For endurance runners with some training background, at least three workouts a week are necessary, depending on the runner's fitness.

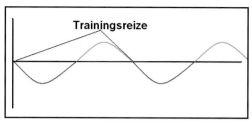

Figure 3: Too great a gap between training stimuli = no performance improvement

6.5   TRAINING SESSION STRUCTURE

"Normal" track and field workouts are composed of three parts. This is largely also true for running and ultrarunning. Like every good class, a workout consists of:

- Introduction
- Main section and
- Conclusion.

In a running workout, the introduction is usually a warm-up. This usually takes the form of a very slow jog. Running drills may also be included here, and ball games or team games are other good warm-up activities.

The main section is when the specific training session is performed. This could be anything from a a long recovery run to interval training.

The final part is usually a warm-down. According to recent sports science research, stretching should be performed in this part, not the warm-up, because stretching before the main training load has no proven benefit.

7　TRAINING MANAGEMENT METHODS

7.1　PERFORMANCE DIAGNOSTICS AND OUT OF COMPETITION TESTS

How do I know if my training is working? Or, how do I determine the right speeds or loading levels? These are the questions I hear most often from those new to training.

There are many ways to monitor training success and discover which training works for you, which I will explore in detail below.

My clear personal favorite is heart rate monitor training because it is the simplest and most effective way for runners to plan structured and targeted training. Heart rate monitors are now inexpensive and accurate. Even if many people are still skeptical, the heart rate doesn't lie!

7.1.1 LACTIC ACID TEST / FIELD TEST

A lactic acid test is a way of determining endurance ability and the establishment of the aerobic/anaerobic threshold enables the runner to set his training zones. Lactic acid is formed in the muscles during physical activity. If it exceeds a concentration of about 4 mmol/l, it can no longer be broken down, resulting in a sudden drop in performance. However, this concentration varies from individual to individual and must be calculated for each runner.

Ideally, the runner should perform this test on a treadmill, as it allows speeds to be run and measured accurately. It is also possible to perform the test on the track, where it is termed a field test. Start at a slow speed, according to the runner's ability. For ultrarunners, the pace is usually increased by 0.5 m/s every 5 minutes. After every stage, a drop of blood is taken (usually from the earlobe) and tested for lactate. The stage test should only end when the athlete is incapable of completing a particular stage.

In some cases, the stage test can already be stopped if the tester thinks that the athlete has reached the aerobic /anaerobic threshold. However, the ideal is always a stage test until exhaustion, i.e., the athlete is unable to maintain the set speed for the set duration.

Although the lactic acid test is considered to be the best way of determining the training zones, errors can be made during the testing process. If the test is not conducted cleanly (which is not always easy as the runner sweats more profusely), the result can be greatly distorted, e.g., by sweat. Taking the wrong amount of blood can also distort results.

The testee should also ensure that the performance diagnostic is conducted properly. In any case, it is always possible to check or compare the result, for example with a Conconi Test (description in the next section). In the case of a significant discrepancy between the two results, the lactic acid test should be repeated.

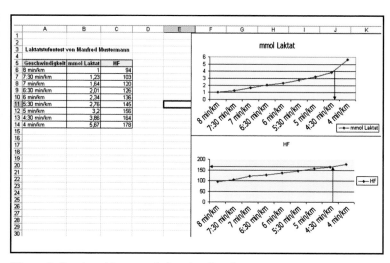

Figure 1: Lactic acid test analysis using Excel

Like the lactic acid test, the spiro ergometric test involves gradually increasing the exercise load, and ideally it should be carried out in a sport-specific way, i.e., runners should perform the test by running. This can also be done on the treadmill. Mobile testing equipment also allows the spiro ergometric test to be done in the field.

As well as measuring heart rate and lactate levels, a VO2max test also analyzes the athlete's exhaled breath, which requires the athlete to wear a mask over the nose and mouth. This enables valuable additional details about the metabolism and respiratory and cardiovascular functions to be obtained.

The test establishes the athlete's maximal oxygen consumption (VO2 max), from which their individual training zones can be calculated. To establish the absolute VO2 max, a short, sharply increasing loading test is necessary. In the spiro ergometric test itself, time periods of about 5 minutes are usually used to obtain the best measurements.

Lactic acid levels are also measured. This is an ideal time to perform this kind of performance diagnostic for training management and monitoring, as the respiratory gas analysis is much less susceptible to error than the lactic acid test using a blood sample.

At the elite level, a spiro ergometric test is normally performed at the start of a workout and then repeated at regular intervals in order to monitor training progress and to adapt the training zones according to the desired performance improvement.

7.1.3   CONCONI TEST

The Conconi Test is a means of establishing the aerobic / anaerobic threshold without taking a blood sample as in the lactic acid test. This method was developed by a biochemist and amateur racing cyclist, Francesco Conconi.

Originally designed for the sport of cycling, it can also be used for running. The results are astonishingly accurate for trained athletes like ultra distance runners.

Based on the assumption that the heart rate increases in a linear fashion in the aerobic zone under stress, Conconi's theory is that in the anaerobic zone, the curve flattens out. This point, called the deflection point, represents the aerobic /anaerobic threshold.

For this point to be determined accurately, eight measurements should be taken in the aerobic zone and three in the anaerobic zone.

Runners should perform the test while running around a 400m track with a second person present, ideally the coach.
    After jogging around the track at a gentle pace (dependent upon the athlete's fitness), the tempo is increased by 0.5 km/h every 200m (enter data in tempo table). After

Track training – also good for the ultrarunner!

every 200 m tempo stage, the heart rate is measured (click the heart rate monitor). The tempo is increased until the athlete is no longer able to maintain the set pace over 200m.

After entering the results in the spreadsheet, a performance curve is produced (this is now easy thanks to Excel, see Figure 2). The point where the curve bends, in this case at 169 bpm, is the aerobic/anaerobic threshold.

This test should be used regularly in workouts to monitor training. It is quite sufficient for all ambitious ultrarunners to do a spiro ergometry test once a year for comparison purposes, and the money saved on performance diagnostics can be spent on new running shoes or other things!

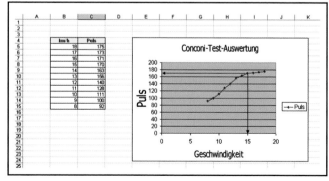

Figure 2: Analysis of the Conconi Test with Excel

km/h	min/km	100m	200m	400m	Puls
8	07:30	00:45	00:90	03:00	
8,5	07:04	00:42	01:25	02:50	
9	06:40	00:40	01:20	02:40	
9,5	06:19	00:38	01:16	02:32	
10	06:00	00:36	01:12	02:24	
10,5	05:43	00:34	01:09	02:18	
11	05:27	00:33	01:05	02:11	
11,5	05:13	00:31	01:03	02:05	
12	05:00	00:30	01:00	02:00	
12,5	04:48	00:29	00:58	01:55	
13	04:37	00:28	00:55	01:51	
13,5	04:27	00:27	00:53	01:47	
14	04:17	00:26	00:51	01:43	
14,5	04:08	00:25	00:50	01:39	
15	04:00	00:24	00:48	01:36	
15,5	03:52	00:23	00:46	01:33	
16	03:45	00:23	00:45	01:30	
16,5	03:38	00:22	00:44	01:27	
17	03:32	00:21	00:42	01:25	
17,5	03:26	00:21	00:41	01:22	
18	03:20	00:20	00:40	01:20	
18,5	03:15	00:20	00:39	01:18	
19	03:09	00:19	00:38	01:16	
19,5	03:05	00:19	00:37	01:14	
20	03:00	00:18	00:36	01:12	
20,5	02:56	00:18	00:35	01:10	
21	02:51	00:17	00:34	01:08	
21,5	02:47	00:17	00:33	01:07	
22	02:44	00:16	00:33	01:06	
22,5	02:40	00:16	00:32	01:04	
23	02:37	00:16	00:31	01:03	
23,5	02:33	00:15	00:31	01:01	
24	02:30	00:15	00:30	01:00	
24,5	02:27	00:15	00:29	00:59	
25	02:24	00:14	00:29	00:58	

Tempo table for the Conconi Test:

If the aerobic / anaerobic threshold is then reached at a higher speed, it indicates that training progress has been made.

7.2 HEART RATE MONITOR TRAINING

7.2.1 ESTABLISHING TRAINING ZONES WITH PERFORMANCE DIAGNOSTICS OR MEASURING HEART RATE VARIABILITY (HRV)

Training zones can be accurately determined by using the heart rate, and training can then be performed according to these heart rate zones. This is the most accurate form of training planning. As the values vary depending on fitness, training must be monitored at regular intervals by further performance diagnostics.

This way of planning training is really only recommended at the elite level, or perhaps for a very ambitious fun runner, whose performance has stopped improving despite very hard training. However, it should be noted that these diagnostics are not easy to carry out.

Another method of almost accurate training management can be achieved by measuring heart rate variability. The market leader in heart rate monitors, POLAR, has developed a method, called the Own Zone and built it into its monitors. This allows the runner to determine his own individual heart rate limits in only 2.5 minutes and then to structure his training based on them.

7.2.2 ESTABLISHING MAXIMAL HEART RATE (HRMAX)

Establishing maximal heart rate can be done anywhere by anyone. In my opinion, the best way is on the track and with at least one other person present. Prerequisites for performing the test are good basic fitness, i.e., running experience, and perfect health! Start by jogging for about 2 km, then run 3000 m at the fastest, even pace that you can, and at least faster than 5 km race pace. Then increase your speed until exhaustion, i.e., until it can't be increased any more and the maximal speed cannot be maintained (final spurt). The heart rate reading at that moment is considered to be the maximal heart rate. Please don't forget to start with a 2, or even better, 3 km jog, to avoid having sore muscles for a few days afterwards.

If you use the HRmax thus established as 100% of the loading level, then the percentage increments can be determined very easily for training plans. These are definitely more effective than speed data, as training conditions (terrain, temperature, weather, etc.) are different every day.

7.3 TEMPO-ORIENTED TRAINING

In tempo-oriented training, training is planned exclusively around the times necessary for each workout, which are derived from the race distance concerned and the target time (as realistic as possible). Simply trying to run pre-set times can quickly lead to over-training, thus making training monitoring all the more important.

If you really do not want to manage your training using your heart rate or sports science methods, but purely based on times, then the only way to monitor training progress is by including races over shorter distances in your training plan. Half marathon and 10km races are suitable for the frequent checking required for setting ultrarunning goals. For distances of 100 km and above, training monitoring races over the marathon or 50 km are recommended, but adequate time for recovery time afterwards is essential!

As a rule of thumb, the following target times can be projected:

- From marathon to 50 km: marathon time plus 10 km best time.
- From marathon to 100 km:
  - marathon pr x 3 (for complete beginners)
  - marathon pr x 2.7 to 2.8 (for experienced and elite athletes who are running a 100 km for the first time)
  - marathon best time x 2.5 to 2.7 (for experienced elite performers).
- From 100 km to 24-hours:
  - 100 km pr below 8 hours – over 230 km
  - 100 km pr below 9 hours – over 210 km
  - 100 km pr below 10 hours – over 180 km
  - 100 km pr below 12 hours – over 150 km.

These are possible km performances. Particularly for the 24-hour event, such figures should be treated with great care. The above figures are calculated from collections of data that I have projected and compared using results lists and especially the best performances of various athletes, but this method does have its weaknesses. For example, a good marathon runner may not be able to transfer his basic speed to the long distances because the mental side is increasingly important the longer the distance run. It is an important difference that determines whether an athlete can perform his best over 2.5 hours or 24-hours.

8 HOW DOES TRAINING CHANGE WITH THE LENGTH OF THE RACE DISTANCE?

The changes required when moving up to ultra-distances are no different than those required required for shorter distances.

The shorter and faster the distance, the shorter and faster the workouts, assuming that the athlete has a solid marathon background. This means that the athlete has successfully competed in a few marathons and he has a training goal and uses a training plan.

Training for the "entry level" ultramarathon distance, the 50 km, is essentially no different than a structured marathon training plan. Ideally, the athlete just extends the long workouts up to 40 km or even 42 km. All other workouts can remain the same, depending on the target performance.

The speed for the first attempt over the 50 km should be roughly 10-15 seconds per km slower than in the marathon. If the athlete moves up from the marathon to the 100 km, then greater adjustments must be made to his training. Apart from the long run, the tempo workouts also change.

They become significantly both longer and slower than is typical for the marathon. For example, if 400 m and 1 km intervals are run in marathon training, for the 100 km distance, intervals of up to 4 x 5 km are run.

Also the tempo endurance run is run over 30 km or more, which "only" corresponds to the

© imago Sportfotodienst

former marathon race tempo. Long weekend runs start at 35 km and go up to 70 km.

There are no strict parameters at the elite level. For example, top athletes may run sessions like 20 x 1 km intervals with 200 m jog recovery where the intervals are run quicker than their actual 10 km best time.

For 24-hour race training, there are no absolutely fixed parameters. One athlete may still be working with a 100 km training plan, while another may train completely differently. In the cross-section of the runners I know of all performance levels, I have noticed that virtually all of them run high mileage on the weekends.

For example, 100-150 miles are run in slow daily stages in one weekend. Multi-day races lasting five days can easily be incorporated into this kind of training plan and seem to be worthwhile both for elite athletes and fun runners (in so far as one can still be a fun runner over these distances). But even for 24-hour race training, tempo running is not completely dispensed with, and long fartlek runs are particularly recommended. Intervals are useful, if they are still run, to avoid "ultra foot slap," as is anything that relieves the monotony of training. Michael Irrgang (German 24-hour-race runner-up in 2009 and member of the 24-hour German national team) swears by 40 x 200 m with 200 m jog recovery (à la Zatopek). Others do really tough interval training on the track with 3 x 10 km intervals.

The longer the distance, the more the choice is left up to the individual runner. Blanket recommendations are useless – it is up to the individual to find out what works for him.

© Stefan Schlett

9   MAINTAINING FLEXIBILITY / STRETCHING

Stretching has been the subject of much discussion. According to the latest scientific research, we are now sure that we are not sure what the purpose of stretching is, in terms of the positive or performance-enhancing effect for runners. One thing that is certain though is that intensive stretching before running, in particular, is actually counterproductive. This is because the muscles and tendons contract under loading. Stretching works in the opposite way and is therefore not good preparation for a subsequent muscular load.

Extensive stretching is also not advisable after an intensive workout. Hard training causes microscopic tears in the muscles and intensive stretching, would only make these tears worse!

So if it cannot be done before training, when is the right time?
Firstly, let me say that if you have had no negative, or even some positive, experiences so far with stretching, then just keep on doing it gently. However, the combination of warm-up, extensive stretching, then racing should be avoided at all costs.

The exercises below show quick and varied ways of including stretching in your workouts. Stretching should not last longer than 15 minutes and 10 minutes are usually adequate. Runners should focus on stretching their leg muscles. So do at least three leg exercises and three more for the rest of the body. Non training days can be used for gymnastics exercises or classes that offer whole body training including whole body stretching exercises.

This kind of supplementary training should be performed at least once a week, ideally twice.

Now for the exercises themselves, which I will divide into categories and present at least two possibilities for each category from which you can choose. Each exercise should be performed at least twice per extremity. You should feel the stretch, but it shouldn't be painful. Do not make any jerky or bouncing movements as you stretch. The second stretch can be held a little longer but should not be painful. Hold the stretches for at least 15 seconds per extremity, ideally 20-30 seconds.

The same is true for the recommended strengthening exercises:
prevention avoids pain and long enforced training breaks. Good flexibility, like well-developed muscles, also enhances performance and therefore your race times!

Lower Leg
• Shin

Adopt a lunge position, with the rear leg bent and your center of gravity under your glutes. The front leg is straight and the toes pulled up as high as possible. You should now feel a stretch in the front of your shin.

Duration: hold for 20 seconds, then changes sides. Each shin should be stretched twice.
This exercise is an excellent way of preventing shin splints.

• Calf / Achilles Tendon

Adopt a lunge position, and lean forward with your front knee slightly bent and your rear leg straight. Lean forward until you can feel a distinct stretch in your calf. Both feet should be flat on the floor with the tips of your shoes or toes pointing forward.

These are used to stretch the calf muscles and the Achilles tendons.

Hold the stretch for 2 x 20 seconds for each leg.

• Quadriceps

Stand up straight. Then hold your right foot in your right hand and pull it up, making sure that your thighs remain parallel. Pull your foot as far up and toward your glutes as possible. You should feel a definite stretch in your quads.

It is also important to perform this exercise correctly. If you lose balance during the exercise, rest your free hand on an object or training partner.

Hold the stretch for 2 x 20 seconds for each leg.

Stand up with your legs crossed and then bend forward until you can feel a stretch in your rear calf muscles, from the back of the knee downwards.

This exercise may be performed in two ways. Firstly, with the arms held against your back and, secondly, with your arms out in front, as in the photo.

• Adductors

Stand with your feet slightly more than shoulder-width apart, then shift your weight to the right and bend your right leg. Keep your left leg straight. Lean to the right until you can feel a definite stretch in your adductor muscles. Then change sides.

Hold the stretch for 2 x 20 seconds on each side.

• Hip Circling

Stand up straight then circle your hips vigorously in a clockwise direction. Keep your legs together and move only your hips.

In the *cat arch*, first kneel down and place your hands behind your knees. Then lean back until your back forms an arch.

Hold this position for 2 x 20 seconds.

Stand with your feet approximately shoulder-width apart and bend your upper body to the left while keeping it straight and holding your right arm up and also pulling it over to the side. Keep your left arm by your side.

Hold this stretch for 2 x 20 seconds on each side of the body.

Stand up straight. First, circle your shoulders gently forward with your arms hanging by your sides. Later you can involve your elbows in the movement also (raise them) and then your whole arm.

- Shrugs

Stand up straight and raise your shoulders trying to touch your ears. Hold this position for 5-10 seconds and then just let your shoulders drop.

Repeat this exercise 3-8 times.

This use to get is also an ideal exercise for office workers to get rid of neck and shoulder stiffness caused by computer work.

- Neck and Head Stretch

Stand up straight. Bring your right arm over your head and place your right hand over your left ear. Then carefully pull your head to the right while pulling your left arm down and pulling your left hand up. Then try to stretch a little further.

Hold the stretch for 2 x 20 seconds on each side of the body.

10 COMPLEMENTARY TRAINING FOR MUSCLES NOT USED IN RUNNING (STRENGTHENING / STABILITY)

Regular strength training is very important when you run very long distances in training, to avoid injuries due to one-sided loading and problems ranging from tension to serious injuries caused by postural misalignments.

Runners who, even when training for the marathon, did no training except running should really consider including at least one weekly strength training session that covers all muscle groups in their ultra running training plan. Well-trained muscles support and encourage good posture, which is the foundation of a good, economical running style.

Expensive equipment is not necessary; you don't even need to join a gym. Below

I will show you a few example exercises that anyone can do at home on a fitness mat or on the carpet. The only other thing I can recommend to strengthen the ankles is a wobble board. This will allow to you to easily incorporate a very useful exercise into your daily routine, e.g., while brushing your teeth, without having to reduce your running mileage.

All other exercises can easily be carried out at home without any costly equipment. There are countless other good exercises that can bring variety to your daily workouts. These can easily be found on the Internet by searching under "proprioception" or "strength training for runners."

So, please remember that injury prevention is better than cure; 20-30 minutes per week are all it takes.

Exercises for the Legs

Tibia (avoidance/prevention of shin splints (see chapter "orthopaedic strain in ultra distance running" by Dr. Göbel)

Lean back against e.g. a wall, then pull the toes of each foot alternately as far up as possible. The exercise can be varied by making it dynamic, i.e., continual change of foot or deliberately long hold of each "hold" phase.

There is no general recommendation for the length of this exercise. In the dynamic version, the exercise is performed until exhaustion. In the "held" version, start with 15-20 seconds per foot and repeat until you can no longer hold the tension for the required time.

one-footed   *two-footed*

one-footed   *two-footed*

- Calf

Stand up straight and raise both heels off the floor at the same time. Then stretch your body up until you are standing on the tips of your toes.

There are also two versions of this exercise. Either dynamic, with a continual up and down motion or with a deliberate hold, as for the shin exercise.

Experts can further increase the difficulty of the exercise by performing it on one leg i.e., one is bent so that the standing leg must then push the entire bodyweight up by itself. As well as more strength, this version also calls for a good sense of balance.

- Hip raise (hamstring, glutes, lower back)

Lie on your back and bend your knees so that you can put your heels on the ground (NOT the whole foot) and pull your toes toward you. Lay your arms out to the side or beside your body (arms straight with tension). Now raise your hips until the thighs and upper body form a line and hold this position.

Vary the exercise by raising one bent leg and performing gentle bouncing movements with the hips.

Prone lie rowing (lower and upper back)

Lie on your front. In this position, raise your upper body about 4.5-7 inches off the floor so that only the hips, lower abdomen and legs are touching the floor. Form a U-shape with your arms bent and then straighten them in front of you again. It is important to perform this calmly and correctly, without rushing.

Plank

Go down on all fours (plank position), with your arms, hands and knees all shoulder-width apart. Now first lift one leg up until it is in line with your back with the knee bent (90°) and the foot pointing up.

Then raise and lower this leg a few inches.

Crunches (front rectus abdominis muscle)

Lie on your back and then raise your legs at a right angle to the mat so that your lower leg is parallel to the mat.

Then raise the upper body slightly until you can feel tension in your front rectus abdominis.

There are several variations on this depending on your fitness levels. In the easier versions, start with your arms stretched out in front of you. Better conditioned athletes can stretch their arms out behind them. As well as holding and extending, the exercise can also be performed dynamically by bouncing slightly in the raised, off-the-floor position.

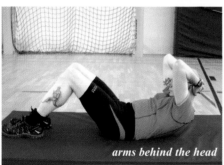
starting position

arms out to the side

arms behind the head

arms back

Don't forget to breathe!

Twisting crunch (oblique abdominal muscles)

The starting position is the same as above, but this time raise the upper body and twist forward slightly, with your arms brought diagonally forward to your knees.

It is also possible to perform this exercise statically, i.e., holding the position, or dynamically with a slight bouncing action, where you must be careful to keep your lower back on the floor. Don't forget to train both sides!

Hip raise (lower abdominals / hip flexors)

The starting position is the same as for the crunches, but the arms are placed on the floor next to the upper body with the palms of the hands on the floor. Then raise the glutes and hips straight up and lower them again.

Take care not to hollow your back and maintain the tension in your trunk muscles.

Dips (shoulders / arms)

Sit up straight with your legs out straight and parallel in front of you. Then place your fists on the mat next to your hips and raise your bottom as high as possible off the mat. Do not let it touch the mat as you lower it.

Increase the difficulty by raising the fists by placing them on a higher surface, e.g., a bench in a gym. Then the whole body must be pushed upward. Lowering the body, during which time the bodyweight must be supported, is another way of increasing the difficulty of the exercise.

Push-ups (arms, chest)

Start in the push-up position, i.e., resting on the toes and hands with the body straight and supported by the hands placed at chest-level.

This exercise entails bending and stretching the arms while keeping the trunk and head aligned. When you lower your body, your nose should almost touch the floor. When you raise your body, your arms should be completely straight, but the body must remain stable and in a straight line throughout.

A considerably easier variant is the knee push-up. The important thing is not the intensity but correct execution. In the knee push-up, you support your body on your knees instead of your feet. In other respects, the execution is identical.

normal push-up

knee push-up

power push-up

More difficult versions are fist push-ups or fingertip push-ups. In the gym, you can also raise your feet by resting them on a box. Even greater difficulty is added by putting a weight on your back or working with a partner who exerts light pressure on your back when you are in the upward phase. Let your imagination run wild here!

10.1 STRENGTH CIRCUIT

Another great strength training method is a strength circuit. This is usually performed in a gym. The number of stations is not fixed; it can vary depending on the number of participants. If you work with one athlete per station, make sure you allow enough recovery time between stations as there will be no waiting time during the activity, if you work with two athletes per station, you can include partner exercises, and while one does the exercise, the other recovers.

Strength circuit training with nine stations

There should be at least six stations, ideally 10. A regular sports hall should usually have all the necessary equipment.

I would suggest just one variation, which can be adapted at will. The exercise time at each station depends on the level of fitness of the athletes. If they are completely new to this type of training, start with a duration of 30 seconds per exercise and then extend this to one minute.

A strength circuit can be an ideal extra workout at the running club, should the necessary facilities be available.

Station 1: Pop-ups
Start from a crouched position, then jump up, stretching your arms straight above your head.

Squat down, squat up

Station 2: Front plank (alternating arm / leg raises)

Adopt the front plank position. Then simultaneously raise the right arm and stretch it forward and stretch the left leg back, then change sides, and stretch the left arm forward and the right leg back.

Station 3: Jumping Rope

I think everyone will be more than familiar with this exercise from their school days.

Station 4: Leg change jumps on bench

From a standing position, place the right and left feet (toes) alternately on a bench.

Station 5: Jumps over the bench

Jump alternately over the bench (left and right). One possible variation is to place the hands on the bench and then jump alternately to the left and right.

Station 6: Push-ups

There are also two versions of this exercise. Firstly, the "normal" push-up where you rest on your toes, and secondly the knee push-up where you rest on your knees.

Station 7: Lower back

One person lies on a bench with their hips directly on the edge and the upper body extending over the edge. The partner holds the exerciser's legs firmly. The exerciser places his hands behind his head and holds his upper body in a horizontal position. At the start of the exercise, the upper body is lowered until it almost touches the floor, and then is gently raised again.

Make sure that the back is not over-extended, i.e., don't raise it beyond the horizontal. The partner corrects appropriately as necessary.

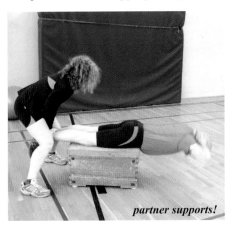
partner supports!

as low as possible!

Station 8: Lower abs (wall bars hang)

The exerciser hangs with his back to the wall bars, then raises his knees (at about 90° angle to the upper body). This exercise may also be performed dynamically or with a "hold" in this position.

Advanced, very fit athletes can even perform this exercise with straight legs.

starting position

bent knee version

straight leg version

Station 9: Crunches on sloping bench

Hang a sloping bench from wall bars, with the slope varying according to the athlete's fitness. Then lie on the bench and fix your feet to the wall bars (your partner supports you here for security). Bend your knees and then roll your upper body forward. Change the exercise intensity by varying the arm position, as mentioned earlier in the section on crunches earlier in this chapter.

© North Face

11 RUNNING DRILLS FOR ULTRA DISTANCE RUNNERS

Running drills are naturally not just useful for ultrarunners. Each track and field event has its own set of drills that focus on the specific needs of that event (e.g., hurdle drills, throwing drills, sprint drills, walking drills, etc.).

However, as there are no specific running drills for ultra distance runners, although many familiar running drills would be suitable.

Running drills are intended to improve coordination and running style. Specific running sequences are practiced in special exercises, e.g., high knees or heel flicks.

Special drills for ultra distance running are needed that focus on economy of running style. The basic racing speed is slower than that in the shorter distances, but the running action must be sustained for longer periods of time (e.g., in a 100 km race roughly 3 times longer than in a marathon). This means that a very powerful push-off or a high knee-lift are less important than in the sprints.

However, good movement execution prevents bad posture and an uneconomic running style. Running drills are therefore a great way of laying the foundations for injury-free, optimal training and racing.

Running drills should be performed at least once per week (in foundation training ideally twice a week) before an easy jogging workout. Six reps of each drill presented below are sufficient. Many more drills can be found on Internet and in specialist books published by Meyer & Meyer.

Running drills should be preceded by a warm-up jog lasting at least 10 minutes. Focus on correct movement execution. Ideally, work with a coach who can observe and correct you. New drills should therefore be "rehearsed" as much as possible before being performed alone in training. As soon as fatigue prevents you from performing a drill, you should stop.

Only move onto the drill variations presented below once you have completely mastered the basic forms.

11.1   DRILLS

High knee skips: jump alternately from the right and left feet, with a vigorous arm action.

Other variations are: vary the jumping sequence (e.g. only jump on every third stride, or deliberately jump for distance), making sure that the arms are deployed in a way that supports the forward movement. Another variation is to jump as high as possible, making sure your arms accompany the movement.

High knee skips

High knee running: the knees are raised as high as possible. Good knee lift is a basic prerequisite for a good running style and essential for good progress.

There are several variations that can be included to add variety. Firstly, you can play with speed, and secondly as with the high knee skips, with the number of steps, work on concentration and rhythm as well as the movement itself. The higher the leg speed, the harder the drill! It is still essential to ensure the movements are still executed correctly. Stop the drill or slow it down if this is no longer possible!

Sideways running: make sure that you don't trip over your own feet. The rear leg is pulled past the front leg and once the former touches the ground, the latter is again placed in the running direction. Make sure that both sides are trained equally.

Possible variations are starting off with running about 50 to 100 yards on each side, then starting to change sides quickly by changing sides every 2 or 3 strides. You can also play around with the stride frequency.

Sideways running

Sideways running with hips

Sideways running with hip twist: in this exercise, the rear leg is placed on the ground in front of the front leg thus causing the hips to twist. Make sure the arm action supports the movement.

Possible variations also involve changing the stride frequency and continual changing of sides.

Heel flicks: heel flicks involve deliberately "throwing" the heels back, trying to touch your glutes. This deliberate swing back is the basic prerequisite for a fast and efficient running style. The quicker the athlete runs, the higher the rear leg swing.

Here too it is possible to vary the stride frequency and play with the number of strides. A good form of coordination training involves performing this drill to command and constantly switching between heel flicks and high knees.

Heel flicks

Running backwards: make sure that the terrain is even and has no tripping hazards. The athlete should look over his shoulder in the direction of movement.

The speed can be varied. If the athlete has good movement execution and good coordination, he can also try hopping backwards.

Running backwards

Heel running: this involves delibe-rately only touching the ground with the heels, i.e., avoiding touching the ground with the balls of the feet as far as possible.

It is also possible to vary the stride frequency and speed of this drill.

Heel running

Toe running: in this drill, you deli-berately run only on your toes and try not to touch the ground at all with your heels.

Variations include changing the fre-quency and changing between heel and toe running on command or other signal.

Toe running

12 ULTRAMARATHON NUTRITION

(Dr. Olaf Hülsman)

The issue of "optimum nutrition" is omnipresent; it is discussed everywhere, from magazines to more or less serious TV documentaries to specialist journals. In his eagerness to be informed, the reader can often get totally confused by contradictory advice, often from self-styled "experts." Things are little better in the field of sports nutrition, particularly in special events like ultra running, where you need to extract useable advice from the often contradictory research findings. However, don't discount your own experience of what works for you, as all bodies react differently to external influences. This principle is equally true for nutrition in general, as well as training and recovery.

The aim of performance-oriented nutrition is, for ultra running as in other sports, a lasting, balanced energy supply that covers the requirement for each individual nutrient. While everyday ultrarunning nutrition is above all a logistical challenge when it comes to making optimal dietary choice for suitable energy intake while combining a high training volume with work or studies, family and other commitments, when it comes to ultradistance racing, the main issue is the maximal possible intake of energy and liquids.

12.1 BASIC NUTRITION

In basic training nutrition, the main priority is meeting the increased energy requirement. Numerous tables exist with which to calculate the amount of energy used, but
given the variations due to training phase, running style, weather conditions and many
other factors, it is only possible to give a rough guide. In general, metabolism shows
down with age, so that from age 50 onward, you must start off with lower values, and
under the age of 30, higher values are also possible. The following figures can be used
for the daily energy requirement, related to bodyweight:

Low activity (sedentary lifestyle with no training): 30-35 kcal/kg,
Average activity (1-2 hours training): 40-50 kcal/kg,
High activity (several hours training): 50-60 kcal/kg,
Ultra distance race (100 km – 24-hours): 80-120 kcal/kg

On race days, even higher figures are possible, particularly in the case of multi-day
races with significantly reduced sleep duration. For example, an accompanying study
of the Sydney to Melbourne Race (960 km) in 1985 for the winner Yiannis Kouros
calculated a total energy turnover of 55,079 kcal in five days and five hours. Because
of the short rest phases, an average consumption of 163 kcal per kg bodyweight was
established for each 24-hours[3]. Peak values of energy consumption of 130-140 kcal
per kg and day have also been calculated during mountain stages of the Tour de France.

The energy turnover for running was determined for shorter distances in studies with
0.89 kcal per kg and km; it is assumed that this consumption is stable up to approximately. the marathon distance. According to these measurements, a person's calculated
consumption for a certain distance is always the same, irrespective of the speed they
run. But the measurements vary between athletes, reflecting variations in terrain,
running technique and training condition[4]. As a rule of thumb, a rounded value of 1
kcal per km and kg bodyweight is often used, which is accurate enough to estimate the
increased demand due to training. An exact calculation of the energy consumption of
an individual is not possible using formulae; instead, laboratory tests are necessary.

Opinions differ as to the ideal ration of nutrients. Key research conclusions show that
the human body can adapt to a wide range of nutrition forms. If a high proportion of
carbohydrates is eaten, it is favored as a source of energy during rest or during exer-

---

[3] Rontoyannis, Skoulis, Pavlou (1989): Energy balance in ultramarathon running. *Am J Clin Nutr* 49 976-79.
[4] di Prampero, Salvadego, Fusi et al. (2009) : A simple method for assessing the energy cost of running
during incremental tests. *J Appl Physiol,* 107, 1068-75.

cise. These adaptations are already measurable after a few days[5]. However, for trained endurance athletes, the fat oxidation during exercise is higher than for an untrained individual. Whether an additional manipulation of the fat oxidation by training phases with a high-fat and low-carb diet or through training on an empty stomach generally leads to enhanced performance, is not conclusively resolved[6]. These kinds of measures can be used in any case to raise the fat burning capacity, which reduces the need for a permanent food intake during a race. However, if enough carbohydrates are available during exercise, the improved fat burning is, at least over the shorter distances, not necessarily accompanied by a better performance. Deliberate training of the fat metabolism is probably a good idea in the preparation for 24-hour races and multi-stage races, as an energy deficit is almost inevitable in these races. This deficit can be withstood under higher loading if loadings with low supply have been trained before-hand. As well as the purely physiological processes, it is also important to learn how to cope mentally with this situation and to develop strategies in training to overcome such phases of weakness.

While in long endurance sessions with both high and low carb intake a worthwhile training is possible high loading intensities such as interval training or tempo running should be performed with full glycogen reserves in the muscles and liver. Due to the high intensity in this type of training, carbohydrates provide the greatest proportion of the energy supply so an inadequate provision can mean reducing the load or having to stop the workout altogether. In order to derive the greatest possible benefit from these workouts, though, a high intensity must be maintained. There is also an increased risk of injury if the musculo-skeletal system is highly stressed despite falling blood sugar levels and the associated loss of concentration.

The key difference between nutrition for ultra distances and other disciplines is the overall higher amount of fat in the energy production. This is caused mainly by the comparatively slow training sessions with low intensity that can often last 4-6 hours, sometimes even 8 hours or more. These loads, in which up to 70% of the energy is obtained from fats, make it possible for ultramarathon runners to add more fat to their diets. This is in addition to the already greater amount of fat that trained athletes consume compared to sedentary individuals, where at the same intensity, less glycogen is consumed[7]. In phases of extreme loading, such as in multi-stage or multi-day races, an increase in fat intake can sometimes be the only way of achieving energy balance. In basic training, a greater amount of fat is welcome because it keeps the daily food consumption smaller than with a very high carbohydrate diet. As long as in the process

---

[5] Cameron-Smith, Burke, Angus, et al. (2003): A short-term, high-fat diet up-regulates lipid metabolism and gene expression in human skeletal muscles. *Am J Clin Nutr* 77, 313 – 8.

[6] Burke (2010): Fuelling strategies to optimize performance: training high or training low? *Scand J Med Sci Sport,* 20, 48 – 58.

[7] Saltin, Astrand (1993): Free fatty acids and exercise. *Am J Clin Nutr,* 57, 752S – 58S.

more energy is not consumed than used and sufficient fiber is also consumed, there will be no negative health effects. The reduction in the amount of food consumed can, on the other hand, enable more fruit and vegetables to be eaten. However, this room for maneuvering is not an open invitation for the unlimited consumption of candy, cakes or pizza. An increase in the fat intake in the basic diet should always be in the necessary quantity and in the form of nutritious foods, such as nuts, olives, fatty fish or vegetable oils. Fatty meat and cold cuts should be avoided even in phases with a high energy requirement as they contain high amounts of arachidonic acid (polyunsaturated omega-6 fatty acid). This fatty acid has an inflammatory effect on the metabolism, which is linked to numerous negative health consequences.

The protein intake is less controversial in the endurance events than in strength sports. Unlike many endurance athletes, the protein requirement of the ultra long endurance disciplines like ultra running, triathlon or cycle racing, are actually higher than that of strength athletes. For example, a frequently quoted study determined the protein requirement of endurance athletes to be 1.4 g.kg per day[8]. However, meeting this increased requirement is in practice only difficult in phases of weight loss due to high training volume and low energy intake, for the usual intake of non-athletes in a normal mixed diet is in the region of 1 g/kg. If the energy intake is significantly reduced, it must be balanced by an increased, regular intake of high-protein food, such as poultry, fish, milk or soya products. During the normal training phases with a balanced energy balance, the higher food intake both with a normal mixed diet and also a vegetarian diet will normally and without special effort provide an optimal protein intake of 1.4 – 1.8 g/kg. So, the timing of the protein intake is more important than the total daily amount (see below). A useful relationship between the macronutrients is described in Table 1.

Table 1: Recommended daily intake of macronutrients according to bodyweight

		General Recommendation General Population	Ultramarathon: Basic Diet Training phase	Ultramarathon: Highly intensive training/multi-stage race
Carbohydrates	[g/kg]	4-5	6-10	10-16
	[En%]	55-60	50-65	50-70
Fat	[g/kg]	1.0	1.0-1.2	1.2-2.5
	[En%]	30	25-35	30-40
Protein	[g/kg]	0.8-1.0	1.4-1.8	1.6-1.8
	[En%]	10-15	10-15	7-12

---

[8] Tarnopolsky, MacDougall, Atkinson (1988): Influence of protein intake and training status on nitrogen balance and lean body mass. *J Appl Physiol,* 64, 187 – 93.

12.2 BASIC NUTRITION SNACKS

Many athletes have become accustomed to snacking during the day. Firstly, this reduces the volume of food eaten at main meals to a more manageable level, and secondly it enables an even distribution of the daily energy intake. To avoid needing to resort to the nearest candy vending machine, it is advisable to always take a few healthy snacks to work or school. This enables the sometimes inconvenient regular fruit and vegetable intake to be achieved relatively easily, if the portions you take with you are already washed and/or chopped up. Below is a selection of easy-to-eat snacks:

- Dried fruit
- Nuts
- Trail mix
- Muesli/fruit bars
- Rice cakes
- Yoghurt / curd cheese / soya desserts
- Rice pudding
- Fruit juice/tomato juice

12.3 WATER BALANCE

Making up for fluid loss is vital in all endurance disciplines. Even over shorter distances, too little or too much fluid can lead to a drastic drop in performance or premature retirement from the race. Uncontrolled drinking of large quantities of water can even have serious health consequences. That is why the development of the correct drinking strategy is important in very long endurance events, such as ultrarunning.

For moderate temperatures and exercise intensities, the sweat loss of most runners lies somewhere between 0.5 and 1 l/hour. However, at race pace and high ambient temperature, the loss can rise to 2.5 l/hour though[9]. A reduction in bodily fluids of around 1-2% leads to a drop in performance, and trained endurance athletes are able to tolerate greater losses without harmful effects than non-athletes. Although accurate monitoring of water lost during exercise is impossible, the fluid balance should not be allowed to drop too low. Perfect balance is usually unrealistic and unnecessary, except during races lasting longer than 24-hours, when the lower intensity of effort makes it possible. Apart from water, the main component of sweat is sodium in a concentration of roughly 1 g/l. Drinking large quantities of pure water can lead to a condition called hyponitremia, due to the dilution of the remaining fluids. The symptoms range from headaches

---

[9] Sawka, Montain (2000): Fluid and electrolyte supplementation for exercise heat stress. *Am J Clin Nutr,* 72, 564S – 72S.

to coordination disturbances to coma, and in extreme cases, even death. This phenomenon is particularly found among less well-trained athletes, who probably tend
to drink excessively due to being told by their coach "drink before you feel thirsty."
Hyponitremia can be prevented by drinking appropriately and consuming sufficient
sodium. Most commercially available sports drinks contain 500-600 mg of sodium per
liter. This is usually suitable, if not drunk in excess and the salt content of the sweat
is normal. "Salty sweater," where high salt loss causes white edges and crusting on
your running top after training, should remind you to watch your sodium intake. When
sports drinks are consumed at high temperatures and by athletes with high losses, the
sodium concentration can be raised to 1 g/l. In a drink with 600 mg of sodium per liter,
add approximately. 1 g of cooking salt (40% of this is sodium) per liter of drink[10]. In
training, the high carbohydrate intake in the form of sports drinks is not always desira-
ble. In this case, 1-2 g of cooking salt/ liter faucet water could be carried in a bottle/
water bladder. To improve the taste, just add a dash of lemon or lime juice. If you are
not sure what kind of drinks will be offered before a race, runners with a high sweat
rate should take salt capsules with them in order to ensure an intake of 500-1000 mg
sodium per hour.

12.4   MICRONUTRIENTS

In general, it is assumed that intensive physical exercise increases the body's micronu-
trient requirements. Official advice is to eat more to cover the higher energy turnover
and, if this extra food is of good quality, the intake of micronutrients will also increase
to meet the increased requirement. Although in theory this sounds plausible, reality
shows that athletes in various events do not, on average, have better diets than the
sedentary population.

With regard to diet, the same advice applies to athletes in terms of a general "healthy"
nutrition. A high intake of whole grain products, fruit and vegetables is important for
an adequate nutrient supply. In general, the recommendation is for five portions per
day to ensure an adequate supply of vitamins and minerals. Actually, the amount of
micronutrients varies greatly according to the type of fruit and vegetables consumed,
and a more realistic intake would be 6-8 portions per day. Even the recommended "5
a day" is not even met in the general population, where 2-3 portions is the norm, and
most athletes do not manage a higher intake on an ongoing basis despite their increased requirements.
   This inadequate consumption means that the actual intake of micronutrients in the
general population is far inferior to the guidelines. For example, 80% of the German
population fails to meet the recommended intake of folic acid, 58% of women that of

---

[10] This amount of salt is contained in standard catering sachets and equates to approximately one heaped
teaspoon or two pinches.

iron and 32% of men that of zinc, and the average consumption of iodine is only 43% of the recommended level[11]. For athletes, the situation is not much better. Although their higher energy intake means that they are more likely to reach the generally recommended consumption of micronutrients than the sedentary population, they do not necessarily meet the increased requirement caused by a high training load.

The increased requirement mainly relates to those nutrients that have key functions in the energy metabolism, as well as those that are lost due to increased sweating. The first group includes the B-vitamins, and the second mainly the trace elements zinc, iron, iodine and copper. Although sodium is the most abundantly found mineral in sweat, it is one of the nutrients that is generally consumed in sufficient quantities. Also, even when sodium losses are high, it tends to be replaced thanks to a greater appetite and salty food. Only during longer workouts with high sweat loss can the sodium supply become critical (see section "Water Balance").

As there is no accurate way of measuring supply levels of many nutrients, regular monitoring and replacement if necessary is not possible. However, many vitamins and minerals can be measured in blood plasma or serum, and many general practitioners can carry out these tests. The concentrations are however largely regulated by the body in a small area, so that the measurement tells you nothing about the supply. Only iron levels can be accurately determined with routine tests, and long distance runners should have these done regularly due to their increased losses.

In order to close the gap between the level of micronutrients contained in the diet and the optimal amounts, a low dose of supplement would be advisable. 100 – 300% of the recommended intake of each vitamin should be taken as well as the amounts of trace elements indicated in Table 2. As in the past, there have been cases where supplements were contaminated with various doping substances; it is essential only to take products that have been tested for purity.

Table 2: Recommended dose of trace elements for basic supply

	Zinc (mg)	Iron (mg)	Copper (mg)	Iodine (µg)	Selenium (µg)
RDA	10	14	1	150	55
Advisable amount in NEM per day	5 - 10	0 - 15	0 - 1	100 - 200	30 - 100

---

[11] Quellenberg, Eissing (2008: Die Enaehrungssituation bei Dortmunder Studierenden. Ernaehrungs-Umschau 55) 202 – 209;
Hamm, Ellrott, Terlinden et al. (2010): NEM in der fachlichen und öffentlichen Diskussion. Dtsch Apothek Z, 150, 3906 – 13

Many athletes mistakenly expect rapid, measurable performance improvement after taking the most diverse nutritional supplements. In studies, nutrients were often given with this goal. However, an improvement in athletic performance or other tangible effects are only possible if the nutrient concerned is replacing a deficiency, which may absolutely be one that has not been discernible due to specific symptoms. In most cases though, no short-term changes are visible. Supplements should instead be seen as a long-term measure to shorten recovery or minimize illness and ensure an optimal intake.

12.5   CARBOHYDRATE LOADING

The jury is out on the value of carbohydrate loading for ultra distances. While many athletes in long distance triathlons deliberately increase their carbohydrate consumption before a race, this measure seems to be less widespread in ultra running. Carbo loading for shorter races, e.g., 50 km, seems to definitely be worthwhile. The longer the race, the lower the carbohydrate turnover per hour that must be replaced and the less the time lost when stopping to eat matters. At distance of 100 km and over, runners eat regularly, maximally filled glycogen reserves usually do not determine the result. Nevertheless, the runner's body should contain at least sufficient supplies for the first phase of the race and for unexpected breaks in supply. Maximal carbohydrate loading before a race is also important for well-trained athletes, as their usage of carbohydrates at the same intensity is higher[14], which can make it hard for these runners to consume the necessary amount of carbohydrate during the race.

One method of carbohydrate loading is to increase the daily carb intake to 8-10 g/kg of bodyweight on the final 3-4 days before the race. You may also see recommendations to increase up to 12 g/kg, but this can often lead to problems of intolerance. Before the loading phase, it is often recommended to empty the glycogen reserves, which can be done by restricting carbohydrate intake for 3-5 days. This should enable maximal glycogen storage and ensure that the final amount stored is higher. In the case of trained athletes, however, with a high carbohydrate proportion of 75% of the energy over three days an identical charge is achieved, irrespective of whether the carbohydrate proportion in the preceding three days constituted 50% or only 15% of the energy[15]. The irksome phase of glycogen depletion before carbo loading appears therefore not to be necessary to obtain an optimally high storage.

As roughly 3 g of water is stored per gram of glycogen, a successful carbohydrate loading shows on the scales. If, for example, 300 g extra carbohydrate is stored, that means more than 1 kg additional weight at the start of the race. For most athletes,

---

[14] Saltin, AStrand (1993): Free fatty acids and exercise. *Am J Clin Nutr,* 57, 752S – 58S.
[15] Sherman, Costill, Fink et al. (1981): Effect of exercise-diet manipulation on muscle glycogen and its subsequent utilization during performance. *Int J Sports Med,* 2, 114 – 8.

this is still beneficial over the shorter distances, especially because this extra weight is quickly lost as the glycogen is used up and the liberated water is then available for the body to use. However, the procedure must absolutely be tested in training as the muscles may feel stiffer than usual and movements may feel more sluggish. To avoid being unsettled by this at the start of a race, you should familiarize yourself with the sensation beforehand. Athletes who otherwise eat low amounts of carbohydrate should, definitely test and if necessary modify this method in training.

12.6 RACE NUTRITION

Due to the wide range of race distances in ultramarathon running, it is even less possible to give "one-size-fits-all" advice for these events than it is for other sports. While a 50 km road race is more similar to a marathon and the needs of most participants are met by the consumption of water and possibly a moderate carbohydrate intake in the form of gels or cola, the demands in 24-hour, multi-day or multi-stage races are completely different and require greater advanced planning and testing.

In general, it is true to say that the longer the race, the more necessary it is to completely replace the calories burned. In long races, an adequate supply can make the difference between dropping out or finishing the race. As there is only limited time available for consuming refreshments and the digestive tract can often only cope with a limited amount of food, the selection of the right kind of food is crucial. So bear in mind these general rules:

- Practice running training with different types of food intake (varying foods and amounts) to allow the digestive tract to get used to them.
- Low fiber and protein content foods are easier to digest.
- In long races (from 100 km), the energy intake should be as similar as possible to the calories consumed. As a guide, 0.9 kcal per km and kg bodyweight, carbohydrate intake up to 1 g per kg bodyweight and hour.
- Start eating early on; don't wait until you feel hungry.
- Find out about the catering arrangements on the course and, if possible, test all foods before the race under race conditions. In races in remote areas with unsafe or untested food supplies, take basic supplies with you.

A realistic fluid intake during a race is roughly 0.5-1 liter; if commercially obtainable sports drinks are available, this is one way of ensuring a carbohydrate intake of up to 70 g.

Catering for Ultra Distance Races

If the race organizer provides a choice of food, here are a few readily available foods with high energy content and good digestibility:

- Sports drinks with 4-7% carbohydrates: combination of maltodextrin/glucose with fructose/sucrose is widely available and advisable.
- Carbohydrate gel: maltodextrin as the main component is usually more easily digested than glucose.
- Sports bars: test how easy they are to eat at the anticipated race temperature.
- Chocolate, chocolate bars.
- Cookies, cakes.
- Currant buns or fruit loaf with butter or margarine.
- Salt sticks, pretzels, crackers.
- Commercially prepared baby drinks.
- Tube feeding formulae with high energy content.

Sports nutrition

Chopped fruit is often provided at aid stations. This is sometimes a welcome change in terms of variety of taste, but the energy content should not be overestimated: an average sized banana or apple contains only 15-20 g carbohydrates. If you eat fruit during the race, particularly dried fruit and fruit bars, don't forget it has a high potassium content. In the metabolism, sodium and potassium act as antagonists, but sodium losses are significantly higher due to sweating Because of the partially antagonistic effects, the potassium intake during loading is controversial. Empirical observation though does show that usual amounts that are consumed in a banana or also with a hot meal are harmless. However, athletes who want to meet the majority of their energy needs during a race with fruit – in whichever form – should be sure to test this beforehand. The high fiber and fructose content in fruit also make it a less than ideal race food.

12.7   RECOVERY

The muscle cells can absorb particularly high amounts of nutrients after exercise. Several studies show that carbohydrate consumption after a workout leads to better storage of glycogen than after a rest phase. This effect can be further enhanced if a small amount of protein or amino acids is added to the carbohydrate[16]. It is important that the protein be easy to digest as otherwise the gastric emptying time is delayed and it takes too long to reach the muscle cells. For optimal use of the time window, consumption should take place no later than 30 minutes after exercise.

Whey and soya proteins are suitable for the recovery phase; existing studies are inconclusive as to whether the consumption of hydrolysates or pure amino acids is more beneficial than these already quickly available intact proteins. It is advisable to consume them in liquid or semi-solid form, as just after exercise most athletes tend not to feel like eating solid food and the dissolved nutrients are quickly available to the body. Try yoghurt, whey or soya drinks, buttermilk and puree or liquid baby food, or even a mixture of cocoa powder based on glucose (= dextrose) or maltodextrine[17] with a simple protein powder from the pharmacy or local store. The powder can be prepared dry in advance and then mixed with water after training. The lack of water means there are no hygiene issues, it is light to carry around and the taste can be varied depending on the choice of ingredients.

The protein intake in the first recovery phase should be in the region of 10-20 g per portion. For a maximal storage of glycogen, the target per kg of bodyweight is an

---

[16] Ivy, Goforth, Damon et al. (2002): Early postexercise muscle glycogen recovery is enhanced with a carbohydrate-protein supplement. *J Appl Physiol,* 93, 1337 – 44.

[17] Maltodextrine is formed from longer chains of glucose building blocks that nevertheless are very quickly available to the body. The chain length is irrelevant, although a supposedly slow splitting of the carbohydrate chain is often cited as an advantage of "complex carbohydrates."

extra 0.8-1 g of carbohydrates. Roughly two hours later, either consume the same combination again or have a full meal. As for training, maximum glycogen storage is not always necessary. Also, such a high energy intake is not wise on a long-term basis; the carbohydrate amounts can be reduced correspondingly.

An intake of 10 g of protein and 8 g of carbohydrates following exercise during an intensive training phase may led to better recovery and reduced vulnerability to infectious illnesses compared with a placebo or a pure carbohydrate intake[18]. A maximal loading with the above-mentioned amounts is mainly useful if the recovery period before the next workout is very short.

© Stefan Schlett

That can be the case if the athlete trains more than once a day but also during multi-stage races in which the time between each stage is limited.

However, in weight reduction phases, it is a good idea to delay post-exercise eating. Endurance exercise liberates increased amounts of fat from the fat tissues and uses it in the energy metabolism. The mobilization of fatty acids through insulin release is halted quickly if available carbohydrates like glucose or maltodextrine are eaten. Besides, as weight loss phases coincide with lower training intensity phases, maximal speed of glycogen synthesis and general recovery are not an issue.

[18] Flakkoll, Judy, Flinn et al. (2004): Postexercise protein supplementation improves health and muscle soreness during basic military training in marine recruits. *J Appl Physiol,* 96, 951 – 56.
[19] Lachterman; Jung (2006): Sport and gastrointestinal system: Einfluss und Wechselwirkungen. Deutsches Ärzteblatt, 103, Ausgabe 31 – 32 vom 07.08.2006, A-2116-20.

13   GASTRO-INTESTINAL DISORDERS DURING LONG ENDURANCE EXERCISE

13.1   INTRODUCTION

Long distance athletes are vulnerable to gastrointestinal disorders. The functional significance of this organ system during physical activity is often underestimated. Stomach and intestines play an important role in the supply of energy, electrolyte and water balance, the production of hormones and immune defense[19]. Intensive endurance exercise can interfere with these functions.

Depending on the type and intensity of exercise, a number of symptoms can develop that can be managed by reducing the exercise intensity, adapting the diet, or through medication. In order to avoid these disorders, moderate aerobic training should predominate, exercise intensity should not be increased too quickly, and an appropriate diet should be adopted. In the case of inflammatory gastrointestinal complaints and duodenal ulcers, the level of sporting activity should depend on the severity of the symptoms.

13.2 EPIDEMIOLOGY

Gastrointestinal disorders are very common in long distance athletes, with up to 80% being affected. Up to 50% of endurance runners suffer from exercise-induced diarrhea, with the worst-affected being cyclists. The problems are more frequent in women and younger athletes, especially after eating a meal 2-3 hours into the race. Dehydration seems to worsen the disorders, as shown in a study of marathon runners. Eighty percent of all runners who lost more than 4% of their bodyweight during the race developed gastrointestinal symptoms.

As a rule of thumb, the longer the race, the more frequently disorders arise, which is particularly relevant for ultramarathoners. These disorders include stomach problems such as rectal tenesmus, diarrhea and lower abdominal pain (e.g., stitch). Less common are heartburn, nausea and vomiting[20].

13.3 HEARTBURN (GASTRIC REFLUX)

The causes of this disorder are not fully understood. On the one hand, there is a suspected link with a delayed gastric emptying and, on the other, it also appears that it may be caused with increased exercise by the associated atony / relaxation of the lower esophageal sphincter. Determined by an altered hormone production, it can lead to a reduction in the secretion of protective mucus factors.

To prevent this disturbance, a change in diet is recommended (less fat, appropriate fluid intake, possibly antacid medication)[21].

Table 1: Frequency of gastrointestinal disturbances in runners

- Queasiness, vomiting, nausea: approx 30%
- Flatulence: approx 20%
- Heartburn, belching, reflux: approx 30%

[20] Riddoch, Trinick (1988): Gastrointestinal disturbances in marathon runners. Br J Sports Med, 22, 71. Worobetz, Gerrard (1985): Gastrointestinal systems during exercise in Enduro athletes: prevalence and speculations on the aetiology. N Z Med J, 98, 644. Sullivan, (1987): Exercise-associated symptoms in triathletes. *Phys Sportsmed,* 15, 105.

[21] Collings, Pierce Pratt, Rodriguez-Stanley, et al. (2003) : Esophageal reflux in conditioned runners, cyclists and weightlifters. Med Sci Sports Exerc, 35, 730. Yazaki, Shawdon, Beasley, Evans, (1996): The effect of different types of exercise on gastro-esophageal reflux. *Aust J Sci Med Sport,* 28, 93.

- Cramps: approx 27%
- Diarrhea: approx 30%
- Rectal tenesmus: approx 45%
- Bleeding: approx 25%

13.4 STOMACH FUNCTION AND EMPTYING (GASTRIC MOTILITY)

Impeded stomach emptying could be triggered by lack of fluids, excess carbohydrate consumption, endorphin release and emotional stress. It leads to queasiness and vomiting. Increased bile acids in the stomach increase the sensation of nausea.

Post-exercise, the nausea usually disappears, which is why the premature termination of a race in the case of severe disturbances should be considered, especially as vomiting can lead to severe dehydration and electrolyte imbalance, particularly due to a high sodium loss, which compounds the discomfort.

To prevent this problem, a suitable pre-race diet is recommended (see above)[22].

Table 2: Triggers for gastrointestinal complaints

- Exercise intensity (> 70% VO2 max)
- Oxygen deficiency (reduced blood flow by more than 70%)
- Mechanical trauma (increased abdominal pressure, concussion)
- Incorrect diet
- Physical and mental stress
- Medication (aspirin, NSAR; antibiotics; doping)

13.5 EXERCISE-INDUCED DIARRHEA

Up to 50% of all endurance runners are affected by this, although fecal incontinence is rare. When questioned, athletes attribute this to race intensity and nervousness or eating too much before the race.

Trigger mechanisms may be a reduction in the mucal blood flow and an increase in hormone release, which lead to a narrowing of the blood vessels in the stomach. Causes could be bad diet, e.g., an excessive intake of concentrated food (carbohydrates, minerals, energy drinks) just before or during exercise.

---

[22] Ryan, Bleiler, Carter, Gisolfi (1989): Gastric emptying during prolonged cycling exercise in the heat. *Med Sci Sports Exerc,* 1, 51 – 8.

The use of anti-diarrhea medication is not advocated and should be done very carefully[23].

Table 3: Dietary errors that can lead to gastrointestinal disturbances

• High osmotic gradients due to the absorption of concentrated food with the release of water in the gastrointestinal tract.
• Long retention time in the gastrointestinal tract by fatty and bulky foods can lead to cramps, bloating, nausea or vomiting.

13.6 GASTRO-INTESTINAL BLEEDING

High exercise intensities can lead to a reduction in the blood supply of the gastrointestinal canal of around 80%, which can result in hemorrhage, ulcers and inflammation. Gastrointestinal tract hemorrhage are actually observed in 8-22% of marathon runners. In even longer distances (i.e., ultramarathon), up to 85% of runners can be affected, depending on the intensity of the race.

The hemorrhage is most frequently located in the large intestine and usually comes from ulcers.

Triggers for the hemorrhage are a temporary displacement of the blood to the working muscles. The resulting reduction in mucal blood flow is further exacerbated by overheating and fluid loss (thickening of the blood) during the race. However, this hemorrhage is almost always harmless and needs no further management.

In a study conducted during the Spartathlon (non-stop race from Athens to Sparta over 246 km), it was shown that in a fecal sample of tested athletes who had previously taken Pantoprazol (a drug that limits the production of gastric acid), less occult blood was present than in those who had taken a placebo (10 to 71%).

A decline in performance and fatigue in conditioned athletes should always be investigated for possible anemia[24].

[23] Riddoch, Trinick (1988): Gastrointestinal disturbances in marathon runners. *Br J Sports Med.* 22, 71.
Worobetz, Gerrard (1985): Gastrointestinal symptoms during exercise in Enduro athletes: prevalence and speculations on the aetiology. *N Z Med J,* 98, 644.
Butcher (1993): Runner's diarrhea and other intestinal problems of athletes. *Am Fam Physician,* 48, 623.
Demers, Harrison, Halbert, Santen, (1981): Effect of prolonged exercise on plasma prostaglandin levels. *Prostaglandins Med,* 6, 413.
[24] Stewart, Ahlquist, McGill, et al. (1984): Gastrointestinal blood loss and enemia in runners. A*nn Intern Med,* 100, 843.
Moses, Baska, Peura, Deuster, (1991): Effects of cimetidine on marathon-associated gastrointestinal symptoms and bleeding. *Dig. Dis Sci, 36, 1390.*
Thalmann, Sodeck, Kavouras, et al (2006): Proton pump inhibition prevents gastrointestinal bleeding in ultramarathon runners: a randomized, double blinded, placebo controlled study. *Br J Sports Med,* 40, 359.

Table 4: General preventive measures for sports-related gastrointestinal disturbances

•	Avoid rapid increases in exercise intensity and duration
•	Avoid excessive anaerobic training
•	Optimize your diet
•	Manage stress
•	Adopt personalized training and nutrition plans and behavioral strategies

13.7 SIDE STITCH

Long distance runners, swimmers, cyclists and ball game players are vulnerable to side stitch. It is usually felt in the lower left or right abdomen, less frequently around the navel and very rarely in the upper abdomen.

The cause is not entirely clear. There are several attempts to explain the phenomenon (disturbance of the diaphragm blood flow, irritation of the peritoneum). Female tri-athletes report increased frequency during menstruation, which would also suggest a hormonal cause.

Typically, the pain subsides once the exercise is finished. It can be prevented by avoiding fatty or high-calorie meals in the three days before the race. Physical measures, such as certain breathing maneuvers or strategic compression of the abdominal wall, appear to have only a limited effect[25].

13.8 INTESTINAL BLOOD DISTURBANCES (INTESTINAL ISCHEMIA)

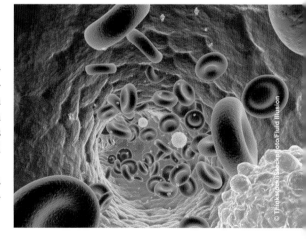

Exercise-related intestinal blood flow disturbances occur most frequently in the large intestine. Typical clinical symptoms are sudden abdominal pain, nausea and blood loss from the anus, which occurs in the first 24-hours post-exercise. A colonoscopy reveals typical changes in the intestinal mucosa.

In most cases, the changes in the mucosa heal up nicely. Only exceptionally is it neces-

---

[25] Morton, Callister, (2000): Characteristics and etiology of exercise-related transient abdominal pain. Med Sci Sports Exerc, 32, 432.
Sinclair, Stitch (1986): the side pain of athletes. *N Z Med J,* 99, 469.

sary to operate to remove the affected section of intestine. However, in the acute phase, physical exercise should be avoided for about four weeks. An extreme blood flow disturbance of the intestine was suffered by Ironman Champion Julie-Ann White in 1993. She suffered an infarction of the large intestine and her life was saved by an emergency operation.

There is currently no known way of preventing this. Athletes who have already suffered from this kind of complaint should ensure an adequate fluid intake before and during the race and monitor their exercise intensity and race length[26].

13.9 EXERCISING WITH GASTROINTESTINAL DISORDERS

In the case of gastrointestinal mucus diseases and gastric and duodenal ulcers, general advice depends on the extent of the disease. While for gastric and duodenal ulcers, exercise has proven to be neither beneficial nor harmful, in the case of the chronic inflammatory intestinal disorders (Crohn's disease and ulceritive colitis), intensive training or racing should be halted during acute inflammatory episodes. There are no concerns about moderate exercise.

Table 5: Exercise advice for selected digestive system disorders

Gastric and duodenal ulcers
In active stage, no racing.
In inactive stage, exercise is possible.

Intestinal inflammation
Rest during periods of severe inflammation.
Exercise is allowed during inactive phases.

Ulcerative colitis – Crohn's disease
No racing in active phases.
In inactive phases, moderate exercise (recovery training, basic endurance training).

[26] Kam, Pease, Thompson (1994): Exercise-related mesenteric infarction. *Am J Gastroenterol*, 89, 1899.
Lucas, Schroy, (1998): 3rd. Reversible ischemic colitis in a high endurance athlete. *Am J Gastroenterol*, 93, 2231.
Moses, (2005): Exercise-associated intestinal ischemia. *Curr Sports Med Rep*, 4, 91.

13.10 SUMMARY AND RECOMMENDATIONS

© Thinkstock/iStockphoto/Fluid Illusion

The majority of endurance athletes suffer from symptoms of the gastrointestinal tract during training or racing (see chapter 14.2 "Epidemiology"). The most common symptoms they suffer are abdominal pain (commonly referred to as side stitch), heartburn, nausea and vomiting, diarrhea and rectal tenesmus.

Athletes with these troublesome symptoms are advised to avoid high-calorie and fatty foods for at least three hours prior to training or racing. Athletes with persistent symptoms should consider temporarily reducing training intensity or duration.

Heartburn and vomiting are reported in up to 17% of athletes, but there is no real proven link to exercise. Athletes with persistent symptoms should manage their condition with antacid medication (aka, proton pump inhibitors).

Long distance running is often associated with anemia, iron deficiency and occult blood loss. The probable source of the bleeding is the stomach. There are no recognized methods of preventing occult blood loss in athletes, although prophylactic antacid medication with a proton pump inhibitor can be effective.

A blood supply disorder of the intestine (intestinal ischemia) is rare and usually disappears without treatment.

© Stefan Schlett

14 ORTHOPEDIC STRAIN IN ULTRARUNNERS

(Dr. Dietmar Göbel)

It should be noted that science is always evolving and that the recommendations published here are just a guide. Nevertheless, everyone is different when it comes to physique, age, and professional and social situation, so the advice given below cannot replace individual training advice and medical care before and during intensive exercise. For these reasons, neither the author nor the publishers can be held responsible for any damages that may result from the advice given.

Running is in man's DNA. From an evolutionary point of view, the time that man has been sitting behind a steering wheel, desk or TV is just a split second. So in theory, we should all be able to run.

This is particularly true for ultrarunning. Man did not catch his prey by sprinting, but patiently chased it to the point of exhaustion.

In this chapter, I would like to just mention in passing the injuries incurred from accidents and falls when "hunting down prey," which if incorrectly treated, can lead to long-term damage. My main focus is directed toward the most frequent injuries to the ultrarunner, and explanations of their causes and treatment so that the athlete is able to avoid these problems by taking appropriate measures. With regard to alternative treatments (which may not be accepted by physicians and the authorities), references to scientific works are given in the text in brackets for the reader to pursue if desired. According to individual statistics, 30-50% of runners are usually injured once a year as follows: 62% – legs; about 18% – lower back; and about 20% in other areas[27].

In our clinic, we treat the following injuries, listed here in order of frequency:

1. Shoulder injuries located in the rotator cuff and shoulder joint
2. Lower back and hip injuries
3. Knee injuries due to ligament overload, meniscus overload and tears, and arthritis
4. Fatigue fractures
5. Achilles tendon injuries
6. Periostitis in different forms
7. Heel spur, rear
8. Heel spur, plantar/plantar fasciitis/overload of foot muscles

14.1 SHOULDER INJURIES

The arm action of the "shoulder" is not the result of one joint alone. The forward and upward arm action is ultimately an interaction of the joints between the head of the ulna and the socket (part of the shoulder blade), the shoulder joint (connection between collar bone and shoulder blade), the joint between the collar bone and the sternum, as well as the connective tissue under the acromion and the movement of the shoulder blade in the upper back area.

Running injuries usually occur in the shoulder, mainly in the area of the muscles below the acromion, the rotator cuffs. The most frequent cause is a shortening of the chest muscles (m. pectoralis). This in turn constricts the movement of the tendons, particularly that of the supraspinatus tendon, and also increases the loading on the AC (acromioclavicular) joint. Injury triggers are often runs in cold weather when wearing a sleeveless top or doing unhabitually long runs holding a hand bottle. The inflammation of the tendon is often accompanied by calcification in the areas of worst blood circulation.

---

[27] Mayer F, et al (2001): Verletzungen und Beschwerden im Laufsport. Deutsches Ärzteblatt, 98A: 1254-1259; Marquardt M (2009): Natural running, quoted according to focus 17-2002.

In acute care, icing and anti-inflammatory tablets (e.g., Diclofenac® and ibuprofen, but be careful to discuss individual dosages with your physician prior to use, as rare side effects can include kidney damage), but also treatment with infiltration can be a good idea in cases of severe inflammation.

Finally, the calcium deposit should be broken down with shock wave therapy. The resulting increased blood circulation to the treated area will ensure the removal of the calcium particles. In this removal process, the body uses, among other things, pluripotent stem cells, which are able to regenerate the tissue so that a "hole" is not left in the area of the former calcium deposit.

This is also how we like to operate: thanks to the high success rate of shock wave therapy, we almost never need to operate to remove calcium deposits, although it can be done by keyhole surgery if necessary. As relapses are possible with both procedures, undergoing the operative risk and the acceptance of post-operative rehabilitation appear to be unnecessary.

14.2   LOWER BACK AND HIP INJURIES

Lower back and hip injuries appear in all sections of the population and are ultimately not a direct consequence of long distance running. No studies prove conclusively that long distance running can damage an otherwise healthy spine and hip girdle. Most injuries arise in the lower back area, radiate into the glutes and sometimes also extend forward into the groin, or to the side or down the back of the hamstring to the foot.

The cause of the pain in distance running must be a relatively hollowed back, i.e., at the base of the spine (fifth vertebra to the sacrum) the hips tilt too far forward. This reduces not only the intervertebral foramina (at this point the nerves leave the spine on their way to the periphery), but the small facet joints are also tilted and forced into a load bearing function. However, these joints are only intended for the purposes of movement and are therefore overtaxed by a load-bearing function. Furthermore, shearing and tractive forces change in this area, which also affects the sacroiliac joint and the area of the hip ligaments and the muscle insertions.

Treatment initially involves alleviating symptoms by means of pain relief. However, in any case, it is essential to analyze the cause of the problem, which usually reveals an often work-associated muscle imbalance and less often, bony "constructional defects."

Common causes are:

In rare cases, if the above-mentioned deficiencies are not rectified by adequate alternative training, injuries cause fatigue fractures at the muscle anchor points, which require an extremely long break from running and rehabilitation (see below). For preventive purposes, the area from the hamstrings to the lower back can be taped (see Figure 1).

14.3 KNEE INJURIES DUE TO LIGAMENT OVERLOADING

Pain in the ultrarunner's knee area not only has many causes but is unfortunately often treated in the same way as for a sedentary individual.

14.3.1 KNEE INJURIES DUE TO OVER-LOADING

Figure 1: Ultrarunner with both hamstrings taped. The tapes start from the back of the knee and continue across the glutes up to the lower back area.

Apart from ligament damage caused by accidents or recurring micro-injuries, e.g., in the context of other sports, in the ultrarunner, the course length and the type of terrain (trails, etc.) can lead to particular stresses on the lateral and cruciate ligaments. Most frequent are pains in the area of the very well supplied neural origin of the intra-articular ligament at the femur and intra-articular ligament insertion at the tibia. It is no coincidence that these two problem areas are also used in acupuncture or neural therapy treatment. After excluding other causes, this treatment should be administered, as well as rest. During recovery time in training, the muscles should be stabilized and stimulated with knee supports or taping. In rare cases, the runner's front cruciate ligament insertion may also be tender. This usually represents a combination of problems though, which should be treated together with arthritis problems (see below) or the above-mentioned intra-articular problems.

In order to prevent these injuries, adequate strengthening of the quadriceps muscles, particularly the inner muscle heads (vastus medialis of the quadriceps, Figure 2) is essential. This is particularly true for women, who commonly suffer from knock-knees and are thus naturally more prone to these problems. Because as a rule the runners' race distance is significantly longer than their longest training distance, suitable footwear is essential. Never run in your oldest shoes just because they are comfortable. Old shoes will offer no support after a few hours and this also causes the pain in the upper tibio-fibular joint (joint between head of the tibia and the fibular) commonly misdiagnosed as a lateral meniscus tear. If the calf muscles are fatigued and the foot muscles increasingly pronate the foot (lowering of the inside of the foot on ground contact), the above-mentioned compression of the lateral malleolus can be the result. A one-off, approximately 20-minute physiotherapy session to monitor the running gait and correct running shoes is a side-effect-free solution.

Dr. Dietmar Göbel

Figure 2: Maximal contraction of the medial section of the quadriceps muscles on gently sloping terrain, preparation for the curve (here to the left) and shortly after complete ground contact by the foot (still eccentric segment of the load).

14.3.2 MENISCUS OVERLOADING AND TEARS

While lateral meniscus tears are usually diagnosed incidentally and very often require no therapy[28], medial meniscus injuries tend to need treatment. In particular, a running gait in which the feet are turned outward is so severely compromising and unphysiologically sound for the medial meniscus with every stride, that eventually the meniscus can be so worn out that further running makes a tear inevitable. This can happen when running or even at the slightest movement if the leg muscles no longer adequately stabilize and support the knee joint. Depending on the type and size of meniscus tear,

---

[28] Schultz W (1983): Research into the possibilities of repairing chronically damaged knee joint cartilage in the case of corrected axial misalignments. Habilitation dissertation of the Georg August University Göttingen, Germany; Schultz, Hedrich, Göbel (1997); Behavior of meniscus tissue in the case of operated varus gonarthroses. Orthopädische Praxis 33: 524-528.

the indicated treatments are either keyhole surgery with partial removal of the detached part of the meniscus or a meniscus suture. In this degenerative type of tear (wear and tear injury), it is not always possible to perform the latter. The assessment of the quality of the knee cartilage is necessary for the success of the operation,as it will be put under even greater stress once part of the meniscus has been removed. It may be advisable to give a hyaluronic acid injection at the same time (Arthritis, below). Depending on the type of operation, gentle jogging should be possible already a week afterwards.

14.3.3 ARTHRITIS

Arthritis pain is often felt behind the knee cap, and less frequently on the medial side of the knee. The first is more typical for women and the second for men. As the development of the injury does not feature a sudden, accidental event, the technical findings of the MRI scan should not be overinterpreted, and runners should not let themselves be told to give up running altogether. In almost all cases, the runner has committed the classic mistake of overtraining, and running despite already suffering a drop in form or another such error. This eventually overloads the shock absorbing properties of the joint cartilage.

Figure 3: Example of awkward running gait that places extreme stress on the medial meniscus and knee joint. The runner on the right of the photo is turning his leg out markedly and "bending" more onto the inner part of the knee joint than if he used the natural roll-slide mechanism of the joint.

In keyhole surgery and in MRI scans, the cartilage damage is categorized first according to quality and second according to size in four stages:

> Stage 1: The cartilage is weakened but the surface is still undamaged so that the striking/loading of the joint surfaces "breaks through" into the bones, but does not dislodge any cartilage particles or reduce the thickness of the cartilage,
>
> Stage 2: The cartilage is already drier and shows some tears. The patient often feels a crunching, e.g., behind the knee cap when bending the knee.
>
> Stage 3: The layer of cartilage has thinned further.
>
> Stage 4: The bone is exposed.

In stage 1, a suitable recovery period, a change of running shoe at least occasionally and intensive build-up training of the medial quadriceps muscles is sufficient. The latter is particularly crucial for women, due to their tendency to be knock-kneed, which makes their knee caps tend to point outward more. This lateralization tendency is reinforced with increasing running distance and fatigue of the leg muscles, as the vastus medialis section of the quadriceps muscles in the leg area is relatively underweight. It is not, like the lateral muscle sections, supported by a kind of ligament tension (tractus), and/or the lateral muscles tend to be shortened. If all the leg muscles are fatigued, the patella (knee cap) moves even further laterally. This results in an asymmetric and unnatural pressure distribution on the joint surface, knee cap to thigh. This asymmetry of the action of the thigh muscles is at least partially compensated in men through their tendency to be slightly bandy-legged.

In arthritis stages 2-4, alongside the elementary component of active muscle balance training, hyaluronic acid injection treatment (usually 3-5 injections) is also recommended. Hyaluronic acid is a naturally occurring substance in the human body that is present in many tissues. It gives synovial fluid its viscous and therefore cushioning and lubricating consistency. Hyaluronic acid molecules are the top protective layer covering cartilage, and by binding with water, they improve the cushioning properties of the cartilage. It has recently been demonstrated that hyaluronic acid injections not only have a pain relieving effect on symptoms, but they also have a disease-modifying effect in that they halt or even partially repair the arthritis[29].

---

[29] Goldberg, et al. (2005): Hyaluronans in the treatment of osteoarthritis of the knee: evidence for disease-modifying activity. Osteoarthritis and Cartilage, 13, 216-224; Jubb, et al. (2001): Structure modifying study of Hyaluronan (500-730kDa, Hyalgan) on osteoarthritis of the knee; *Arthritis Rheum* 2001; 44, P9; 155; Barrett, et al. 2002 retrospective study of outcomes in Hyalgan treated patients with osteoarthritis of the knee *Clim Drug Invest* 22: 87-97.

Runners who know that they are suffering from arthritis may already use magnetic field therapy for prophylactic and recovery purposes and to increase the exercise tolerance of the joint[30]. Acupuncture treatment can relieve pain in acute cases but should not be seen as disease-modifying.

To what extent nutritional supplements can prevent or inhibit arthritis is still open to debate. The best researched active agents, glucosamine and chondroitin have been linked to positive effects. However, a current study of the *British Medical Journal*[31] now questions this based on the findings of a meta-analysis.

14.4 FATIGUE FRACTURES

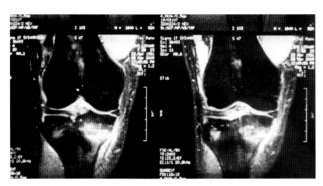

Figure 4: Fatigue fracture of the medial (inner) head of the tibia in an MRI scan.

Fatigue fractures occur as a result of long-lasting and unaccustomed exercise. Obviously, for a well-conditioned ultrarunner, the exercise should not be unfamiliar. However, fatigue fractures are increasingly common, mainly in the foot and knee joints (Figure 4). In my opinion, the cause is "pot hunting," i.e. running too many races too close to each other without allowing adequate recovery for the muscles whose job it is to protect bones and joints. Problems are particularly likely if all races are run flat out, instead of approaching some as just a chance to meet friends and enjoy running. The slave of the training plan is also at risk. So be flexible: if your professional or social situation changes to become more stressful, your training plan should be adapted accordingly.

[30] Nikolakis, et al. (2002): pulsed magnetic field therapy for osteoarthritis of the knee – a double-blind sham-controlled trial. Wiener Klinische Wochenschrift 114: 678-684; Fischer, Pelka, Barociv (2005): Adjuvant Behandlung der Gonarthrose mit schwachen pulsierenden Magnetfeldern. Z. Orthop 143: 544-550; Fischer, Pelka, Baravic (2006): Adjuvant Treatment of osteoarthritis of the knee with weak magnetic fields. Aktuelle Rheumatologie 31: 226-233; Trock, Bollet, Markvoll (1994): The effect of pulsed electromagnetic fields in the treatment of osteoarthritis of the knee and cervical spine. Report of randomized, double blind, placebo controlled trial. *Journal of Rheumatology* 21. 1903-1911.
[31] Wandel et al.: Effects of glucosamine, chondroitin, or placebo in patients with osteoarthritis of hip or knee: network meta-analysis. *BMJ* 341: 711.

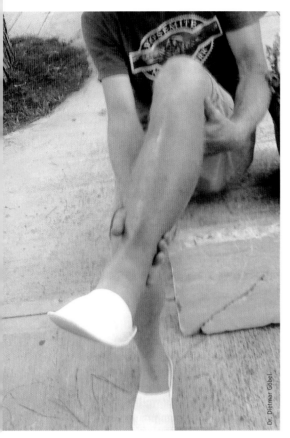

Unsuitable running shoes in terms of hardness and support, a sudden increase in mileage (both training runs or race distance), or steep downhill running are the most frequent causes of periostitis in the front of the tibia or inflammation of the surrounding muscles and their toe / foot extensor tendons (Figure 5). In addition to swelling, the runner may also feel a rubbing of the extensor tendon over the ankle joint. The lower leg is swollen and. As well as local icing, lymph taping, antiphlogistic medication and injection treatment can bring rapid healing and quickly get the athlete running again. In terms of prevention, the shoes should not be laced too tightly and particularly in the case of very smooth synthetic fiber socks (such as compression socks), rubbing in the shoe due to overly narrow shoes should be avoided. If treatment is begun too late, the result can be longer, sometimes even permanent, damage caused by chronic compartment syndrome of the muscles of the lower leg (chronic lack of space for the muscles in their compartments).

Figure 5: Extreme shin splints after the Spartathlon (153 miles nonstop)

14.7   HEEL SPUR, DORSAL

The dorsal heel spur below the Achilles tendon insertion can be an incidental finding in the context of an X-ray indicated for other reasons but can also be painful in itself. This is usually caused by an asymmetric pulling effect of the Achilles tendon in the case of increased pronation of the foot (over-pronation) and a weakness of the muscles that stabilize the medial foot-edge (e.g., tibialis posterior tendon). Increased pressure of the heel cap can intensify or prolong the pain. Eventually, periostitis in this location leads to increased bony growth and the spur that can be seen in X-rays, and then to bursitis. The bursitis responds well to injection treatment but the footwear should also be checked and any weakness in the foot stabilizing muscles should be eliminated by targeted physiotherapy. Only in extremely rare cases is an operation needed to remove the spur.

14.8   PLANTAR HEEL SPUR PLANTAR FASCIITIS/ OVERLOADING OF THE FOOT MUSCLES

Plantar heel spur, plantar fasciitis and overloading of the foot muscles have one thing in common: the overloading of the longitudinal foot arch and the structures responsible for stabilizing the rear of the foot during touchdown, foot roll and push-off.

What usually happens is that initially the foot muscles can no longer withstand the continuous load giving rise to an inflammation in particular of the inner (medial) tibialis posterior tendon that supports the edge of the foot.

This inflammation often exists with no discernible symptoms for the runner, i.e. it is discovered due to the pain in the plantar fascia, directly below the longitudinal arch or at the heel bone anchor point (plantar heel spur). The chronic inflammation of the plantar fascia origin leads ultimately to the spur visible on an X-ray. It is important to realize that it is not just the typical overpronated / flat-footed runner who is vulnerable to this type of injury; a runner with normal gait who trains over very long distances with no pronation support can also be affected.

The same is true for runners who persistently train when they are tired, i.e., directly after running an ultra distance race or having to train for 2-3 hours in the evening after having worked for 12 hours on their feet. The other extreme is the runner with high foot arches: a rigid, high midfoot arch and curvature of the metatarsal causes increased tension of the toe flexor tendons so that the natural rolling motion and pushing off action of the foot creates a significantly increased tension in the plantar fascia. Also this foot type may also need an orthotic support of the inner (medial) edge of the foot.

The initial therapy is the temporary or permanent (depending on the shape of the foot) wearing of insoles and corrective running shoes, alongside anti-inflammatory medication, as well as in acute cases of inflammation 2-3 injections. As far as possible, targeted physiotherapy should eliminate any muscular imbalance, e.g., the above-mentioned weakness of the tibialis-posterior-muscle, but also shortenings of the calf muscles or weaknesses of the upper leg muscles, which affect the natural rolling motion of the foot when running.

Shock wave therapy has been shown to be successful and is the therapy of choice for chronic injuries and for speeding up recovery from injury, before the above-mentioned physiotherapy measures can take effect. Around three 5-10 minute sessions are usually sufficient.

14.9   FINAL REMARKS

Running shoes are a topic of constant discussion among runners, trainers and physicians. I have already given a few tips above, which perhaps may help you to avoid the occasional injury or trip to the doctor's office.

However, I would like to remind you that Western civilized man originally ran in bare feet, but it is obviously to relearn this skill when running just 8-10 hours per week. Barefoot running is in my opinion a good idea for proprioceptive training in small doses, e.g., on the beach, or in case you have to train at the track, on the grass in the center, etc. Ultrarunners in particular, however, should not forget what happens on a long race course after 8, 10, 12 or more hours, when the body gets tired. I myself run in supported shoes at the end of the week in order to avoid overloading my feet after a long week standing up at work, maybe even on night shifts.

But on Mondays, I run in unsupported shoes. The experienced ultrarunner will feel this himself over the years. If you are unsure, ask an experienced coach who is knowledgeable about running.

Just one more piece of advice to end with: slightly bow-legged runners should consider how their feet strike the ground; there is usually a tendency to over-pronate the foot, so that a gait analysis by the inexperienced in some sports store may give a completely incorrect result even after 30 minutes on the treadmill, while the coach would be able to spot this in 30 seconds.

© imago Sportfotodienst

15 MENTAL ASPECTS OF ULTRA DISTANCE RUNNING

Mental preparation is an essential component of ultra distance running, for if the mind is not willing, the body will never attain its goals.

Let me begin with a quote from Goethe: "Circumstances don't control us; we control them!"

The longer the distance, and therefore the longer the race lasts, the more important the runner's mental strength. If a marathon is run 80% with the legs and 20% with the head, in a 24-hour race, the ratio changes to 50%-50%. For even longer races, the mental strength required to master the distance exceeds 50%.

It goes without saying that a first class physical preparation is essential to accomplish a sporting goal (that's what training is for), for even the strongest mind cannot achieve much without a fit body.

So why did I choose that quote by Goethe?

I think that it corresponds exactly to the situation of the ultrarunner. The sheer length of the race makes us vulnerable to a much greater range of uncertainties than would the "normal" marathon, when you can usually put your feet up after about 4.5 to 6 hours. For ultra distance races longer than 100 km, things start to get interesting. Not only does the race last about three times longer than the marathon, but there is also the changing weather conditions to take into account. For example, in the early morning, it may still be very cold, then at midday it can really heat up. If, in a marathon, drinks are sufficient to ensure an adequate energy supply, I need something more substantial in a 24-hour race. The gastrointestinal area is sensitive to movement, food intake, processing and digestion, etc.

It is up to me to prepare for all these things in advance. I can't just turn up at a race and think that I'm fit and everything will be ok. That may work for a 10 km race as it's over in 30-40 minutes. But what happens when my stomach suddenly starts to rebel after 15 hours' running? Or my legs get heavy and my muscles hurt? Or I haven't brought enough food and I run in what's know as a "bonk?"

I need a solution fast! And I can't just wait until the situation has arisen to think about it. WE control our circumstances; they don't control us!

So I really need to prepare specifically for these situations. I have already mentioned many eventualities above, but a lot can happen in 24-hours. How do I deal with low points?

Preparation for an ultra distance race must include mental preparation or even mental training. There many ways of doing this, and you need to choose what works best for you. Just as in physical training, there isn't a "one size fits all plan" that works for everyone.

For those runners who start off from a position of good mental health, a meticulously prepared contingency plan should suffice. This involves contemplating what could happen during the race and preparing a coping strategy for such eventualities.

I personally am one of those who needs to prepare very carefully for a specific race, such as the Spartathlon. In the year that I managed to finish the Spartathlon, I planned the sequence of events meticulously and mentally rehearsed the race over a one-year period. I knew at which aid stations I had left my things, and I knew how I wanted to deal with stomach problems and the heat, etc.

On my laptop, the background photo was the Spartathlon logo. On my office door was a 2-yard long banner with the word "SPARTAAAAAA!!!!!" on it.

And I trained like I had never trained before.

So I devoted my entire year just to this event and made everything else subordinate to this goal. I planned how to deal with every difficulty that I had experienced, or heard of others experiencing, during a race, and the most important thing was that I had a solution ready in my head should any of these things actually happen. I would not be suddenly faced with a problem and wonder what to do. I wanted to control circumstances and not be controlled BY them!

I therefore worked on:
- goal-setting
- appropriate running training (targeted yearly training plan)
- confronting the uncertainties of the race, the weather conditions (external conditions) and my body
- preparing solutions for all possible problems,
- visualizing the race beforehand
- positive thinking.

Every ultrarunner should be clear that:
- at some point there will be pain – that's just the way it is!
- nobody is immune to uncertainties, either self-caused or other-caused.

However, every ultrarunner should also know that:
- at some point the pain will stop
- you can do it because you WANT to
- circumstances are foreseeable and we can control them

While doing research for this chapter, I read a book by Professor Sigurd Baumann (*Psychology in Sport*), in which he highlights the importance of psychology in sport in general. He also presents a number of coping strategies, and I recommend this book to those ultrarunners who are forced to retire from races prematurely due to "head problems."

The chapters on
- mental training
- relaxation
- visualization
- motivation training

Are particularly worth reading, both for coach and athlete.

There is no universal, generic solution; instead the mental aspects are so multifaceted and individual that on we can work out what helps us and how to cope.

So, anyone who still believes that they will be at the mercy of circumstances despite intensive analysis of their upcoming race, needs solutions.

Most people only look to their training for answers, saying that they had the wrong training plan. However, very often, failure is caused by inadequate mental preparation and finding the wrong solution to problems that arise!

Always remember:

It is inevitable that problems will crop up during the race, but there are also always solutions. So be prepared. When a problem arises, just solve it and move on!

Set goals. I don't just mean one goal, but ideally a minimum goal, an ambitious goal and a dream goal. These goals must be realistic; even the dream goal must be achievable when the external conditions are ideal.

Memorize your solutions and goals. Go to the starting line and **KEEP IT SIMPLE!**

16   BASIC TRAINING

People always ask about training plans, but they usually mean the "final" program before a special race. Depending on the coach and training philosophy, this type of program is provided for between 6 and 12 weeks or even longer.

But how do you train between these training plans? Assuming a double periodization, i.e., I plan to peak twice in one year, then with a 12-week training plan, I have just covered 6 months. In my plans, I prefer an 8-week rhythm, which means that I have covered 4 months.

As we know, the main competition phase is followed by a recovery phase, where the priority is the recovery of the muscles, ligament and bone systems, and also psychological recovery (see previous chapter). This lasts between two and four weeks per annual peak.

After this, comes basic training, in which training content and intensity are slowly increased again. This implies that even basic training already follows a structure that is oriented toward the future main race, and even at this early stage, all training already has a purpose and is not just done for its own sake.

From fun runners to ambitious ultrarunners, this means increasing training volume and intensity for three weeks then recovery training for one week, i.e., in the fourth week, the volume is half that of the previous week.

Unlike the middle and long distances in track and field, it is during this phase that ultrarunners work on increasing basic speed because the emphasis in special preparation training is more focused on very long runs. Even the interval sessions are not performed at maximal speed due to their length (up to 4 x 5km intervals), in order to practice speed endurance over long distances.

This means that a lot of work is done during interval or intensive sessions specifically with short intervals and a high number of repetitions (e.g., 20 x 200 m with 200 m jog at over 95% HRmax). Also very suitable are races over 5 and 10 km and the half marathon, which should be run at or even (over the short distances) above the aerobic/anaerobic threshold.

While I cannot present a separate program for every performance level, I can describe, by way of example, a four-week cycle that would be appropriate for a 100 km runner aiming to run below 12 hours. One can say, roughly, that the weekly volume should be about 75-80% of what it would be in the main special preparation phase.

Example:
Week 1 (23.61 miles / 38 km)

Day	Session	Comment
Monday	Rest day / cross training	Strengthening
Tuesday	10 km endurance run	75-80% HRmax
Wednesday	Rest day / cross training	
Thursday	10 x 200 m intervals	Up to 97% HRmax
	2 km jog warm-up and warm-down, 200 m jog recovery between intervals	Running drills (after warm-up jog)
Friday	Rest day / cross training	
Saturday	Rest day / cross training	
Sunday	20 km recovery endurance run	65-80% HR max

Week 2 (26.72 miles / 43 km)

Day	Session	Comment
Monday	Rest day / cross training	Strengthening
Tuesday	10 km endurance run	75-80% HRmax
Wednesday	Rest day / cross training	
Thursday	12 x 200 m intervals 2 km jog warm-up and warm-down, 200 m jog recovery between intervals	Up to 97% HRmax Running drills (after warm-up jog)
Friday	Rest day / cross training	
Saturday	15 km endurance run	approx. 7:15 min/km, 75-80% HRmax
Sunday	10 km race	over 90% HRmax

Week 3 (36.66 miles / 59 km)

Day	Session	Comment
Monday	Rest day / cross training	Strengthening
Tuesday	10 km endurance run	75-80% HRmax
Wednesday	Rest day / cross training	
Thursday	14 x 200 m intervals 2 km jog warm-up and warm-down, 200 m jog recovery between intervals	Up to 97% HRmax Running drills (after warm-up jog)
Friday	Rest day / cross training	
Saturday	15 km endurance run	75-80% HRmax
Sunday	25 km endurance run	75-80% HR max

Week 4 (21.75 miles /35 km, recovery week)

Day	Session	Comment
Monday	Rest day / cross training	Strengthening
Tuesday	10 km extensive endurance run	75-80% HRmax
Wednesday	Rest day / cross training	
Thursday	10 km fartlek	At least 3 different tempos
Friday	Rest day / cross training	
Saturday	Rest day / cross training	
Sunday	15 km extensive endurance run	75-80% HRmax

In subsequent cycles, the volume and intensity can be further increased, particularly in the race lengths or the number of shorter races.

If a level is reached that is in the region of 80% of the special training plan, then the time is usually right to embark on the special preparation. If this level is attained much sooner, you could consider making your goals slightly more ambitious (if your speed and heart rate are at appropriate levels). Alternatively, you could continue at this level and work to improve your best time over the shorter distances.

It is extremely important not to do race training for the shorter distances. The idea is to do fast runs and improve your basic speed. Above all, make sure you do not overtrain or get injured.

© Thinkstock/iStockphoto/Fluid Illusion

17 TRAINING PLANS FOR DISTANCES FROM 50 KM TO MULTI-DAY RACES

17.1 MISCELLANEOUS

The goal of any ambitious athlete should be to get a personalized training plan provided by a coach. Training should also be constantly monitored and analyzed, and changed if necessary.

In ultrarunning in particular, training is very individual and every athlete has different requirements in terms of training stimuli and volume, and even recovery. However, I have decided to write a section on this and include possible training sessions that can be treated as general pointers, and while I am at it, I also wanted to turn it into a little book. Structured training plan with appropriate targets is usually much more effective than just training from day to day.

First, have a clear goal before working on an appropriate training plan. Also be sure how much time you have available for training aside from other commitments, such as work or family.

Below, I have presented example training plans from 50 km to 24-hour race. Over the years, I have had a great variety of feedback from the athletes that I manage, who range from fun runners to runners on the national team, who have followed my suggested training plans. Using this feedback and my own experience as an ultrarunner, I have constantly reevaluated and, when necessary, adapted the programs over the years.

17.2 TRAINING ZONES

In the training plans I use the following terminology to refer to the different training zones:

Training type	Heart Rate
Long recovery jog	< 70%
Extensive endurance run	75-80%
Intensive endurance run	80-85%
Tempo endurance run	85-90%
Interval	> 90%
Fartlek	Varies between 70-90%

17.3 PREREQUISITES

For the "normal" runner, the best way of managing and monitoring training is to use a heart rate monitor. These are readily available on the market and range in price from about $20 to several hundred dollars, depending on functionality and quality.

A good benchmark for efficient training is the resting heart rate (i.e., the pulserate in the morning before getting out of bed). This should drop as your fitness improves. By documenting your training in a training diary, you can establish at which intensity levels to train (when you can run over the same distance under roughly the same conditions with a lower heart rate at the same speed – on an ongoing basis).

The comparison of the speed with the heart rate measurement also makes it possible to establish a training and race pace that is both realistic and prevents possible overtraining (overloading due to over-intensive training or too little recovery leading to enforced rest).

From reading and from my experience, the following possible heart rates can be transferred to the appropriate race distances (appropriate training is a prerequisite).

Race	Average HR as% of personal HRmax
10 km	@ 92% (90-95%)
13.11 miles (half marathon)	@ 90% (88-91%)
26.22 miles (marathon)	@ 86% (84-90%)
50 km	@ 85% (82-88%)
100 km	@ 80% (75-83%)
24-hours	@ 70% (60-80%) > no literature available

For distances in excess of 50 km, there is little to no scientifically based training advice available, so I have drawn on my own experience and that of other ultrarunners ranging from fun runners to elite level athletes.

For all the training suggestions presented here, several year of marathon training is a basic prerequisite, as are a knowledge of training structure and diverse training methods. Basic conditioning training must be completed before embarking on the individual training plans.

Before embarking on a training plan, all athletes are reminded of the importance of having a medical check that, at the very least, includes a stress ECG test and an echo-cardiogram test!

The training plans assume a reasonable performance level so that the given time goals can be attained. Another prerequisite for reaching the goals is the appropriate basic conditioning training.

For the 100 km distance, this means that the given required marathon time can be pro-duced at any time. For the 50 km distance, this means that training runs of at least 30 km have been performed, and that the current performance level over the half marathon distance can be produced.

For the 24-hour race, this means that runs longer than the marathon distance are regu-larly completed.

17.4   YOUR FEEDBACK PLEASE!

Should you want to try out the suggested training plans, and if you have already done so, I would really appreciate your feedback. Please let me know at which plan you used, how you implemented it, and what the result was.

17.5   TRAINING PLAN FOR 50 KM – ENTRY LEVEL

Current marathon level:	5hrs
Weekly time available:	4-9 hrs
Training days per week:	3-4
Weekly mileage:	40-87 km
Total mileage, incl. race:	490 km
Cross training:	e.g., cycling, ergometer, swimming, but at recovery pace!

The strengthening and running drills mentioned in the "comments" section are part of the training plan. About 20-30 minutes should be allowed for the strengthening exercises. Each muscle group should be worked on. At least six types of running drill should be performed (e.g., three basic drills plus one appropriate variant of each). Drills can be found in the relevant chapter of this book.

Flexibility/stretching exercises should be carried out twice weekly after the extensive or recovery runs.

Week 1 (45 km)

Day	Session	Comments
Monday	Rest day / cross training	Strengthening
Tuesday	10 km extensive endurance run	@ 7:15 min/km, 75-80% HR max
Wednesday	Rest day / cross training	
Thursday	4 x 1 km intervals 2 km warm-up and warm-down, 600 m jog recovery	@ 6:30 min/km, up to 90% HR max running drills
Friday	Rest day / cross training	
Saturday	Rest day / cross training	
Sunday	25 km extensive endurance run	@ 7:15 min/km, 75-80% HRmax

Week 2 (59 km)

Day	Session	Comments
Monday	Rest day / cross training	Strengthening
Tuesday	10 km extensive endurance run	@ 7:15 min/km, 75-80% HRmax
Wednesday	Rest day / cross training	
Thursday	2 x 2 km intervals 2 km jog warm-up and warm-down, 1 km jog recovery	@ 6:30 min/km, up to 90% HRmax running drills
Friday	Rest day / cross training	
Saturday	10 km extensive endurance run	@ 7:15 min/km, 75-80% HRmax
Sunday	30 km Extensive endurance run	@ 7:15 min/km, 75-80% HRmax

Week 3 (72 km)

Day	Session	Comments
Monday	Rest / cross training	Strengthening
Tuesday	10 km intensive endurance run	@ 6:50 min/km, 80-85% HRmax
Wednesday	Rest / cross training	
Thursday	2 x 3 km intervals 2 km warm-up and warm-down jog, 2 km jog recovery between intervals	@ 6:30 min/km, up to 90% HRmax, running drills
Friday	Rest / cross training	
Saturday	15 km extensive endurance run	@ 7:10 min/km, 75-80% HRmax
Sunday	35 km Extensive endurance run	@ 7:10 min/km, 75-80% HRmax

Week 4 (40 km, recovery week)

Day	Session	Comments
Monday	Rest day / cross training	Strengthening
Tuesday	10 km extensive endurance run	@ 7:10 min/km, 75-80% HRmax
Wednesday	Rest day / cross training	
Thursday	10 km fartlek	At least 3 different tempos
Friday	Rest day / cross training	
Saturday	Rest day / cross training	
Sunday	20 km extensive endurance run	@ 7:10 min/km, 75-80% HRmax

Week 5 (74 km)

Day	Session	Comments
Monday	Rest day / cross training	Strengthening
Tuesday	10 km intensive endurance run	@ 6:50 min/km, 80-85% HRmax
Wednesday	Rest / cross training	
Thursday	3 x 2 km Intervals 2 km warm-up and warm-down jog, 2 km jog recovery between intervals	@ 6:30 min/km, up to 90% HR max running drills
Friday	Rest / cross training	
Saturday	15 km extensive endurance run	@ 7:10 min/km, 75-80% HRmax
Sunday	37 km extensive endurance run	@ 7:10 min/km, 75-80% HRmax

Week 6 (87 km)

Day	Session	Comments
Monday	Rest / cross training	Strengthening
Tuesday	13 km intensive endurance run	@ 6:50 min/km, 80-85% HRmax
Wednesday	Rest / cross training	
Thursday	3 x 3 km Intervals 2 km warm-up and warm-down jog, 2 km jog recovery between intervals	@ 6:30 min/km, up to 90% HRmax Running drills
Friday	Rest / cross training	
Saturday	15 km extensive endurance run	@ 7:10 min/km, 75-80% HRmax
Sunday	42 km extensive endurance run OR Training marathon at extensive endurance run pace!	@ 7:10 min/km, 75-80% HRmax

Week 7 (45 km, tapering)

Day	Session	Comments
Monday	Rest / cross training	Strengthening
Tuesday	10 km extensive endurance run	@ 7:10 min/km, 75-80% HRmax
Wednesday	Rest / cross training	
Thursday	15 km extensive endurance run	@ 7:10 min/km, 75-80% HRmax, running drills
Friday	Rest / cross training	
Saturday	Rest / cross training	
Sunday	20 km extensive endurance run	@ 7:10 min/km, 75-80% HRmax

Week 8 (68 km, tapering, race)

Day	Session	Comments
Monday	Rest / cross training	Strengthening
Tuesday	10 km Extensive endurance run	@ 7:10 min/km, 75-80% HRmax
Wednesday	Rest / cross training	
Thursday	5 km Extensive endurance run	@ 7:10 min/km, 75-80% HRmax, running drills
Friday	Rest / cross training	
Saturday	3 km Extensive endurance run	@ 7:10 min/km, 75-80% HRmax
Sunday	50 km Extensive endurance run / race	@ 7:20 min/km = 6:06:40h

Personally, I would run at 7:10 min/km split pace as the tempo in the training plan dominates and should not cause any problems at all. This would produce a finish time of 5:58:20 hrs!

17.6 TRAINING PLAN FOR 50 KM IN/UNDER 5 HOURS (6:00 MIN/KM)

Prerequisites

Current marathon performance level:	4 hrs
Weekly training time:	5-10 hrs
Training days per week:	3-5
Mileage:	from 49-89 km
Total mileage, including race:	540 km / 355.5 miles
Cross training:	e.g., cycling, ergometer, swimming, but at recovery pace!

The strengthening and running drills mentioned in the "comments" section are part of the training plan. About 20-30 minutes should be allowed for the strengthening exercises. Each muscle group should be worked on. At least six types of running drills should be performed (e.g., three basic drills plus one appropriate variant of each). Drills can be found in the relevant chapter of this book.

Flexibility/stretching exercises should be carried out twice weekly after the extensive or recovery runs.

Week 1 (56.4 km)

Day	Session	Comments
Monday	Rest / cross training	Strengthening
Tuesday	10 km intensive endurance run	@ 5:35 min/km, 80-85% HRmax
Wednesday	Rest / cross training	
Thursday	5 x 1 km intervals 2 km warm-up and warm-down jog, 600 m jog recovery between intervals	@ 5:10 min/km, over 90% HRmax Running drills
Friday	Rest / cross training	
Saturday	10 km extensive endurance run	@ 5:50 min/km, 75-80% HRmax
Sunday	25 km extensive endurance run	@ 5:50 min/km, 75-80% HRmax

Week 2 (64 km)

Day	Session	Comments
Monday	Rest / cross training	Strengthening
Tuesday	10 km tempo endurance run	@ 5:20 min/km, 85-90% HRmax
Wednesday	Rest / cross training	
Thursday	3 x 2 km intervals 2 km warm-up and warm-down jog, 1 km jog recovery between intervals	@ 5:10 min/km, over 90% HRmax, running drills
Friday	Rest / cross training	
Saturday	12 km extensive endurance run	@ 5:50 min/km, 75-80% HRmax
Sunday	30 km Extensive endurance run	@ 5:50 min/km, 75-80% HRmax

Week 3 (74 km)

Day	Session	Comments
Monday	Rest / cross training	Strengthening
Tuesday	12 km tempo endurance run	@ 5:20 min/km, 85-90% HRmax
Wednesday	Rest / cross training	
Thursday	2 x 3 km intervals 2 km warm-up and warm-down jog, 2 km jog between intervals	@ 5:10 min/km, over 90% HRmax, running drills
Friday	Rest / cross training	
Saturday	15 km extensive endurance run	@ 5:50 min/km, 75-80% HRmax
Sunday	35 km extensive endurance run	@ 5:50 min/km, 75-80% HRmax

Week 4 (49 km, recovery week)

Week	Session	Comments
Monday	Rest / cross training	Strengthening
Tuesday	12 km extensive endurance runs	@ 5:50 min/km, 75-80% HRmax
Wednesday	Rest / cross training	
Thursday	Rest / cross training	
Friday	12 km fartlek	At least three different tempos
Saturday	Rest / cross training	
Sunday	25 km extensive endurance run	@ 5:50 min/km, 75-80% HRmax

Week 5 (80 km)

Week	Session	Comments
Monday	Rest / cross training	Strengthening
Tuesday	15 km tempo endurance run	@ 5:20 min/km, 85-90% HRmax
Wednesday	Rest / cross training	
Thursday	3 x 2 km intervals 2 km warm-up and warm-down jog, 1 km jog recovery between intervals	@ 5:10 min/km, over 90% HRmax, running drills
Friday	Rest / cross training	
Saturday	15 km extensive endurance run	@ 5:50 min/km, 75-80% HRmax
Sunday	38 km extensive endurance run	@ 5:50 min/km, 75-80% HRmax

Week 6 (89 km)

Day	Session	Comments
Monday	Rest / cross training	Strengthening
Tuesday	15 km tempo endurance run	@ 5:20 min/km, 85-90% HRmax
Wednesday	Rest / cross training	
Thursday	3 x 3 km Intervals 2 km jog warm-up and warm-down, 2 km jog recovery between intervals	@ 5:10 min/km, over 90% HRmax, running drills
Friday	Rest / cross training	
Saturday	15 km extensive endurance run	@ 5:50 min/km, 75-80% HRmax
Sunday	42 km extensive endurance run OR training marathon at extensive endurance run pace	@ 5:50 min/km, 75-80% HRmax

Week 7 (52 km, tapering)

Day	Session	Comments
Monday	Rest / cross training	Strengthening
Tuesday	10 km intensive endurance run	@ 5:35 min/km, 80-85% HRmax
Wednesday	10 km extensive endurance run	@ 5:50 min/km, 75-80% HRmax, running drills
Thursday	Rest day / cross training	
Friday	12 km extensive endurance run	@ 5:50 min/km, 75-80% HRmax
Saturday	Rest / cross training	
Sunday	20 km extensive endurance run	@ 5:50 min/km, 75-80% HRmax

Week 8 (76 km, tapering and race)

Day	Session	Comments
Monday	Rest / cross training	Strengthening
Tuesday	10 km extensive endurance run	@ 5:50 min/km, 75-80% HRmax
Wednesday	8 km extensive endurance run	@ 5:50 min/km, 75-80% HRmax, running drills
Thursday	Rest / cross training	
Friday	5 km extensive endurance run	@ 5:50 min/km, 75-80% Hrmax
Saturday	3 km extensive endurance run	@ 5:50 min/km, 75-80% Hrmax
Sunday	50 km extensive endurance run – race	@ 6:00 min/km = 5:00:00h

Personally, I would probably run at 5:50 min/km split pace, as the pace in the training dominates and should not cause any problems at all. This would produce a time of 4:51:40hrs!

17.7 TRAINING PLAN FOR 50 KM IN/UNDER 4:30 H (5:24 MIN/KM)

Prerequisites

Current marathon performance level:	3:30-3:40 h
Weekly training time:	6-10 h
Training days per week:	4-5
Mileage:	from 71-108 km
Total mileage including race:	694.4 km (431.5 miles)
Cross training:	e.g., cycling, ergometer, swimming, but at recovery pace

The strengthening and running drills mentioned in the "comments" section are part of the training plan. About 20-30 minutes should be allowed for the strengthening exercises. Each muscle group should be worked on. At least six types of running drills should be performed (e.g., three basic drills plus one appropriate variant of each). Drills can be found in the relevant chapter of this book.

Flexibility/stretching exercises should be performed three times per week after the extensive or recovery runs.

Week 1 (71.4 km)

Day	Session	Comments
Monday	Rest / cross training	Strengthening
Tuesday	15 km intensive endurance run	@ 5:05 min/km, 80-85% HRmax
Wednesday	Rest / cross training	
Thursday	5 x 1 km intervals, 2 km jog warm-up and warm-down, 600 m jog recovery between intervals	@ 4:45 min/km, over 90% HRmax, running drills
Friday	Rest / cross training	
Saturday	15 km extensive endurance run	@ 5:20 min/km, 75-80% HRmax
Sunday	30 km extensive endurance run	@ 5:20 min/km, 75-80% HRmax

Week 2 (89 km)

Day	Session	Comments
Monday	Rest / cross training	Strengthening
Tuesday	12 km tempo endurance run	@ 4:55 min/km, 85-90% HRmax
Wednesday	15 km extensive endurance run	@ 5:20 min/km, 75-80% HRmax
Thursday	3 x 2 km intervals, 2 km jog warm-up and warm-down, 1 km jog recovery between intervals	@ 4:45 min/km, over 90% HRmax, running drills
Friday	Rest / cross training	
Saturday	15 km extensive endurance run	@ 5:20 min/km, 75-80% HRmax
Sunday	35 km extensive endurance run	@ 5:20 min/km, 75-80% HRmax

Week 3 (95 km)

Day	Session	Comments
Monday	Rest / cross training	Strengthening
Tuesday	15 km tempo endurance run	@ 4:55 min/km, 85-90% HRmax
Tuesday	15 km extensive endurance run	@ 5:20 min/km, 75-80% HRmax
Thursday	2 x 3 km intervals, 2 km jog warm-up and warm-down, 2 km jog recovery between intervals	@ 4:45 min/km, over 90% HRmax, running drills
Friday	Rest / cross training	
Saturday	15 km extensive endurance run	@ 5:20 min/km, 75-80% HRmax
Sunday	38 km extensive endurance run	@ 5:20 min/km, 75-80% HRmax

Week 4 (71 km, recovery week)

Day	Session	Comments
Monday	Rest / cross training	Strengthening
Tuesday	15 km intensive endurance run	@ 5:00 min/km, 80-85% HRmax
Wednesday	Rest / cross training	
Thursday	16 km fartlek	At least three different tempos
Friday	Rest / cross training	
Saturday	15 km extensive endurance run	@ 5:20 min/km, 75-80% HRmax, running drills
Sunday	25 km extensive endurance run	@ 5:20 min/km, 75-80% HRmax

Week 5 (102 km)

Day	Session	Comments
Monday	Rest / cross training	Strengthening
Tuesday	15 km tempo endurance run	@ 4:55 min/km, 85-90% HRmax
Wednesday	15 km extensive endurance run	@ 5:20 min/km, 75-80% HRmax
Thursday	4 x 2 km intervals, 2 km jog warm-up and warm-down, 1 km jog recovery between intervals	@ 4:45 min/km, over 90% HRmax, running drills
Friday	Rest / cross training	
Saturday	15 km extensive endurance run	@ 5:20 min/km, 75-80% HRmax
Sunday	42 km extensive endurance run OR training marathon at extensive endurance run pace	@ 5:20 min/km, 75-80% HRmax

Week 6 (108 km)

Day	Session	Comments
Monday	Rest / cross training	Strengthening
Tuesday	17 km tempo endurance run	@ 4:55 min/km, 85-90% HRmax
Wednesday	15 km extensive endurance run	@ 5:20 min/km, 75-80% HRmax
Thursday	3 x 3 km intervals, 2 km jog warm-up and warm-down, 2 km jog recovery between intervals	@ 4:45 min/km, over 90% HRmax, running drills
Friday	Rest / cross training	
Saturday	17 km extensive endurance run	@ 5:20 min/km, 75-80% HRmax
Sunday	42 km extensive endurance run OR training marathon at extensive endurance run pace	@ 5:20 min/km, 75-80% HRmax

Week 7 (72 km, tapering)

Day	Session	Comments
Monday	Rest / cross training	Strengthening
Tuesday	15 km intensive endurance run	@ 5:05 min/km, 80-85% HRmax
Wednesday	15 km extensive endurance run	@ 5:20 min/km, 75-80% HRmax
Thursday	Rest / cross training	
Friday	17 km extensive endurance run	@ 5:20 min/km, 75-80% HRmax, running drills
Saturday	Rest / cross training	
Sunday	25 km extensive endurance run	@ 5:20 min/km, 75-80% HRmax

Week 8 (86 km, tapering and race)

Day	Session	Comments
Monday	Rest / cross training	Strengthening
Tuesday	15 km extensive endurance run	@ 5:20 min/km, 75-80% HRmax
Wednesday	10 km extensive endurance run	@ 5:20 min/km, 75-80% HRmax
Thursday	Rest / cross training	
Friday	8 km extensive endurance run	@ 5:20 min/km, 75-80% HRmax, running drills
Saturday	3 km extensive endurance run	@ 5:20 min/km, 75-80% HRmax
Sunday	50 km extensive endurance run – race	@ 5:24 min/km = 4:30h

Personally, I would run 5:20 min/km splits, as the tempo in the training plan dominates and should not present no problems at all. This would produce a time of 4:26:40 h!

17.8 TRAINING PLAN FOR 50 KM IN/UNDER 4:00 H (4:48 MIN/KM)

Prerequisites

The following program differs from the previous ones in this performance category because the extensive tempo is not run in the race. At this level, the race is run in the aerobic/anaerobic threshold area, similar to the marathon. Using this framework program, significantly better times have been run. It is important to evaluate yourself accurately and not to overload yourself, paying particular attention to your heart rate data. Make sure you get enough sleep and that your private and professional lives are as stress-free as possible!

Current marathon performance level:	3:15 h
Weekly training time:	7-11 h
Training days per week:	5
Mileage:	from 75-124 km
Total mileage:	759.6 km (472 miles)
Cross training:	e.g., cycling, ergometer, swimming, but at recovery pace

The strengthening exercises and running drills referred to in the "comments" below are part of the training plan and essential in the long term for this very demanding training plan if you want to run long and injury-free. Allow at least 30 minutes for the strengthening exercises and work on every muscle group. For the running drills, do at least six drills (e.g., three basic ones with another suitable variant). Descriptions of these exercises and drills can be found in the relevant chapters of this book.

Flexibility/stretching exercises should be done three times a week after the extensive or recovery runs.

© Thinkstock/iStockphoto/Fluid Illusion

Week 1 (89.4 km)

Day	Session	Comments
Monday	Rest / cross training	Strengthening
Tuesday	15 km intensive endurance run	@ 4:45 min/km, 80-85% HRmax
Wednesday	15 km extensive endurance run	@ 4:55 min/km, 75-80% HRmax
Thursday	10 x 1 km intervals, 2 km jog warm-up and warm-down, 600 m jog recovery between intervals	@ 4:15 min/km, over 90% HRmax, running drills
Friday	Rest / cross training	
Saturday	10 km extensive endurance run	@ 4:55 min/km, 75-80% HRmax
Sunday	30 km extensive endurance run	@ 4:55 min/km, 75-80% HRmax

Week 2 (97 km)

Day	Session	Comments
Monday	Rest / cross training	Strengthening
Tuesday	15 km tempo endurance run	@ 4:35 min/km, 85-90% HRmax
Wednesday	15 km extensive endurance run	@ 4:55 min/km, 75-80% HRmax
Thursday	3 x 3 km intervals, 2 km jog warm-up and warm-down, 2 km jog recovery between intervals	@ 4:15 min/km, over 90% HRmax, running drills
Friday	Rest / cross training	
Saturday	15 km extensive endurance run	@ 4:55 min/km, 75-80% HRmax
Sunday	35 km extensive endurance run	@ 4:55 min/km, 75-80% HRmax

Week 3 (104 km)

Day	Session	Comments
Monday	Rest / cross training	Strengthening
Tuesday	17 km tempo endurance run	@ 4:35 min/km, 85-90% HRmax
Wednesday	15 km extensive endurance run	@ 4:55 min/km, 75-80% HRmax
Thursday	2 x 5 km intervals, 2 km jog warm-up and warm-down, 3 km jog recovery between intervals	@ 4:15 min/km over 90% HRmax, running drills
Friday	Rest / cross training	
Saturday	15 km Extensive endurance run	@ 4:55 min/km, 75-80% HRmax
Sunday	40 km Extensive endurance run (5 km final acceleration at or 5 s/km faster than race pace)	@ 4:55 min/km, 75-80% HRmax

Week 4 (75 km recovery week)

Day	Session	Comments
Monday	Rest / cross training	Strengthening
Tuesday	15 km intensive endurance run	@ 4:45 min/km, 80-85% HRmax
Wednesday	10 km extensive endurance run	@ 4:55 min/km, 75-80% HRmax
Thursday	15 km fartlek	At least three different tempos
Friday	Rest / cross training	
Saturday	10 km extensive endurance run	@ 4:55 min/km, 75-80% HRmax, Running drills
Sunday	25 km extensive endurance run	@ 4:55 min/km, 75-80% HRmax

Week 5 (109 km)

Day	Session	Comments
Monday	Rest / cross training	Strengthening
Tuesday	20 km tempo endurance run	@ 4:35 min/km, 85-90% HRmax
Wednesday	15 km extensive endurance run	@ 4:55 min/km, 75-80% HRmax
Thursday	4 x 3 km intervals, 2 km jog warm-up and warm-down, 2 km jog recovery between intervals	@ 4:15 min/km, over 90% HRmax, running drills
Friday	Rest / cross training	
Saturday	15 km extensive endurance run	@ 4:55 min/km, 75-80% HRmax
Sunday	40 km extensive endurance run (10 km final acceleration at or 5 s/ km faster than race pace)	@ 4:55 min/km, 75-80% HRmax

Week 6 (124 km)

Day	Session	Comments
Monday	Rest / cross training	Strengthening
Tuesday	22 km tempo endurance run	@ 4:35 min/km, 85-90% HRmax
Wednesday	15 km extensive endurance run	@ 4:55 min/km, 75-80% HRmax
Thursday	3 x 5 km intervals, 2 km jog warm-up and warm-down, 3 km jog recovery between intervals	@ 4:15 min/km, over 90% HRmax, running drills
Friday	Rest / cross training	
Saturday	20 km extensive endurance run	@ 4:55 min/km, 75-80% HRmax
Sunday	42 km extensive endurance run (15 km final accelaration at or 5 s/ km faster than race pace)	@ 4:55 min/km, 75-80% HRmax

Week 7 (80 km, tapering)

Day	Session	Comments
Monday	Rest / cross training	Strengthening
Tuesday	20 km intensive endurance run	@ 4:45 min/km, 80-85% HRmax
Wednesday	10 km extensive endurance run	@ 4:55 min/km, 75-80% HRmax
Thursday	Rest / cross training	
Friday	10 km recovery endurance run	@ 5:30 min/km, up to 70% HRmax, running drills
Saturday	15 km extensive endurance run	@ 4:55 min/km, 80-85% HRmax
Sunday	25 km extensive endurance run	@ 4:55 min/km, 75-80% HRmax

Week 8 (81.2 km, tapering and race)

Week	Session	Comments
Monday	Rest / cross trainiang	Strengthening
Tuesday	8 x 1 km intervals, 2 km warm-up and warm-down, 600 m jog recovery between intervals (run intervals at race pace)	@ 4:45 min/km, 80-85% HRmax
Wednesday	10 km Extensive endurance run	@ 4:55 min/km, 75-80% HRmax, running drills
Thursday	Rest / cross training	
Friday	5 km Extensive endurance run, last km at race pace	@ 4:55 min/km, 75-80% HRmax
Saturday	Rest / cross training	
Sunday	50 km race	@ 4:48 min/km, @ 80% HRmax

Personally, I would probably run 7 min/km splits, as the pace in the training plan dominates and should not present any problems at all.

17.9   TRAINING PLAN FOR 100 KM IN/UNDER 11 H (6:36 MIN/KM)

Prerequisites

Current marathon performance level:	3:44 h
Weekly training time:	7-15 h
Training days per week:	4-5
Mileage:	from 68-131 km
Total mileage including race:	754 km (468.5 miles)
Cross training:	e.g., cycling, ergometer, swimming, but at recovery pace

Week 1 (68 km)

Day	Session	Comments
Monday	Rest / cross training	
Tuesday	15 km intensive endurance run	@ 5:55 min/km, 80-85% HRmax
Wednesday	Rest / cross training	
Thursday	6 x 1 km intervals, 2 km jog warm-up and warm-down, 600 m jog recovery between intervals	@ 5:30 min/km, over 90% HRmax
Friday	Rest / cross training	
Saturday	10 km extensive endurance run	@ 6:30 min/km, 75-80% HRmax
Sunday	30 km extensive endurance run	@ 6:30 min/km, 75-80% HRmax

Week 2 (87 km)

Week	Session	Comments
Monday	Rest / cross training	
Tuesday	10 km tempo endurance run	@ 5:42 min/km, 85-90% HRmax
Wednesday	15 km extensive endurance run	@ 6:30 min/km, 75-80% HRmax
Thursday	3 x 2 km Intervals, 2 km jog warm-up and warm-down, 600 m jog recovery between Intervals	@ 5:30 min/km, over 90% HRmax
Friday	Rest / cross training	
Saturday	15 km extensive endurance run	@ 6:30 min/km, 75-80% HRmax
Sunday	35 km extensive endurance run	@ 6:30 min/km, 75-80% HRmax

Week 3 (99 km)

Day	Session	Comments
Monday	Rest / cross training	
Tuesday	15 km tempo endurance run	@ 5:42 min/km, 85-90% HRmax
Wednesday	15 km extensive endurance run	@ 6:30 min/km, 75-80% HRmax
Thursday	3 x 2 km intervals, 2 km jog warm-up and warm-down, 600 m jog recovery between intervals	@ 5:30 min/km, over 90% HRmax
Friday	Rest / cross training	
Saturday	15 km extensive endurance run	@ 6:30 min/km, 75-80% HRmax
Sunday	40 km extensive endurance run OR training marathon at extensive endurance run pace	@ 6:30 min/km, 75-80% HRmax

Week 4 (70 km, recovery week)

Day	Session	Comments
Monday	Rest / cross training	
Tuesday	15 km tempo endurance run	@ 5:55 min/km, 80-85% HRmax
Wednesday	Rest / cross training	
Thursday	15 km fartlek	At least three different tempos
Friday	Rest / cross training	
Saturday	15 km extensive endurance run	@ 6:30 min/km, 75-80% HRmax
Sunday	25 km extensive endurance run	@ 6:30 min/km, 75-80% HRmax

Week 5 (107 km)

Day	Session	Comments
Monday	Rest / cross training	
Tuesday	15 km tempo endurance run	@ 5:42 min/km, 85-90% HRmax
Wednesday	15 km extensive endurance run	@ 6:30 min/km, 75-80% HRmax
Thursday	4 x 2 km intervals, 2km jog warm-up and warm-down, 1 km jog recovery between intervals	@ 5:30 min/km, over 90% HRmax
Friday	Rest / cross training	
Saturday	17 km extensive endurance run	@ 6:30 min/km, 75-80% HRmax
Sunday	45 km extensive endurance run OR training marathon at extensive endurance run pace with extra 2.8 km (1.74 miles)	@ 6:30 min/km, 75-80% HRmax

Week 6 (117 km)

Day	Session	Comments
Monday	Rest / cross training	
Tuesday	15 km tempo endurance run	@ 5:42 min/km, 85-90% HRmax
Wednesday	15 km extensive endurance run	@ 6:30 min/km, 75-80% HRmax
Thursday	3 x 3 km intervals, 2 km jog warm-up and warm-down, 2 km jog recovery between Intervals	@ 5:30 min/km, over 90% HRmax
Friday	Rest / cross training	
Saturday	20 km extensive endurance run	@ 6:30 min/km, 75-80% HRmax
Sunday	50 km extensive endurance run OR training ultramarathon over 50 km at extensive endurance run pace	@ 6:30 min/km, 75-80% HRmax

Week 7 (75 km, tapering)

Day	Session	Comments
Monday	Rest / cross training	
Tuesday	15 km intensive endurance run	@ 5:55 min/km, 80-85% HRmax
Wednesday	15 km extensive endurance run	@ 6:30 min/km, 75-80% HRmax
Thursday	Rest / cross training	
Friday	25 km extensive endurance run	@ 6:30 min/km, 75-80% HRmax
Saturday	Rest / cross training	
Sunday	20 km e xtensive endurance run	@ 6:30 min/km, 75-80% HRmax

© Thinkstock/iStockphoto/Fluid Illusion

Week 8 (131 km, tapering, race)

Day	Session	Comments
Monday	Rest / cross training	
Tuesday	12 km extensive endurance run	@ 6:30 min/km, 75-80% HRmax
Wednesday	10 km extensive endurance run	@ 6:30 min/km, 75-80% HRmax
Thursday	Rest / cross training	
Friday	6 km extensive endurance run	@ 6:30 min/km, 75-80% HRmax
Saturday	3 km extensive endurance run	@ 6:30 min/km, 75-80% HRmax
Sunday	100 km extensive endurance run – race	@ 6:35 min/km = 10:58:20h

Personally, I would run 6:30 min/km splits, as pace dominates in the training plan and should not present any problems at all. This would produce a time of 10:50 h!

17.10 TRAINING PLAN FOR 100 KM IN/UNDER 10H (6:00 MIN / KM)

Prerequisites

Current marathon performance level:	3:29 h
Weekly training time available:	7-15 h
Training days per week:	4-6
Mileage:	from 80-139 km
Total mileage including race:	862 km (535.6 miles)
Cross training:	e.g., cycling, ergometer, swimming, but at recovery pace

Week 1 (93 km)

Day	Session	Comments
Monday	Rest / cross training	
Tuesday	15 km intensive endurance run	@ 5:20 min/km, @ 80-85% HRmax
Wednesday	15 km extensive endurance run	@ 5:50 min/km, @ 75-80% HRmax
Thursday	8 x 1 km intervals, 2 km jog warm-up and warm-down, 600 m jog recovery between intervals	@ 4:45 min/km, over 90% HRmax
Friday	Rest / cross training	
Saturday	10 km extensive endurance run	@ 5:50 min/km, @ 75-80% HRmax
Sunday	35 km extensive endurance run	@ 5:50 min/km, @ 75-80% HRmax

Week 2 (100 km)

Day	Session	Comments
Monday	Rest / cross training	
Tuesday	15 km tempo endurance run	@ 5:00 min/km, 85-90% HRmax
Wednesday	15 km extensive endurance run	@ 5:50 min/km, @ 75-80% HRmax
Thursday	4 x 2 km intervals, 2 km jog warm-up and warm-down, 1 km jog recovery between intervals	@ 4:45 min/km, over 90% HRmax
Friday	Rest / cross training	
Saturday	10 km extensive endurance run	@ 5:50 min/km, @ 75-80% HRmax
Sunday	45 km extensive endurance run OR training marathon at extensive endurance run pace plus extra 2.8 km (1.74 miles)	@ 5:50 min/km, @ 75-80% HRmax

Week 3 (107 km)

Day	Session	Comments
Monday	Rest / cross training	
Tuesday	15 km tempo endurance run	@ 5:00 min/km, 85-90% HRmax
Wednesday	15 km extensive endurance run	@ 5:50 min/km, @ 75-80% HRmax
Thursday	3 x 3 km intervals, 2 km jog warm-up and warm-down, 2 km jog recovery between intervals	@ 4:45 min/km, over 90% HRmax
Friday	Rest / cross training	
Saturday	15 km extensive endurance run	@ 5:50 min/km, @ 75-80% HRmax
Sunday	45 km extensive endurance run OR Training marathon at extensive endurance run pace plue extra 2.8 km (1.74 miles)	@ 5:50 min/km, @ 75-80% HRmax

Week 4 (80 km, recovery)

Day	Session	Comments
Monday	Rest / cross training	
Tuesday	10 km intensive endurance run	@ 5:20 min/km, @ 80-85% HRmax
Wednesday	15 km extensive endurance run	@ 5:50 min/km, @ 75-80% HRmax
Thursday	15 km fartlek	At least three different tempos
Friday	Rest / cross training	
Saturday	15 km extensive endurance run	@ 5:50 min/km, @ 75-80% HRmax
Sunday	25 km extensive endurance run	@ 5:50 min/km, @ 75-80% HRmax

Week 5 (125 km)

Day	Session	Comments
Monday	Rest / cross training	
Tuesday	15 km tempo endurance run	@ 5:00 min/km, 85-90% HRmax
Wednesday	15 km extensive endurance run	@ 5:50 min/km, @ 75-80% HRmax
Thursday	4 x 2 km intervals, 2 km jog warm-up and warm-down, 1 km jog recovery between intervals	@ 4:45 min/km, over 90% HRmax
Friday	15 km recovery endurance jog	@ 6:15 min/km, up to 70% HRmax
Saturday	15 km extensive endurance run	@ 5:50 min/km, @ 75-80% HRmax
Sunday	50 km extensive endurance run OR training ultramarathon over 50 km at extensive endurance run pace	@ 5:50 min/km, @ 75-80% HRmax

Week 6 (139 km)

Day	Session	Comments
Monday	Rest / cross training	
Tuesday	17 km tempo endurance run	@ 5:00 min/km, 85-90% HRmax
Wednesday	15 km extensive endurance run	@ 5:50 min/km, @ 75-80% HRmax
Thursday	3 x 3 km intervals, 2 km jog warm-up and warm-down, 2 km jog recovery between intervals	@ 4:45 min/km, over 90% HRmax
Friday	15 km recovery endurance jog	@ 6:15 min/km, up to 70% HRmax
Saturday	15 km extensive endurance run	@ 5:50 min/km, @ 75-80% HRmax
Sunday	60 km extensive endurance run, OR training ultramarathon over 60 km at extensive endurance run pace	@ 5:50 min/km, @ 75-80% HRmax

Week 7 (85 km, tapering)

Day	Session	Comments
Monday	Rest / cross training	
Tuesday	15 km intensive endurance run	@ 5:20 min/km, @ 80-85% HRmax
Wednesday	15 km extensive endurance run	@ 5:50 min/km, @ 75-80% HRmax
Thursday	Rest / cross training	
Friday	25 km extensive endurance run	@ 5:50 min/km, @ 75-80% HRmax
Saturday	10 km recovery endurance jog	@ 6:15 min/km, up to 70% HRmax
Sunday	20 km extensive endurance run	@ 5:50 min/km, @ 75-80% HRmax

Week 8 (133 km, tapering, race)

Day	Session	Comments
Monday	Rest / cross training	
Tuesday	15 km extensive endurance run	@ 5:50 min/km, @ 75-80% HRmax
Wednesday	10 km extensive endurance run	@ 5:50 min/km, @ 75-80% HRmax
Thursday	Rest / cross training	
Friday	5 km extensive endurance run	@ 5:50 min/km, @ 75-80% HRmax
Saturday	3 km extensive endurance run	@ 5:50 min/km, @ 75-80% HRmax
Sunday	100 km extensive endurance run – race	@ 5:58 min/km = 9:56:40h

Personally, I would run 5:50 min/km splits, as pace dominates in the training plan and should not present any problems any all. This would even produce a time of 9:43:20!

17.11 6 AND 12-HOUR RACES

On the racing scene, shorter versions of the 24-hour race (i.e., 6-hour and 12-hour races) are common.

While they were originally considered to be good ways for the race organizer to increase the number of starters and thus the finacial income in the very long ultradistance races, a good racing scene has now developed in its own right, at least in 6-hour racing. As has become usual in the 24-hour races, the 6-hour and 12-hour races usually are run on circuits between 1 and 3 km long.

The 6-hour race in particular is suitable for those runners who want a very relaxed introduction to ultrarunning. There is no set distance that must be covered within a certain time limit. Instead, everyone runs for 6 hours and at the end, the distance they have covered is calculated. Everyone, no matter how far they have run, is classified. Also, all the runners start and finish at the same time, elite and fun runners alike.

The world's best 6-hour performance was set by Tomasz Chawawko from Poland. He ran 92.188km in Stein, Netherlands, on March 7, 2004. The women's best performance of 81.896m was set by Ricarda Botzon of Germany on February 15, 2002, in Amelinghausen, Germany.[33]

---

[33] Source: http://statistik.d-u-v.org/bestenlisten/WBP_IAU_201104.pdf and http://statistik.d-u-v.org/getresulteventalltime.php?event=7524

It is precisely these types of distances achieved at the elite level that work against the 6-hour race. The performances achievable there are very close to the distance of 100 km, which is raced at the World, European and Asian Championships level, and also usually in national championships. So therefore an elite level race for many top athletes is rather counterproductive because these performances cannot be used to qualify for international races, while a completed 6-hour race is just as exhausting as a 100 km race run in a personal best time.

However, the 6-hour race is eminently suitable as an entry-level distance for interested marathon runners. Here, the runner gets a flavor of what ultrarunning is like, the runners are the same as in the long runs as the 6-hour race is very suitable as a stepping stone to a 24-hour race, for example. Last but not least, every runner is classified, even if they need to walk or stop for a while.

Also the precedence of circuits run over time measured allows many senior runners to continue their running careers and the whole point of the races is for people to run in them without being in constant fear of the sweeper bus or being told by an announcer that they have to drop out because they cannot achieve the cut-off times. Given the demographic trends of Western industrial nations, this kind of race definitely has a good future!

In the 12-hour race, the world's best performance is 161.800 km, set by the Greek Yiannis Kouros on May 4, 1997, in Adelaide, Australia. The women's record of 140.672 was set by Angela Mertens of France on May 8, in Moreuil, France.[34]

There is no real racing scene for the 12-hour race, and the performances in the ranking lists are often split times from longer races, in cases where they were recorded during the longer race, which is nowadays easily done to the nearest circuit thanks to electronic lapcounters.

For the fun runner, the 12-hour race is comparable to the 100 km, whereas top athletes, as seen above, can achieve distances approaching 100 miles. However, as a stepping stone to a 24-hour race, it is suited to both fun runners and top athletes. This is why, ideally, the number of races organized should be increased. It would also be ideal if these races took place at night, to practice running at "antisocial" hours and get used to struggling with the body's natural biorhythms. At the same time, these stepping stone races allow the runner to experiment in the areas of nutrition, planned or unplanned breaks, race pace planning, equipment, etc.

---

[34] Source: http://statistik.d-u-v.org/bestenlisten/WBP_IAU_201104.pdf

When preparing equipment / catering, make sure that the equipment, etc., can be reached from a standing position. If you want to run as many miles as possible, make sure that your own aid station is not too comfortably equipped. For example, do not put anything to lie on or a comfortable chair with a back rest, etc. Make it as Spartan as possible and as good as necessary. A stool to sit on, so that if necessary you can change your shoes and a table for equipment are all you need. If appropriate, also ensure that the table is waterproof and that should be enough.

That is incidentally also the case up to and including the 24-hour race, in which no rest phases must or should be planned. For 48-hour races and beyond, a different kind of planning again is required.

Presented below are two example training plans for beginners and fun runners. Of course, the programs for 50 km-100 km are also suitable for the 6 and 12-hour races. So, if my goal is to run 100 km in 12 hours, the 100 km program is definitely also a good way to achieve it.

The following programs are therefore presented so that the runner can run or walk the course as continuously as possible without being able to take long breaks. This is also why instructions are given in terms of time in the plans and not in distance.

© Thinkstock/iStockphoto/Fluid Illusion

Prerequisites

Current marathon performance level:	@ 5 hrs
Weekly training time available:	7-14 hours
Training days per week:	5
Training time per week:	4-7.5 hours
Total time including race:	43.25 hours
Cross training:	e.g., cycling, ergometer, swimming, but at recovery pace

Week 1 (@ 240 minutes)

Day	Session	Comments
Monday	Rest / cross training	
Tuesday	Extensive endurance run, 60 mins	80% HRmax
Wednesday	Rest / cross training	Stabilizing/flexibility 45-60 mins
Thursday	Extensive endurance run, 60 mins with 3 accelerations 100m from the finish	80% HRmax
Friday	Rest / cross training	
Saturday	Rest / cross training	
Sunday	Recovery endurance jog, 120 mins	70% HRmax

Week 2 (@ 260 Minutes)

Day	Session	Comments
Monday	Rest / cross training	
Tuesday	Extensive endurance run, 70 mins	80% HRmax
Wednesday	Rest / cross training	Stabilizing/flexibility 45-60 mins
Thursday	Extensive endurance run, 60 mins, incl. 5 mins tempo run at @ 85% HRmax	80% HRmax
Friday	Rest / cross training	
Saturday	Rest / cross training	
Sunday	Recovery endurance jog, 120 mins	70% HRmax

Week 3 (@ 280 minutes)

Day	Session	Comments
Monday	Rest / cross training	
Tuesday	Extensive endurance run, 80 mins	80% HRmax
Wednesday	Rest / cross training	Stabilizing/flexibility 45-60 Mins
Thursday	Extensive endurance run, 60 mins, incl. 10 mins tempo run at @ 85% HRmax	Rest: 80% HRmax
Friday	Rest / cross training	
Saturday	Rest / cross training	
Sunday	Recovery endurance jog, 140 mins	70% HRmax

Week 4 (@ 270 minutes, recovery)

Day	Sessions	Comments
Monday	Rest / cross training	
Tuesday	Recovery endurance jog, 60 mins	70% HRmax
Wednesday	Rest / cross training	Stabilizing/flexibility 45-60 mins
Thursday	Extensive endurance run, 60 mins	80% HRmax
Friday	Rest / cross training	
Saturday	Rest / cross training	
Sunday	Recovery endurance jog, 150 mins	70% HRmax

Week 5 (@ 350 minutes)

Day	Session	Comments
Monday	Rest / cross training	
Tuesday	Extensive endurance run, 90 mins	80% HRmax
Wednesday	Rest / cross training	Stabilizing/flexibility 45-60 mins
Thursday	60 mins, incl. 3x5 mins tempo run at 85-90% HRmax, 5 mins jog between each (easy interval training)	Rest 80% HRmax
Friday	Rest / cross training	
Saturday	Rest / cross training	
Sunday	Recovery endurance jog, 200 mins	70% HRmax

Week 6 (@ 415 minutes)

Day	Session	Comments
Monday	Rest / cross training	
Tuesday	Extensive endurance run, 100 mins	80% HRmax
Wednesday	Rest / cross training	Stabilizing/flexibility 45-60 mins
Thursday	Intervals, 75 minutes, incl. 4x5 mins tempo run with 85-90% HRmax 5 mins jog in between	Rest; 80% HRmax
Friday	Rest / cross training	
Saturday	Rest / cross training	
Sunday	Recovery endurance jog, 240 mins	70% HRmax

Week 7 (@ 330 minutes, initial tapering)

Day	Session	Comments
Monday	Rest / cross training	
Tuesday	Extensive endurance run, 90 mins	80% HRmax
Wednesday	Rest / cross training	Stabilizing/flexibility 45-60 mins
Thursday	Fartlek, 60 mins, at least 3 different intensive tempos	80-90% HRmax
Friday	Rest / cross training	
Saturday	Rest / cross training	
Sunday	Recovery endurance jog, 180 mins	70%

Week 8 (@ 450 minutes, tapering and race)

Day	Session	Comments
Monday	Rest / cross training	
Tuesday	Recovery endurance jog, 60 mins	70% HRmax
Wednesday	Rest / cross training	Stabilizing/flexibility 45-60 mins
Thursday	Extensive endurance run, 30 mins	80% HRmax
Friday	Rest / cross training	
Saturday	Rest / cross training	
Sunday	Race, 360 mins	70-80% HRmax

This framework training plan should enable you to run between 45 und 65 km in 6 hours.

© Thinkstock/iStockphoto/Fluid Illusion

17.11.2 TRAINING PLAN 12-HOUR RUN

Prerequisites

Current performance level:	6-7 hours split time is possible
Weekly training time available:	7-14 hours
Training days / week:	4
Training time per week:	6.35-15.5 hours
Total time incl. race:	81.83 hours
Cross training:	e.g., cycling, ergometer, swimming, but at recovery pace

Week 1 (@ 381 minutes)

Day	Session	Comments
Monday	Rest / cross training	
Tuesday	Extensive endurance run, 60mins	80% HRmax
Wednesday	Rest / cross training	Stabilizing/flexibility 45-60 mins
Thursday	Intervals, 10 mins warm-up, 8x5 mins at 85-90% HRmax, 3 mins jog between intervals, 10 mins warm-down	
Friday	Rest / cross training	Stabilizing/flexibility 45-60 mins
Saturday	Extensive endurance run, 60 mins	80% HRmax
Sunday	Recovery jog, 180 mins	70% HRmax

Week 2 (@ 494 minutes)

Day	Session	Comments
Monday	Rest / cross training	
Tuesday	Extensive endurance run, 70 mins	80% HRmax
Wednesday	Rest / cross training	Stabilizing/flexibility 45-60 mins
Thursday	Intervals, 10 mins warm-up, 10x5 mins at 85-90% HRmax 3 mins jog between intervals, 10 mins warm-down	
Friday	Rest / cross training	Stabilizing/flexibility 45-60 mins
Saturday	Extensive endurance run, 90 mins	80% HRmax
Sunday	Long recovery jog, 240 mins	70% HRmax

Week 3 (@ 615 minutes)

Day	Session	Comments
Monday	Rest / cross training	
Tuesday	Extensive endurance run, 90 mins	80% HRmax
Wednesday	Rest / cross training	Stabilizing/flexibility 45-60 mins
Thursday	Intervals, 10 mins warm-up, 6x10 mins at 85-90% HRmax 5 mins jog between intervals, 10 mins warm-down	
Friday	Rest / cross training	Stabilizing/flexibility 45-60 mins
Saturday	Extensive endurance run, 120 mins	80% HRmax
Sunday	Extended recovery jog, 300 mins	70% HRmax

Week 4 (@ 435 minutes, recovery)

Day	Session	Comments
Monday	Rest / cross training	
Tuesday	Long recovery jog, 60 mins	70% HRmax
Wednesday	Rest / cross training	Stabilizing/flexibility 45-60 mins
Thursday	Intervals, 10 mins warm-up, 8x10 mins at 85-90% HRmax, 5 mins jog between intervals, 10 mins warm-down	
Friday	Rest / cross training	Stabilizing/flexibility 45-60 mins
Saturday	Long recovery jog, 60 mins	70% HRmax
Sunday	Long recovery jog, 180 mins	70% HRmax

Week 5 (@ 735 minutes)

Day	Session	Comments
Monday	Rest / cross training	
Tuesday	Extensive endurance run, 90 mins	80% HRmax
Wednesday	Rest / cross training	Stabilizing/flexibility 45-60 mins
Thursday	Intervals, 10 mins warm-up, 10x10 mins at 85-90% HRmax, 5 mins jog between intervals, 10 mins warm-down	
Friday	Rest / cross training	Stabilizing/flexibility 45-60 mins
Saturday	Extensive endurance run, 120 mins	80% HRmax
Sunday	Long recovery jog, 360 mins	70% HRmax

Week 6 (@ 930 minutes)

Day	Session	Comments
Monday	Rest / cross training	
Tuesday	Extensive endurance run, 120 mins	80% HRmax
Wednesday	Rest / cross training	Stabilizing/flexibility 45-60 mins
Thursday	Intervals, 10 mins warm-up, 8x15 mins at 85-90% HRmax, 10 mins jog between intervals, 10 mins warm-down	
Friday	Rest / cross training	Stabilizing/flexibility 45-60 mins
Saturday	Long recovery jog, 180 mins	70% HRmax
Sunday	Long recovery jog, 420 mins	70% HRmax

Week 7 (@ 450 minutes, tapering)

Day	Session	Comments
Monday	Rest / cross training	
Tuesday	Extensive endurance run, 90 mins	80% HRmax
Wednesday	Rest / cross training	Stabilizing/flexibility 45-60 mins
Thursday	Intervals, 10 mins warm-up, 5x10 mins at 85-90% HRmax, 5 mins jog between intervals, 10 mins warm-down	
Friday	Rest / cross training	Stabilizing/flexibility 45-60 mins
Saturday	Long recovery jog, 90 mins	70% HRmax
Sunday	Long recovery jog, 180 mins	70% HRmax

Week 8 (@ 870 minutes, tapering and race)

Day	Session	Comments
Monday	Rest / cross training	
Tuesday	Extensive endurance run, 60 mins	80% HRmax
Wednesday	Rest / cross training	Stabilizing/flexibility 45-60 mins
Thursday	Extensive endurance run, 60 mins with 3 accelerations 100 m from the finish	80% HRmax
Friday	Rest / cross training	Stabilizing/flexibility 45-60 mins
Saturday	Long recovery jog, 30 mins	Shake out legs
Sunday	Race, 720 minutes	

Depending on your level of fitness, this training plan should enable you to cover between 80 and 110 km in the 12 hours.

17.12 TRAINING FOR THE 24-HOUR RUN AND BEYOND

Prerequisites

For the 24-hour run and beyond, there is no universal training plan that works for everyone. This event cannot simply be approached with one single program. There are actually two different "camps" of 24-hour runners.

One camp trains exactly the same as for a 100 km, except that the long runs are extended slightly (to 80 or even 100 km). The other camp swears by high mileage on three or four consecutive days.

Neither camp excludes tempo training completely, although it is advisable to replace the interval workout with a longer run. The longer workouts on the weekend should be run at the target race pace.

The example training plan below is not based on my own experience but on the preparations of athletes I know, all of whom train according to a similar philosophy and aim for similar race results, which are usually well beyond 230 km in 24-hours.
This program therefore allows you to train for a goal of 180+ km.

Current performance level:	100 km below 10 hours should be achievable before starting the training plan.
Weekly time available:	7-20 hours
Training days per week:	5-6
Mileage:	80-205 km (50-127.4 miles)
Total mileage, incl. Race:	1,110 km (690 miles)
Cross-training:	e.g., cycling, ergometer, swimming, but at recovery pace

Week 1 (95 km)

Day	Session	Comments
Monday	Rest / cross training	
Tuesday	15 km intensive endurance run	80-85% HRmax
Wednesday	15 km extensive endurance run	75-80% HRmax
Thursday	15 km extensive endurance run	75-80% HRmax
Friday	Rest / cross training	
Saturday	20 km long recovery jog	Up to 70% HRmax
Sunday	30 km long recovery jog	Up to 70% HRmax

Week 2 (110 km)

Day	Session	Comments
Monday	Rest / cross training	
Tuesday	15 km tempo endurance run	85-90% HRmax
Wednesday	20 km extensive endurance run	75-80% HRmax
Thursday	15 km intensive endurance run	80-85% HRmax
Friday	Rest / cross training	
Saturday	30 km long recovery jog	Up to 70% HRmax
Sunday	30 km long recovery jog	Up to 70% HRmax

Week 3 (155 km)

Day	Session	Comments
Monday	Rest / cross training	
Tuesday	20 km tempo endurance run	85-90% HRmax
Wednesday	20 km extensive endurance run	75-80% HRmax
Thursday	15 km intensive endurance run	80-85% HRmax
Friday	20 km long recovery jog	Up to 70% HRmax
Saturday	40 km long recovery jog	Up to 70% HRmax
Sunday	40 km long reecovery jog	Up to 70% HRmax

Week 4 (80 km, recovery week)

Day	Session	Comments
Monday	Rest / cross training	
Tuesday	15 km intensive endurance run	80-85% HRmax
Wednesday	15 km extensive endurance run	75-80% HRmax
Thursday	10 km extensive endurance run	75-80% HRmax
Friday	Rest / cross training	
Saturday	20 km long recovery jog	Up to 70% HRmax
Sunday	20 km long recovery jog	Up to 70% HRmax

Week 5 (170 km)

Day	Session	Comments
Monday	Rest / cross training	
Tuesday	20 km tempo endurance run	85-90% HRmax
Wednesday	20 km extensive endurance run	75-80% HRmax
Thursday	20 km intensive endurance run	80-85% HRmax
Friday	20 km long recovery jog	Up to 70% HRmax
Saturday	40 km long recovery jog	Up to 70% HRmax
Sunday	50 km long recovery jog	Up to 70% HRmax

Week 6 (200 km)

Day	Session	Comments
Monday	Rest / cross training	
Tuesday	20 km tempo endurance run	85-90% HRmax
Wednesday	20 km extensive endurance run	75-80% HRmax
Thursday	20 km extensive endurance run	75-80% HRmax
Friday	30 km long recovery jog	Up to 70% HRmax
Saturday	50 km long recovery jog	Up to 70% HRmax
Sunday	60 km long recovery jog	Up to 70% HRmax

Week 7 (95 km, tapering)

Day	Session	Comments
Monday	Rest / cross training	
Tuesday	20 km intensive endurance run	80-85% HRmax
Wednesday	15 km extensive endurance run	75-80% HRmax
Thursday	10 km extensive endurance run	75-80% HRmax
Friday	Rest / cross training	
Saturday	20 km long recovery jog	Up to 70% HRmax
Sunday	30 km long recovery jog	Up to 70% HRmax

Week 8 (215 km, tapering and race –at least 180 km)

Day	Session	Comments
Monday	Rest / cross training	
Tuesday	15 km extensive endurance run	75-80% HRmax
Wednesday	10 km extensive endurance run	75-80% HRmax
Thursday	10 km long recovery jog	Up to 70% HRmax
Friday	Rest / cross training	
Saturday	Race	Up to 70% HRmax
Sunday	Race	Up to 70% HRmax

I wish you the best of luck in both training and racing!

I would prefer to start at 6:30 min/km pace, I would also monitor my heart rate and, if possible, not let it rise above 70% HRmax.. Wait and see what happens to it near the end of the race; in my experience, it is actually hard to get it to 70% at this point.

17.13 EXAMPLE TRAINING PLAN FOR A MULTIDAY RACE

Prerequisites

Several years of marathon training. Good basic conditioning training. The athlete(s) should be capable of running 2 marathons/ultras on the weekend occasionally ("double decker").

This training plan is intended for those who just want to finish, although successful multiday runners use very similar plans in terms of mileage, they run at different tempos. Vital in the preparation of multiday races, as well as getting used to running long distances every day, is the prevention of typical injuries such as shin splints and other orthopedic problems. To this end, it is worth counteracting any malposture and associated abnormal biomechanical stress by doing appropriate exercises and/or targeted strengthening exercises for the antagonist muscles that work against the "used" muscles (see also the chapters entitled "Maintaining Flexibility" and "Strengthening Exercises" in this book).

The tempo is deliberately kept slow. I have only included one workout that deliberately contained tempo work and which the athlete can run more or less intensively according to his needs and how he feels.

Core workouts are scheduled for the two weeks with high mileage (weeks 4 and 6). I have deliberately split the training in week 4 into two in order to be able to fit in such high mileage, and also to give the body the chance to recover a little between workouts. The week can in this way also be integrated into a "normal" working week, which still requires a great deal of discipline. I once incorporated such a week into my normal daily life and was quite flat the following week. Please remember to get enough sleep during these weeks.
The training plan is also ideally suited for the preparation of a 24-hour run and should allow you to achieve a thoroughly respectable result beyond the 160 km mark (it is hard to make a prognosis as much depends on the individual).

I have also deliberately scheduled Sunday as a rest day to allow you to spend time with your family, as such a time-intensive program requires a great deal of tolerance and understanding on their part.

Before starting training, you are strongly advised to undergo a sports medical check that should include at least a stress ECG and a heart ultrasound check.

Current performance level:	marathon level – "double-decker" level
Weekly training time available:	10-25 hrs
Training days per week:	4-6
Mileage:	from 70-210 km (43.5-130.5 miles)
Total mileage, incl. race:	1173 km (728.9 miles)
Cross training:	e.g., cycling, ergometer, swimming, but at recovery pace

Week 1 (105 km)

Day	Session	Comments
Monday	20 km recovery/extensive endurance run	
Tuesday	20 km recovery/extensive endurance run	
Wednesday	15 km fartlek	
Thursday	Rest / cross training	
Friday	20 km recovery/extensive endurance run	
Saturday	30 km recovery/extensive endurance run	
Sunday	Rest / cross training	

Week 2 (115 km)

Day	Session	Comments
Montag	20 km recovery/extensive endurance run	
Tuesday	20 km recovery/extensive endurance run	
Wednesday	15 km fartlek	
Thursday	Rest / cross training	
Friday	20 km recovery/extensive endurance run	
Saturday	40 km Long recovery jog	
Sunday	Rest / cross training	

Week 3 (125 km)

Day	Session	Comments
Monday	20 km recovery/extensive endurance run	
Tuesday	25 km recovery/extensive endurance run	
Wednesday	15 km fartlek	
Thursday	Rest / cross training	
Friday	25 km recovery/extensive endurance run	
Saturday	40 km Long recovery jog	
Sunday	Rest / cross training	

Week 4 (210 km)

Day	Session	Comments
Monday	10 km extensive endurance run	
Tuesday	20 km recovery/extensive endurance run	
Wednesday	2 x 20 km recovery/extensive endurance run (morning and evening)	
Thursday	2 x 20 km recovery/extensive endurance run (morning and evenings)	
Friday	2 x 25 km recovery/extensive endurance run (morning and evenings)	
Saturday	2 x 25 km recovery/extensive endurance run (morning and evenings)	
Sunday	Rest / cross training	

Week 5 (90 km)

Day	Session	Comments
Monday	Rest / cross training	
Tuesday	10 km extensive endurance run	
Wednesday	15 km fartlek	
Thursday	Rest / cross training	
Friday	20 km recovery/extensive endurance run	
Saturday	45 km long recovery jog	
Sunday	Rest / cross training	

Week 6 (160 km)

Day	Session	Comments
Monday	25 km extensive endurance run	
Tuesday	25 km recovery/extensive endurance run	
Wednesday	15 km fartlek	
Thursday	20 km recovery/extensive endurance run	
Friday	25 km recovery/extensive endurance run	
Saturday	50 km recovery/extensive endurance run	
Sunday	Rest / cross training	

Week 7 (70 km, tapering)

Day	Session	Comments
Monday	Rest / cross training	
Tuesday	15 km Recovery/Extensive endurance run	
Wednesday	25 km Recovery/Extensive endurance run	
Thursday	Rest / cross training	
Friday	20 km Recovery/Extensive endurance run	
Saturday	10 km long recovery jog	
Sunday	Rest / cross training	

Week 8 (298 km race)

Day	Session	Comments
Monday	Rest / cross training	
Tuesday	1st Stage Lindlar (55 km)	
Wednesday	2nd Stage Solingen (75 km)	
Thursday	3rd Stage Remscheid (58 km)	
Friday	4th Stage Kürten (65 km)	
Saturday	5th Stage Wipperfürth (45 km)	
Sunday	Sleep!	

© Thinkstock/iStockphoto/Fluid Illusion

18   (ULTRA) TRAIL RUNNING

Trail running means running off-road through the countryside. It really doesn't matter if the terrain is hilly or not, or even what the running surface is like. The important thing is to run through the countryside.

Trail running is currently undergoing something of a boom worldwide. Usually the surface underfoot is in its natural state and the terrain is hilly.

For the "trail community," though, a real trail race is longer, steeper and more difficult to run. For me personally, a good trail run is made by the surrounding countryside and the impressions that I gain there. It must of course be longer than 42,195 km (26.22 miles).

If we take the Ultratrail Mont Blanc (UTMB), for example, I find it hard to appreciate the surrounding countryside when running at night. I have run there through two nights and the focus was on the physical and mental challenge and less on the enjoyment of nature. However, during the daytime, the breathtaking beauty of the Mont Blanc massif more than compensated for the hardships.

I found other events that take place over several days and which are also signficantly shorter and more enjoyable, at least in terms of the enjoyment of nature.

So, if the terrain is not hilly, then we do not need a special chapter devoted to ultra trail training. The same training principles are applicable as for all flat courses as presented in this book.

Therefore, a specific preparation is only necessary if:

• the course is on uneven terrain and
• has a hilly profile.

The aim of training is to orient one's self to the conditions of the race. In other words, informing one's self about the elevation profile of the course and what the terrain is like underfoot. All this information can be found on the internet, just by entering the name of the race in a search engine. Better still, get in touch with somebody who has already run the race. Make sure that this person also actually finished the race; if they didn't, they can't tell you about the whole course! First browse through the reports of non-finishers in order to find the causes of their failure in order to avoid making the same mistakes yourself by making sure you have your own coping strategies in place (see also the Chapter on "Mental Aspects").

Once you have found out what the course is like, the next step is to study the local weather conditions. What should I expect at which altitude, time of year and time of day? What should I take with me? What can I leave or have left at the aid stations? Do I need a support crew? When and where?

And now the $64,000 question: **How do I train for the race?**

Which brings us back to the subject of this book. If I live in a similar environment (mountains), then it is of course easy to train in the mountains. I just leave my house and start running. Depending on my training condition and goal, I can incorporate altitude running into my endurance training.

If I have enough mountains, then I also usually have access to trails similar to those that must be mastered during the race. I just take a training plan that vaguely corresponds to the running time (planned race duration), eliminate the interval workout and embark on some intensive mountain workouts.

Unfortunately, not everyone lives in an area that resembles the race course, so I would like to give some alternatives. What do you do if you live in a lowland area but want to take part in the K78 Swiss Alpine Marathon, for example?

In this case, targeted training of the muscles solicited when running in the mountains is essential and should be trained at least once a week. If you live in hilly terrain or have hills nearby with a 5-15% gradient that you can train on that are about 500m long, it is a great idea to integrate them into your training plan. Just run up and down them several times (depending on your training condition and program). They are also a great place to do part of the long weekend run to prepare your muscles at least for the type of inclines in the race.

If you don't have this, you must find other ways of familiarizing your running muscles with the upcoming load. I prepared for the Ultratrail Mont Blanc (UTMB) with intensive step running. I found a high-rise building with at least five floors and just ran up and down the steps.

One training session consisted of a 2 km warm-up, 30-90 mins step running and at least 2 km warm-down jog. My heart rate during the step running was significantly higher than 90% HRmax. It is important to tackle each step individually, both going up and going down. I used this workout instead of the interval session, and it fulfilled its purpose admirably. It is often forgotten that it is actually running downhill that is the performance limiting factor in mountain ultrarunning, for the shock load for muscles, joints and tendons is huge. You should therefore be careful that the flight phase when running downhill is not too long so that the bodyweight (now several times your normal bodyweight!) is also cushioned well. You can only do this if you prepare the relevant muscles beforehand, which is precisely what running down steps does.

For the long run, if possible, include training races over hilly courses, or training runs over hilly terrain that may be in the vicinity (around 1 – 2 hours' drive away).

Your **running style** also requires special attention. Your posture should be as upright as possible. Runners often bend over and lean forwards, especially when running uphill. This reduces the funcionality of the diaphragm and therefore also that of the lungs. This in turn reduces the amount of oxygen that can be inhaled, which adversely affects performance and is particularly noticeable when running at altitudes where there is less oxygen in the atmosphere or the physical effort is high and the body needs more oxygen.

Hence the great importance of running with as upright a posture as possible when running uphill. So start during training and try to keep your upper body at an angle of 90° to the ground (as when running on the flat). Depending on the slope, that is not always possible. But try to maintain an optimal breathing volume. It is particularly important to focus on this when running very long distances.

When running downhill, your running speed can be easily controlled by your upper body posture. If you lean forward, i.e., let yourself fall, your speed increases. If you deliberately lean backward, your speed automatically drops. When running downhill, take into account that even it if is easier, the strain on your muscles is greater as they must absorb multiples of your bodyweight. Particularly in ultradistances, this can overload the muscles involved, possibly even causing you to retire prematurely from the race. It is therefore essential to practice running downhill in training in order to prepare these muscles in advance.

As far as the running surface is concerned, you should try to run on a similar surface to that in the race at least once a week. This may mean running beside the paths in a park, or in soft sand, or even along agricultural tracks where tractors have made the ground very uneven. Bridle paths are also an excellent training location. Everyone should be able to find something of this nature, wherever they live, so that regional disadvantages are made up for by ingenuity.

The last important point that is not so easy to prepare for is the altitude! However well trained you are, if you cannot cope with the altitude during the race, you will not be able to finish. So you need to know how to deal with the type of altitude you will encounter during the race. If you have never been at a high altitude before and the race is held at 6,000 feet above sea level, you must absolutely acclimatize yourself to a similar altitude before the race. It takes two or three weeks to acclimatize yourself, similar to altitude training. If this is unreastic time-wise, you should allow at least one week and get a feel for what running is like at a moderate speed at altitude. Should the time during the race at that altitude not be that long (e.g., the UTMB, where the altitude quickly drops to below 6,000 feet), then the race can be mastered by running at an appropriate pace on these sections of the course. Otherwise, acclimatization is essential and must be part of your race preparation. Ideally, you should familiarize yourself with the altitude with a stay in the mountains before the race.

    As far as equipment is concerned, you need to find out how you will be on the move and the weight of the equipment required. In the specialist stores, you will find that the lighter the kit, the more expensive it is. It is essential to plan beforehand what you need to take with you and for which reason. Is this a one-off experience for you or do you plan to run many trail runs in the future? I can tell you that most runners enjoy this kind of experience of nature so much that they can't wait for the next race!

    Finally, I would like to present two training plans for the ultratrail distances to help you prepare for the K78 Swiss Alpine (79 km / 49.1 miles and 2370 m / 7777.56 feet) and for the Western States 100 miles (100 miles and 5500 m / 18,044.62 feet).

Training plan for K 78 Swiss Alpine Marathon
Prerequisites

Current marathon performance level:	@ 3:30 hrs
Weekly training time:	7-14 hrs
Training days / week:	5
Weekly mileage:	68-116 (42.25-72.08 miles)
Total mileage incl. race:	@ 693 km (430.6 miles)
Cross training:	e.g., cycling, ergometer, swimming, but at recovery pace

NB: If possible, one of the sessions, ideally the step running, can be replaced by a suitable length run in hilly terrain.

Week 1 (@ 68 km / 42.25 miles)

Day	Session	Comments
Monday	Extensive endurance run, 10 km	80% HRmax
Tuesday	2 km warm-up jog, 20 mins step running, 2 km warm-down jog.	Step running up to 90% HRmax
Wednesday	Rest / cross training (whole body strengthening exercises, 30 mins)	
Thursday	2 km warm-up jog, 6 x 200m uphill runs, jog back (200 m), 2 km warm-down jog.	uphill runs up to 90% HRmax
Friday	Rest / cross training (whole body stretching program, 30 mins)	
Saturday	Extensive endurance run 15 km	80% HRmax
Sunday	Long recovery jog 30 km, hilly terrain if possible.If on the flat, include bridges, steps, etc., anywhere you must run up and down.	70% HRmax

Week 2 (@ 75 km / 46.6 miles)

Day	Session	Comments
Monday	Extensive endurance run, 12 km	80% HRmax
Tuesday	2 km warm-up jog, 30 mins step running, 2 km warm-down jog	Step running up to and exceeding 90% HRmax
Wednesday	Rest / cross training (whole body strengthening program, 30 mins)	
Thursday	2 km warm-up jog, 8 x 200m uphill runs, jog back (200 m), 2 km warm-down jog.	Uphill runs up to 90% HRmax
Friday	Rest / cross training (whole body stretching program, 30 mins)	
Saturday	Extensive endurance run 15 km	80% HRmax
Sunday	Long recovery jog 35 km, hilly terrain if possible. If on the flat, include bridges, steps, etc., anywhere you must run up and down.	70% HRmax

Week 3 (@ 89 km / 55.3 miles)

Day	Session	Comments
Monday	Extensive endurance run, 15 km	80% HRmax
Tuesday	2 km warm-up jog, 40 mins step running, 2 km warm-down jog.	Step running up to and exceeding 90% HRmax
Wednesday	Rest / cross training (whole body strengthening program, 30 mins)	
Thursday	2 km warm-up jog, 10 x 200m uphill runs, jog back (200 m), 2 km warm-down jog.	Uphill runs up to 90% HRmax
Friday	Rest / cross training (whole body stretching program 30 mins)	
Saturday	Extensive endurance run 20 km	80% HRmax
Sunday	Long recovery jog 40 km, hilly terrain if possible. On the flat, include bridges, steps, etc., anywhere you must run up and down.	70% HRmax

Week 4 (@ 70 km / 43.5 miles, recovery)

Day	Session	Comments
Monday	Extensive endurance run, 10 km	80% HRmax
Tuesday	2 km warm-up jog, 50 mins step running, 2 km warm-down jog.	Step running up to and exceeding 90% HRmax
Wednesday	Rest day / cross training (whole body strengthening program, 30 mins)	
Thursday	2 km warm-up jog, 12 x 200m uphill runs, jog back (200 m), 2 km warm-down jog	Uphill runs up to 90% HRmax
Friday	Rest / cross training (whole body stretching program, 30 mins)	
Saturday	Extensive endurance run 15 km	80% HRmax
Sunday	Long recovery jog 30 km, hilly terrain, if possible. If on the flat, include bridges, steps, etc., anywhere you must run up and down.	70% HRmax

Week 5 (@ 100 km / 62.14 miles)

Day	Session	Comments
Monday	Extensive endurance run, 17 km	80% HRmax
Tuesday	2 km warm-up jog, 60 mins step running, 2 km warm-down jog	Step running up to and exceeding 90% HRmax
Wednesday	Rest / cross training (whole body strengthening program, 30 mins)	
Thursday	2 km warm-up jog, 14 x 200m uphill runs, jog back (200 m), 2 km warm-down jog	Uphill runs up to 90% HRmax
Friday	Rest / cross training (whole body stretching program, 30 mins)	
Saturday	Extensive endurance run 20 km	80% HRmax
Sunday	Long recovery jog 45 km, hilly terrain, if possible. If on the flat, include bridges, steps, etc., anywhere you must run up and down.	70% HRmax

Week 6 (@ 116 km / 72.1 miles)

Day	Session	Comments
Monday	Extensive endurance run, 20 km	80% HRmax
Tuesday	2 km warm-up jog, 70 mins step running, 2 km warm-down jog.	Step running up to and exceeding 90% HRmax
Wednesday	Rest / cross training (whole body strengthening program, 30 mins)	
Thursday	2 km warm-up jog, 16 x 200m uphill runs, jog back (200 m), 2 km warm-down jog	Uphill runs up to 90% HRmax
Friday	Rest / cross training (whole body stretching program, 30 mins)	
Saturday	Extensive endurance run 25 km	80% HRmax
Sunday	Long recovery jog 50 km, hilly terrain, if possible. If on the flat, include bridges, steps, etc., anywhere you must run up and down.	70% HRmax

Week 7 (@ 75km / 46.6 miles, start tapering)

Day	Session	Comments
Monday	Extensive endurance run, 15 km	80% HRmax
Tuesday	2 km warm-up jog, 80 mins step running, 2 km warm-down jog.	Step running up to and exceeding 90% HRmax
Wednesday	Rest / cross training (whole body strengthening program, 30 mins)	
Thursday	2 km warm-up jog, 18 x 200m uphill runs, jog back (200 m), 2 km warm-down jog	Uphill runs up to 90% HRmax
Friday	Rest / cross training (whole body stretching program, 30 mins)	
Saturday	Extensive endurance run 15 km	80% HRmax
Sunday	Long recovery jog 30 km, hilly terrain, if possible. If on the flat, include bridges, steps, etc., anywhere you must run up and down.	70% HRmax

Week 8 (@ 100km, 62.14 miles, tapering and race)

Day	Session	Comments
Monday	Extensive endurance run, 10 km	80% HRmax
Tuesday	2 km warm-up jog, 20 mins step running, 2 km warm-down jog.	Step running up to and exceeding 90% HRmax
Wednesday	Rest / cross training (whole body strengthening program, 30 mins)	
Thursday	2 km warm-up jog, 6 x 200m uphill runs, jog back (200 m), 2 km warm-down jog	Uphill runs up to 90% Hrmax
Friday	Rest / cross training (whole body stretching program, 30 mins)	
Saturday	Swiss Alpine Marathon K78, 79.1 km / 49.15 miles	Good luck!
Sunday	Relax!	

Training plan for Western States 100 Mile Run

Prerequisites

Current performance level:	100km in 10 hours
Weekly training time:	8-17 hours (excluding race week)
Trainingstage/Woche:	5
Mileage:	86-150 km / 53.4-93.2 miles (excluding race week)
Total mileage, including race:	975 km / 605.84 miles
Cross training:	e.g., cycling, ergometer, swimming, but at recovery pace

Week 1 (@ 88km / 54.7 miles)

Day	Session	Comments
Monday	Extensive endurance run, 15 km	80% HRmax
Tuesday	2 km warm-up jog, 60 mins step running, 2 km warm-down jog.	Step running up to 90% HRmax
Wednesday	Rest / cross training (whole body strengthening exercises, 30 mins)	
Thursday	2 km warm-up jog, 14 x 200m uphill runs, jog back (200 m), 2 km warm-down jog.	uphill runs up to 90% HRmax
Friday	Rest / cross training (whole body stretching program, 30 mins)	
Saturday	Extensive endurance run 15 km	80% HRmax
Sunday	Long recovery jog 40 km, hilly terrain if possible. If on the flat include bridges, steps, etc., anywhere you must run up and down.	70% HRmax

Week 2 (@ 97km / 60.3 miles)

Day	Session	Comments
Monday	Extensive endurance run, 17 km	80% HRmax
Tuesday	2 km warm-up jog, 70 mins step running, 2 km warm-down jog.	Step running up to 90% HRmax
Wednesday	Rest / cross training (whole body strengthening exercises, 30 mins)	
Thursday	2 km warm-up jog, 16 x 200m uphill runs, jog back (200 m), 2 km warm-down jog,	uphill runs up to 90% HRmax
Friday	Rest / cross training (whole body stretching program, 30 mins)	
Saturday	Extensive endurance run 15 km	80% HRmax
Sunday	Long recovery jog 45 km, hilly terrain if possible. If on the flat, include bridges, ste1ps, etc., anywhere you must run up and down.	70% HRmax

Week 3 (@ 118km / 73.3 miles)

Day	Session	Comments
Monday	Extensive endurance run, 20 km	80% HRmax
Tuesday	2 km warm-up jog, 80 mins step running, 2 km warm-down jog.	Step running up to 90% HRmax
Wednesday	Rest / cross training (whole body strengthening exercises, 30 mins)	
Thursday	2 km warm-up jog, 18 x 200m uphill runs, jog back (200 m), 2 km warm-down jog,	uphill runs up to 90% HRmax
Friday	Rest / cross training (whole body stretching program, 30 mins)	
Saturday	Extensive endurance run 20 km	80% HRmax
Sunday	Long recovery jog 55 km, hilly terrain if possible. If on the flat include bridges, steps, etc., anywhere you must run up and down.	70% HRmax

Week 4 (@ 86km / 53.4 miles, recovery)

Day	Session	Comments
Monday	Extensive endurance run, 10 km	80% HRmax
Tuesday	2 km warm-up jog, 90 mins step running, 2 km warm-down jog.	Step running up to 90% HRmax
Wednesday	Rest / cross training (whole body strengthening exercises, 30 mins)	
Thursday	2 km warm-up jog, 20 x 200m uphill runs, jog back (200 m), 2 km warm-down jog.	uphill runs up to 90% HRmax
Friday	Rest / cross training (whole body stretching program, 30 mins)	
Saturday	Extensive endurance run 15 km	80% HRmax
Sunday	Long recovery jog 35 km, hilly terrain if possible. If on the flat include bridges, steps, etc., anywhere you must run up and down.	70% HRmax

Week 5 (@ 128km / 79.5 miles)

Day	Session	Comments
Monday	Extensive endurance run, 20 km	80% HRmax
Tuesday	2 km warm-up jog, 100 mins step running, 2 km warm-down jog.	Step running up to 90% HRmax
Wednesday	Rest / cross training (whole body strengthening exercises, 30 mins)	
Thursday	2 km warm-up jog, 22 x 200m uphill runs, jog back (200 m), 2 km warm-down jog.	uphill runs up to 90% HRmax
Friday	Rest / cross training (whole body stretching program, 30 mins)	
Saturday	Extensive endurance run 20 km	80% HRmax
Sunday	Long recovery jog 60 km, hilly terrain if possible. If on the flat include bridges, steps, etc., anywhere you must run up and down.	70% HRmax

Week 6 (@ 150km / 93.2 miles)

Day	Session	Comments
Monday	Extensive endurance run, 25 km	80% HRmax
Tuesday	2 km warm-up jog, 110 mins step running, 2 km warm-down jog.	Step running up to 90% HRmax
Wednesday	Rest / cross training (whole body strengthening exercises, 30 mins)	
Thursday	2 km warm-up jog, 24 x 200m uphill runs, jog back (200 m), 2 km warm-down jog.	uphill runs up to 90% HRmax
Friday	Rest / cross training (whole body stretching program, 30 mins)	
Saturday	Extensive endurance run 25 km	80% HRmax
Sunday	Long recovery jog 70 km, hilly terrain if possible. If on the flat, include bridges, steps, etc., anywhere you must run up and down.	70% HRmax

Week 7 (@ 119km / 73.9 miles, tapering)

Day	Session	Comments
Monday	Extensive endurance run, 20 km	80% HRmax
Tuesday	2 km warm-up jog, 120 mins step running, 2 km warm-down jog.	Step running up to 90% HRmax
Wednesday	Rest / cross training (whole body strengthening exercises, 30 mins)	
Thursday	2 km warm-up jog, 25 x 200m uphill runs, jog back (200 m), 2 km warm-down jog,	uphill runs up to 90% HRmax
Friday	Rest / cross training (whole body stretching program, 30 mins)	
Saturday	Extensive endurance run 20 km	80% HRmax
Sunday	Long recovery jog 50 km, hilly terrain if possible. If on the flat, include bridges, steps, etc., anywhere you must run up and down.	70% HRmax

Week 8 (@ 189km / 117.44 miles, tapering and race)

Day	Session	Comments
Monday	Extensive endurance run, 10 km	80% HRmax
Tuesday	2 km warm-up jog, 60 mins step running, 2 km warm-down jog.	Step running up to 90% HRmax
Wednesday	Rest / cross training (whole body strengthening exercises, 30 mins)	
Thursday	2 km warm-up jog, 10 x 200m uphill runs, jog back (200 m), 2 km warm-down jog.	uphill runs up to 90% HRmax
Friday	Rest / cross training (whole body stretching program, 30 mins)	
Saturday	Western States 100 miles / 161 km	Good luck!
Sunday	Western State 100 miles / 161 km	Enjoy your success!

© Thinkstock/iStockphoto/Fluid Illusion

19   EQUIPMENT

Heart rate monitor, clothing, shoes, GPS device/watch, evaluation software ... enough could be written on the subject of equipment to fill a whole bookcase.

However, I have restricted myself to presenting a brief overview of the topic and giving my personal recommendations. It makes no difference how far we run, whether in training or racing; when our equipment wears out, we can either buy new stuff more often or think about investing in higher quality products.

Running apparel

The right clothing is, of course, essential, and so-called functional clothing is now commonplace. These clothes are made of special man-made fibers that are very wind and water resistant but also breathable. This combination is hard to achieve. If on top of this, the fabric did not stink of sweat after every workout and one could wear it two or three times before it needed washing, it would be perfect!

We should be so lucky, for the clothing should also last as long as possible.

The fact is that this type of quality does not come cheap. It is also quite pointless to wear an outrageously expensive and very functional running top and put a jacket on top that might be wind and water proof but is not breathable. If the sweat cannot evaporate anywhere, then your clothes will end up sweaty, wet and stained with salt from your sweat.

In my opinion, at least for workouts lasting over 3 hours, proper clothing is essential. It should follow the onion principle, i.e., many layers that can be removed or put back on as required. The advantage of proper clothing is that it is very light and can easily be tied around your waist if necessary.

Jacket/Vest

This must be very high quality. A jacket should be wind and water proof but also keep you fresh. A cheap jacket just cannot do this, so unfortunately your wallet must take a hit. You should buy one jacket for summer and another for winter. The summer jacket should ideally have detachable sleeves so that it can also be worn as a vest between seasons.

The advantage of a high-quality jacket is definitely its durability. I have been using my favorite GORE running vest for five years with no problems.

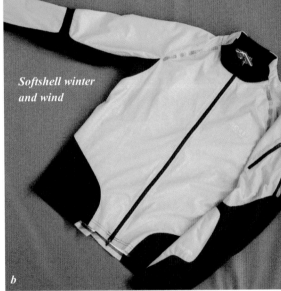

Softshell winter and wind

a   b

Tights/Tops

Here too, quality is key. A good fit (not too tight, not too loose) is essential. Also the seams should not be in places where blisters and possibly injuries can be caused by friction. Always try items of clothing on before purchasing and don't just rummage in the sale bin.

Tops should include at least 5 sleeveless tops, 2 long-sleeved tops and 2 winter long-sleeved tops, and more if training is very frequent. These items are sufficient for 3-5 workouts per week.

Summer clothing

Between seasons clothing

Winter clothing

For the trousers, I recommend at least 3 pairs of shorts (ideally tights), 2 long, light summer tights (or alternative/additional ¾ length tights) and at least one pair of warm winter tights.

Sports underwear should also be purchased if you regularly run for more than 60 minutes at a time. Cotton underwear soon gets stained with sweat, as do cotton socks or cotton bras for women. Bras should always be tried on for size. For unfamiliar items, just buy one first all and test it over a typical training distance.

Accessories

As well as clothing, there are also useful accessories for ultrarunners that can make training and racing a lot easier.

These include practical items such as caps, gloves or oversleeves. In my opinion, the cap should have a visor. One very light and thin one for summer and a warmer one for the winter is quite sufficient. Choose a cap with neck flap to protect the back of your neck from the sun. As for gloves, you will need a thinner pair for the between season period and a warmer pair for winter. Make sure they are functional too (i.e., wind and water resistant). Now very popular are the oversleeves worn by

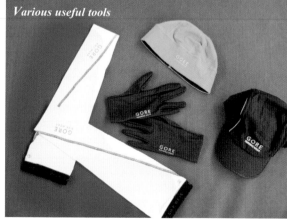

Various useful tools

Running in the snow and ice: snow chains for the feet

See and be seen; it might save your life one day

a

b

cyclists. Particularly in ultrarunning, races can start very early in the morning or even at night (e.g., Biel), when it can be quite chilly. As there is no time to change or take off clothes during a race, these oversleeves are a great way of converting a t-shirt into a long-sleeved top. They can easily be removed, folded up and put in a pocket or hydration pack or belt when no longer needed.

Recently, compression garments have become very popular. They are intended to improve lymph flow, thus allegedly increasing performance levels and speeding up recovery if they are worn for a while after the end of the race. I had good experiences with CEP socks when I had slight calf muscle problems during a multi-day race once. During the stage the following day, I put these socks on again and was able to complete the following 3 stages with no problems at all. Fellow runners tell me that they only put the socks on after a race and wear them for several hours. they feel that this significantly enhances recovery. I think that each person should experiment to see if they benefit or not.

Drinking bottle/belt/backpack

Essential for long training runs.

In your hand or in your belt, whichever you prefer

The longer the course, the more problematic the issue of fluid and food intake. Of course, I can choose my training runs so that I run past my house every 5 km. But I think that this would become boring after a while. Especially in summer, it is advisable to take a bottle of water even for a 60-minute run.

Drinking bottles usually have a capacity of about 1 pint / 0.5 liter. It is a good idea to include a gas station or grocery store in your training route. If you are out in the forest, the bottle will be empty after about 10 km at the latest and, if there is no good spring handy, the return or onward journey will be agony.

For such long runs, a hydration pack is particularly suitable. For the ultrarunner, a hydration pack with a drink bladder capacity of at least 4 pints (usually enough for 30 km, except during extreme heat). Ideally, as well as the compartment for the drinks bladder, it should also have another storage compartment in which to put paper tissues, vaseline or bag balm and the odd energy bar or gel. Also proven to be very useful if the backpack is suitably constructed, are perhaps one or two small storage pockets in the front where you keep a camera or cell phone as well as the next snack easily at hand. I personally swear by the NATHAN hydration pack, which has all these features. It is also important to be able to try out the pack before buying, or at least to wear it for a while inside the store.

Heart rate monitors and GPS watches

There are a great many different models on the market. As the price range is very wide, you should work out exactly what you need and want before you buy.

Cell phone or heart rate monitor, the choice is yours...

If you still have a cheap discount model when you start running because you don't want to run above a certain heart rate, models that are suitable for ambitious ultrarunners are more sophisticated and more expensive.

It is a good idea to do a needs analysis. The ultrarunner the following features are usually essential:

- good display readability, even in rain or darkness,
- long battery life / measuring time,
- accurate data (ECG-accurate measurement),
- adjustable heart rate zones,

- easy to use, even when running and wearing gloves,
- coded transmitter (important when running in a group and in races) and
- possibility for subsequent training and race analysis on the computer.

Also important for ultrarunners who like to run off-road are:
- distance measurement and
- distance recording by GPS or other system.

For elite runners:
- training planning,
- training management and
- implementation

It is important to have the right programming methods for the right workouts.

If in the past it was enough to just keep a handwritten training diary/log, nowadays everything is analyzed and recorded on computer. Usually the heart rate manufacturer provides a compatible software program that generally also contains the all-important training management and analysis features.

On the Internet, there are many free or very reasonably priced software solutions for this purpose. Of course there are also a number of smart phone apps, but these are often unsuitable for ultradistances due to their limited battery life.

Version 2 is still available as a free download, but a fee of €35 must be paid for the latest version 3, which is still very reasonable. Check out the website: http://zone-fivesoftware/sporttracks for more information about the features of the software. It is possible to import to almost all training computers.

Shoes must withstand a lot, especially for ultra-runners.

Running shoes

The runner's most important piece of equipment? Yes, very probably.

Although it is pointless if my shoes are comfortable

and functional if I get friction burns from wearing the wrong clothing.

The market is simply enormous. Go for a high quality product, but remember that appearances can be deceptive and all that glitters is not gold.

Running shoes should be bought in a specialist store, ideally where you can get professional advice and there is a treadmill on which to try out the shoes.

So how can you tell if the sales assistant is knowledgeable? First, you can ask him which sports he practices, and if he says running, you can also ask which kind of running and how long for. I have often received slightly irritated answers to these questions and in those cases, I have just left the store. Why do I ask these questions? For example, if the sales assistant is just a track or middle distance runner (up to 800m), he will have a great knowledge of spikes but his personal experience of the "right" road racing shoes will be rather limited. He may well have run the odd 10 km, but that is usually it for the average middle distance runner.

If he is a serious 10 km runner, or even farther, you can assume that he knows what road racing shoes feel like. If he runs the marathon or longer, he definitely has the right experience to be able to advise an ultrarunner.

A good running shoe sales assistant will also ask about your old shoes. Why? It is important to know what type of shoes you have used before and the sole profile will also give information about your running style. So take your old running shoes with you!

A treadmill analysis is essential to help you select the right shoes. You should start by running barefoot (with socks) on the treadmill. Run at your usual running speed and hold it for 3-4 minutes. You should be used to running on a treadmill so that you are able to run smoothly and naturally. This should be followed by a thorough analysis of the video recording of the test. The sales assistant should be able to describe the running gait accurately, including any foot misalignment and recommend appropriate running shoes based on the analysis.

There are various different types of running shoes:
• neutral shoes
• stability shoes
• shoes for overpronation
• shoes for supination
• racing shoes (also called lightweight trainers) and
• spikes

The selection of running shoes is not without controversy.

I would only rarely recommend shoes for overpronation (rolling inward of the ankle) and supination (marked foot strike with the outside edge of the foot). This should only happen in the case of a very slight malposition. For more severe misalignment, an orthopedic specialist or podiatrist should be consulted. When selecting an orthopedic specialist or podiatrist, it is important that he asks about your old shoes and that he too is a serious runner. He will usually prescribe the wearing of orthotic insoles that are individually adapted to your feet. However, be careful not to just get a prescription, you also need a diagnosis. Ideally the orthopedist should observe your running gait on a treadmill. There are also specialized running stores that offer regular, free diagnoses by orthopedists and orthopedic shoe manufacturers. Just look out for them.

If you do have a foot misalignment, you need to buy neutral shoes. Heavier runners (over 176 lb) require a stabilizing shoe. The regular insole should then be replaced with your personalized orthotic insole.

If you do not have a foot misalignment, go for neutral or stabilized shoes (for runners weighing more than 176 lb).

Even ultrarunners weighing less than 176 lb should consider buying a pair of stabilized shoes. As training and racing time can exceed five or six hours, shoes may need to be changed, and the constant stress on the feet is very tiring for the foot muscles and the sensitive ligament system and bone structure. Stabilized shoes are recommended as a way of preventing this fatigue and resulting injuries via a gentle minimal medial support (see also Chapter 14).

The ultrarunner should possess at least four pairs of running shoes:
• two pairs of neutral shoes
• one pair of stabilizing shoes
• one pair of trail shoes

You should also buy several brands so your feet can alternate between different kinds of footbed. The serious ultrarunner who also likes to run the odd fast 10 km or half-marathon should also purchase a pair of racing shoes that are considerably lighter than the usual, well-cushioned running shoes.

When it comes to cushioning, it doesn't matter whether it is made of gel, foam or air. It is also important that the shoes are a good fit from the start and that there are no pressure points. Ignore the advice: "you can run them in, it's rubbish! Your running shoes should feel comfortable straightaway.

As a general rule, shoes should not be reworn for at least 24 (and up to 48) hours after running, as it takes this long for the shoe material to "recover". So, daily runners, don't wear the same shoes two days in a row.

20   RACE ANECDOTES

20.1   SPARTATHLON 2009

I am standing in front of the Acropolis for the third time waiting for the start of the Spartathlon. On the two previous occasions (2006 and 2007), I didn't manage to finish the race. I had to throw in the towel very early on. Last year, I also registered to take part, but as my preparation training wasn't going very well, I didn't fly to Greece at all.

This year, training didn't go according to plan either. After a very good start to the year with a new best time over 50 km in Hanau-Rodenbach (Germany)

and successfully finishing the "Über die Höhen im Bergischen Land" (a 5-day multi-stage race starting in Cologne, Germany), the middle of the year went anything but according to plan. I wanted to use the German 24-hour Championships is Stadtoldendorf to gain self-confidence for my participation in the Spartathlon. Runners had to cover at least 180 km, and my pre-race target was 200 km. I had run farther in training than ever before, lots of long runs and occasional speed work. So all in all, a good combination for my planned success.

But it was not to be. After 8-9 hours, the problems started. Aching feet, empty head and motivation gone. After more excruciating hours, I dropped out. I then rejoined the race and walked for another lap, but was totally disappointed with myself and my apparent lack of motivation for the whole race.

I made up my mind that I would never return to Sparta this or any other year. After I took my socks off, my ankle also swelled up the size of a handball. I had had enough of running.

After resting for a week at home with a zinc oxide bandage and my feet up, then I took my first running steps, and I felt pretty good. So, as I had entered the Berlin 24-hour race, I just did gentle training for the next 12 days with no problems and then traveled to Berlin for the race. Famous last words; after 3 hours the pain returned and I dropped out after 8. Not exactly motivating either.

My Spartathlon dream was now dead. The following day I went to see Dr. Dietmar Göbel in Donaueschingen and had my problem with the dorsal flexor looked at for the first time. It was a 10-hour journey just to see a doctor, but I would do it again in an instant! Dietmar did not make any promises and say that I shouldn't write off the Spartathlon. But there was no way I could complete my training plan as it was. My dorsal flexor would not hold up. For the following four weeks, I received strict mileage targets that I had to meet. Then, Dietmar allowed me to run no more than 120 km (75 miles) per week to prepare for the Spartathlon. I did not think this was enough, but I stuck to it. But then my performance started to improve and I thought: "Well, maybe you can go after all, just wait and see. And if you don't run, just go to support Dagmar."

Then, on a training run around Wipperfürth, Dagmar was bitten on the heel by a stupid dog. The whole thing swelled up and Dagmar had to forget about the Spartathlon. She had just won the STUNT 100

in Sibesse and shortly afterward finished the Cologne Path nonstop race over 171 km (106.26 miles), so was in really good shape and now this.

Yes, I was now faced with the decision of whether to drop the whole thing altogether or just carry on training and hope that things would work out. Dagmar left me completely free to train and every week I grew more confident that maybe I could make it. I just trained to Dietmar's mileage targets. As a final test for Sparta, at the last minute, I entered the Six Hours Bachtal Run in Remscheid-Lennep, a challenging circular course that I wanted to run quite gently. The first four hours I ran very evenly just below 6 min / km split times and then increased the pace a little for the final hours of the race. I managed over 63 km, without pushing myself at all. So I decided that I would definitely fly to Greece.

Everything was paid for. One week later there was another easy marathon during the Liège 24-hours in Belgium, and I was counting the days until the plane took off.

Somehow it was now clear to me that I would be able to do it. I have no idea why. Also, mentally I tried to approach the event differently than usual. I kept saying to myself: "Everyone goes through bad times, it's normal and when it's your turn, just get through it and don't get bogged down in negative thoughts!" It sounds easy, but I really had to believe it before I could start the race after such bad experiences.

A few days before the flight, we arranged that Dagmar's older daughter Myriam would look after my little girl Fabienne. Next we found ourselves in Cologne airport on September 23, 2009, where we met with Nina Schumacher, who was supporting Dr. Göbel. We also met up with Ulrich Meiniger and Holger Sakuth. We were all very excited already about our upcoming adventure.

After checking in at the Hotel London, Dagmar and I were assigned a room at the Palmyra Beach Hotel.

So we had to walk another 500 yards from one hotel to the other with all our luggage where we finally checked in. In 2006 and 2007, I stayed in different hotels. I think that I would be a good hotel guide for the Glyfada area!

As the reception area of the Hotel London is a regular meeting point. We spent some time there chatting with old running friends. Oh yes, the race packs were there too, of course! But they didn't want to give them out at first. I still had not submitted my doctor's certificate. How embarrassing! Me, of all people, the team manager of the German Ultramarathon Foundation for the Spartathlon office where I had the task of checking these for the German participants and then making sure they were aware of them. Luckily, this year too we were able to take part in a medical study for which we needed to give blood here in the hotel and then after the finish of the race in Sparta. In return, after a short medical check-up, I got the "ok" to run in the Spartathlon and my race pack was handed over. So it is true that you can pay for many things with blood!

The time until we left by bus for the start on the Acropolis I just spent resting and eating. We had planned no sightseeing activities so that I could just concentrate on the race. Our great sightseeing tour was buying my cola bottle in the nearby supermarket.

Otherwise, our thoughts just revolved around not missing the mealtimes and giving in the drop bags.

Based on my experience from previous years, from km 30 onward I prepared a drop bag every 10 km. Each plastic bag contained a 1 pint bottle of Coca-Cola, 1 g of salt and an imported snack from Aldi, Germany! Also, every 40 km I included bag balm in case I needed to anoint myself again and new plasters for my nipples, as well as a sachet of magnesium every 60 km. I put my night clothing at km 100.5, which consisted of long tights, a long-

Depositing the drop bags with personal items

sleeved top, a thin jacket and finally a headlamp. At base camp at the Sangaspass, I also left another pair of trail shoes and a thicker jacket, while at km 202.1, I left a complete running outfit, including socks and underwear.

For the race itself, I decided against a hydration pack, like the last time, but instead went for a drink belt with a bottle compartment in which I could always store the bottle of Coke from km 30 onward, and I wanted to hold a drinking bottle in my hand. Luckily, Dagmar had given me an original Amphipod bottle that was shaped to fit my hand perfectly. I could carry this with me the whole time without it bothering me! In this bottle, I just put water that I could sip as I ran to avoid overloading my stomach. At the same time, I used it for cooling my head by splashing it on my face from time to time.

So, the whole race was prepared for. It didn't matter if the aid stations were now as well equipped as in 2006, or if there would still be water after 40 km, as in 2007; I had left what I needed along the course and was, apart from the water, completely self-sufficient. I also had €20 cash with me so that I could buy something if necessary.

My conclusion before the race: I would always be this organized in the future! Also the reassurance of knowing that I would find something nice every 10 km, even if I didn't need it, made me much more relaxed!

And so on Friday morning at 6am on September 25, 2009, we travelled in the bus to the Acropolis. Dagmar had decided not to take the bus to Sparta but to accompany Nina in supporting Dietmar.

In this way, we thought we might get to see each other occasionally, and Dagmar could familiarise herself with the course in preparation for her participation the following year. So both of them traveled to the Acropolis in a rental car behind the buses. Nina followed an empty bus that had nothing to do with the Spartathlon! After 20 minutes, she realized her mistake and they both arrived at the start in time but in a real panic! I was equally stressed while I was waiting for Dagmar and a few running friends, because they wanted to give her some valuables for her to take with her to Sparta. Dagmar also had the German flag for the German team photo in front of the Acropolis. Luckily, they both turned up about 8-9 minutes before the start of the race. We quickly took the team photo and joined the throng at the starting line. I managed to snatch a good luck kiss for the 153 miles that were to come and then we were off.

The start in front of the Acropolis theatre. Only 153 miles to go!

On the path down from the Acropolis, we ran on large flag stones that required us to take care that we didn't trip. I had decided to run strictly by heart rate right from the start, at a maximum of 140 bpm. With a maximum heart rate of 197 bpm, this was 72%, and I could always run well below 6 min/km splits like this in training.

It was still quite cool (68° F), and I hoped that the temperature wouldn't rise too much before km 40. Unfortunately, this was not to be. Already at km 20 the sun was blazing down and the temperature rose constantly. So I decided to increase my limit to 150 bpm. If this meant that I couldn't achieve the time limit for the first station, then so be it.

However, I was able to run 6 min/km splits quite easily and reached km 40 after 4:02 h. It was now very hot and the temperature must have been around 86°F. The sun burned and shadows were practically non-existant. My long training runs in the mid-day heat were paying off. I normally hated the heat but my idea of running with my "cooling bottle" in my hand and the preparation seemed to be working out, because I covered the next 40 km with 1:30 h to spare. I deliberately took my foot off the gas and kept my heart rate below 150 bpm, even significantly below 145 bpm. From then on, I could take the hills in my stride, which also saved a bit of energy that I would definitely need later on.

Meanwhile, I had also been able to see Dagmar on the coast road. Nina and Dagmar had made a quick stop and it was hard for me not to run up to them but that could have been classified as unfair assistance. We could only be looked after at quite specific points, so just wave and run on. I went on to run past my previous exit points at km 60 (2006) and km 70 (2007). Not this time!

Then at 3.50 pm, the great moment arrived. I was running across the streets of Corinth. My first important intermediate goal. Running over the bridges and seeing this imposing building was a very special experience. Somehow I knew here that I had done it and I said to myself: "Don't get too cocky, still a few more miles to go!"

Then things went a little less well after Corinth. At the first big control station where supporters are allowed to care for their runners, I was hoping to see Dagmar but unfortunately she had already left. Dietmar seemed to have got off to a good start. I reached Corinth at about 4:03 pm, i.e., 27 minutes before the cut-off! This was already 15 minutes better than I had anticipated. I was amazed at how many people settled down and made themselves comfortable here. Massages, long breaks, change of clothing, etc. I didn't see the point. Firstly, I was able to gain a good cushion here and then I would waste all that time to be just within the cut-off? No, I treated Corinth just like any other aid station and just kept on going. So, while I was in 274th place at km 40, at Corinth I myself up in 222nd place.

The following section of the course was really very pleasant to run found past olive and citrus groves, slightly hilly and varied terrain. My next goal was the 100 km mark. At the checkpoint at km 100.5, I had deposited my first "night kit" I arrived there after about 11:40 h and therefore had a cushion of about 30 minutes before the cut-off. I changed my running vest, smeared bag balm on the "important" places and donned the head lamp, even though it was still light. That was actually my only longish pit stop on the whole course. I estimate that the whole procedure took 7-10 minutes.

After 15:01 h I reached ancient Nemea, (km 124). It was now pitch black and I found myself in 156th place. I think that in Corinth alone I had made up at least 30 places because I had just treated it as a normal aid station.

Streets of Corinth

I now had the Sangas Pass in my sights as the next goal, firstly, because I had never run farther than 158 km before (UTMB) and secondly, because there were more rumors about these mountain trails than about any other part of the course. At around km 150, Thomas Eberhardt was lying on a lounger at a aid station. He had unfortunately returned his race number, which meant he could not return to the course. He wished me good luck and shortly afterward I began the long climb to the Sangas base camp. The trail twisted and turned up the mountain. Somewhere there in a village (I can't remember the name), I met Regina Berger-Schmitt, who had quite a few circulation problems and was unfortunately forced to drop out shortly afterward. Even though I cursed the long climb, things were still going well for me, and I really enjoyed running the mountain trail. On the climb, you could see almost the whole time where you were going and somehow the pass never seemed to get any nearer. Then the trail went down under the highway and the base camp lay before me. Here I was very pleasantly surprised. Dagmar was still there, and I was so pleased to see her. Dietmar had to stay there a little longer and he had stomach problems. Finally a kiss and back off to the mountains. As I had not yet had any problems with my shoes, I kept my trail shoes on and just took a thicker jacket with me.

Now came the infamous 2 km of the Sangas Pass, and in hindsight, I must say that it was a very beautiful section of the course. If I were to run the Spartathlon again, I would really look forward to it. I covered the 2 km climb in less than 30 minutes and overtook a few runners on the way. Just before I ran over the crest, we ran under a power line and a strong wind blew up. I quickly put the thin jacket on and did not stop for long at the checkpoint but started the descent immediately. It is not very pleasant up there now. I admired the volunteers who stayed up there the whole night! The way down is a nightmare. Although the trail is wider, it is very uneven with a lot of scree that made it almost impossible to run. I swear almost as much as during the ascent on the hairpin trails. But better to arrive cautiously down in the village of Sangas than to run a risk and perhaps twist an ankle or fall. In Sangas, we went back to running on the roads, which is a bit more boring but at least we could run again. I now alternated constantly between running and walking, making sure that I always arrived 30 minutes before the cut-off and take no risks time-wise. What good would that do? Over 160 km now lay behind me, I have conquered Sangas and nothing is going to jeopardize my chance of success!

My next goal is the transit performance for 24 hours. I had calculated beforehand that ideally I could be in Nestani, at km 172, at 7 am. And so it happened. I reached Nestani at 6:48 am. As well as the joy of seeing Dagmar again there, I hear that Dietmar has had to drop out. I was convinced before the race that he would finish, but that is the Spartathlon for you. Even for "certain finishers," there is no guarantee. I change my long-sleeved top for the DUV Spartathlon running shirt.

Another kiss of encouragement and here too I am wary of stopping and resting for too long. I am now in 132nd place. It is slowly getting light. I run past Ralf Simon at some point, who has had to drop out. On the course section between Corinth and Nestani, I was constantly passing Bertram Glogger, Ulrich Meiniger and Holger Sakuth[35]. We did not run far together but gave each other some words of encouragement. The kids in the towns and villages along the way were great too. Who else would ask runners for their autographs well into the night?!

My next intermediate goal is the 200 km mark. A magical figure. Running and/or walking 200 km without stopping. Maddness! After about 28 hours, I reach this mark and rejoice. What will keep me going now? And, I still feel good!

Now, just over the distance of a marathon left. Unfortunately, coming up is a section of the course that cannot be considered one of the nicest. It starts with a few more miles uphill, and running up is out of the question. Then absolutely endless hilly up and down sections. The whole time we ran along these highways, sometimes with and sometimes without breakdown lanes. Great care is required around the curves because the truck and automobile drivers like to take them very tightly. It has also been raining for a while.

Sometimes it's just showers and sometimes pouring. I have stopped swearing. On a few bridges, I stop for a moment and yell: "I don't give a ****! I am coming, so rain as hard as you want!" Followed by a loud: "SPARTAAAAAAA!" Something inside

---

[35] Bertram Glogger, from Augsburg: the database specialist is not only a passionate cross-country skiier, but he also helps actively in the work on the DUV statistics database; Ulrich Meiniger and Holger Sakuth: they know each other through their work as tax consultant and auditor, but come from Cologne and Eisenach and can very often be found running together in various running events of all sorts of lengths.

Statue of King Leonidas in Sparta
(Finish of the Spartathlon)

It took me 35:24:46 hours and I finished in 117th place. 190 out of 320 did not finish. This time, I've done it! Never again! Never again? Whoknows?

Then off to the medical tent. My shoes and socks are taken off and my feet washed with a disinfectant. Slippers on and plastic covers over the shoes. But what's this? I am weighed and a lady I know from the London Hotel from the medical team wants to take a blood sample. Damn! They haven't forgotten. For my medical certificate, I also promised to give a blood sample after the finish! And a promise is a promise!

We then got a taxi back to our hotel. Dagmar had already taken our things up to the room. I slowly get ready, for afterward on the marketplace, is the victory ceremony and this time, as a finisher, I have to go right in front of the stage. In 2006 and 2007, we looked on and admired these finishers. Now I would be sitting there with others admiring us.

The finale is a huge victory ceremony in Athens, which takes place on Monday evening at a lovely venue. Each and every finisher is called up and honored. A very fitting finale.

me wants to say: "Olbrich, you have a screw loose!" and then I say: "So what? I want to finish!"

I have now been running for a while with blisters on my softened feet. Shall I take a look? No! Just keep going. After 222.5 km, I have moved up to 117th place. At this point, 190 runners are no longer in the race and there are only 24 km to go until Sparta. I have no more than 4 hours to go. Fantastic! I meet Anke Drescher on this section of the course. She is having problems but somehow she manages to produce a final spurt. She will get to the finish well before me. I don't want to race her. Up to now, I have run mainly alone and set my own pace and that's how I want to carry on.

Then at some point it arrives – the final incline! I had been expecting it a few miles back. Unfortunately, the course profile on the Sparta side doesn't really add up? For the last 11 km are mainly downhill! It doesn't matter. I realize that suddenly I have only another 20 minutes to go until the limit. I am constantly overtaken by a small group and then I overtake them again at the aid stations.

155 km (96.31 miles), at an altitude of 8,500 m (27887 feet), non-stop

After a year's wait, we are finally returning to Chamonix. My friend Frank, who intends to run, Walter, who will support us, and I leave Cologne on Wednesday morning. After Frank dropped out last year at km 117 in Champex Lac, and I dropped out at km 42 in Les Chapieux, this year we were determined to finish the whole course. Walter also said that he was prepared to take care of us during the race this year.

After a long trip, we arrived in Chamonix that evening. Frank excelled himself once again as quartermaster and found a very nice apartment in the town center. We dropped off our bags

In the rooms, we and gazed in awe at Mont Blanc and the fantastic mountain scenery. For the first time, I started to feel uneasy. As we knew from the previous year how expensive it was to stay in Chamonix, this time we were better prepared and had brought all our food for a week with us. Of course, including the most important food of all, Kölsch beer!

The next day, we were able to collect our starting documents from the Chamonix ice rink. After checking with Walter that morning about which aid stations he would be able to meet us at during the race, we went to the starting card desk. This year, the compulsory equipment had to be checked before we could be given our starting number. Luckily, Kunibert Schmitz, the soldier from Cologne (see Isarlauf anecdote) had phoned us to warn us, otherwise we would have had to go back to our apartment, as there was no reference to it in the information we had received.

At the desk, t-shirts were being given out again. No one could say that this race was not good value for money. The price of ▯70 ($90) included 44 hours of care and course service, as well as an appropriate finishers' present from The North Face (expensive) at each stage stop. This year, there was even electronic timing and monitoring by a chip on the back of the starting number. After having my equipment checked, we had to sign a form saying that we had not used any doping products (did the imported Kölsch count?) and also that we promised to take the compulsory equipment to the race. Then off to collect our starting numbers and latest information about the race, try on our t-shirts and then quickly check out the small ultrarunning trade fair.

The next day we had a lie-in, then a quick visit to Les Houches (the first of the aid stations), lunch in the apartment and a nice afternoon nap. We were gradually getting nervous. We wanted to skip the official briefing. Edgar Kluge, who had been staying with us since the previous day, went along, which was a good thing as we learned that before the start, every runner had to be scanned, so we had to allow enough time for this. So, the lesson is to never miss a briefing!

We slowly got ourselves ready, packed our bags for the two stage stops to where they would be transported (Courmayeur, at km 73 and Champex Lac at km 117). We dropped off our bags and then headed for the start, which this year was directly in front of the Tourist Office, about 160 yards from last year's start.

We had arranged not to meet Walter until La Fouly, at km 100. Frank and I thought that until then we should make it under our own steam in order to have a realistic chance of finishing the race. Initially ,I was skeptical, as in the previous year, the aid stations were sometimes badly equipped,

But, Frank was right. So after the start, Walter was free until the late afternoon of the following day, and he wanted to use it for a mountain tour. We calculated that it would take us about 20 hours to reach La Fouly.

Then before we knew it, we were standing at the start. The starting signal was given after a delay of about 5 minutes, and we slowly moved off. Frank and I wanted to try to run together the first night, but then we discussed that each of us should do his own thing if the other's pace wasn't right.

It was an impressive sight; well over 1,000 starters were setting off in the evening twilight. Frank and I enjoyed the start. We went through Chamonix and then toward Les Houches, the location of the first aid station, and we knew that directly afterward was the first steep uphill section of the course. So, we ran very prudently, as this was not the place to make up time.

During this section, we were overtaken by Stefan, Markus and Wolfgang from Cologne. Stefan's wife Andrea was also running with them but only wanted to run part of the course. Wolfgang had decided to run the first 117 km up to Champex Lac. We greeted each other and carried on running.

After the first aid station, we had to climb about 650 m (2132.5 feet) in 5 km. I was glad to see the excellently equipped aid station at the Col de Voza (at about 1,653 m / 5 423.22 feet above sea level) the start of the climb. Fantastic! Frank was just too strong on the mountain and the idea of running together during the first night was forgotten. Frank stormed ahead on, and I crawled up slowly!

From the Col de Voza, the course descended to Les Contamines (km 24), at an altitude of about 1,121m (3,677.82 feet) above sea level, the location of the second aid station and of the first cut-off time to be observed (up to 2am). Here I had an absolutely uneasy feeling as it was where I had torn my ligaments the previous year and then had to retire at km 42. Shortly before Les Contamines,

Andrea overtook me. She seemed to be going well and trotted nimbly past me. At the aid station itself, Frank was waiting, and we wanted to try and see if we could run a few miles together. Andrea agreed and off we went. Until km 28, we ran relaxed on the flat along a stream. The other two were just a touch too fast for me, and I let them go on ahead without me. After all, I knew what was coming ... from km 28, there was another 1,250 m (4101 feet) to climb over a distance of about 9 km (5.6 miles). So stay cool, Wolfgang!

The third big aid station in La Balme, at km 32, was also really appreciated. Here there was a fabulous night scene of runners equipped with headlamps. So many crazy people! The view up the mountain, on the other hand, was rather sobering!

At km 37 we reached Croix Bonhomme (around 2,479 m / 8133.2 feet above sea level. The previous year, I enjoyed a nice hot soup in the cabin there, because it was soooo cold at the time. But this time I was going really well and I just wanted to keep going after passing the check point there. The course now went downhill toward Les Chapieux, at km 42 (about 1,549 m / 5082 feet above sea level), where I dropped out last year. But in hindsight, this wasn't all bad, as I met Elisabeth Herms-Lübbe and Bernhard Sesterheim from Leiwen. This year, I enjoyed the "run-in" there and feasted on a hot meal and, of course, delicious beer! ☺

But what comes next after running downhill from altitude? That's right, another uphill climb to the Col de la Saigne (ca. 2,516 m / 8255 feet above sea level). This time, a climb of just 1,000 m / 3281 feet and more over about 11 km / 6.8 miles. The Col de la Saigne is also on the Italian border.

As I ran down the mountain, the sun rose slowly to reveal a breathtaking view. Up to Lac Combal, at km 59, we descended another 500 m / 1640 feet down to an altitude of 1,975 m / 6480 feet above sea level and the location of the next big aid station. The downside: afterward there was another 2 km / 1.25 mile climb up to Arète Mont Favre at about 2435 m / 7989 feet. Ouch!

Now downhill to km 72 at Courmayeur. The only downer in ideal running weather and mountain scenery: the aid station at Col Chécruoi. There, along with the usually running nutrition, was a collection of different Italian wines, bread and at least 6 different types of cheese. I was first in line anyway! It was pure torture to have to leave it!

Then came Courmayeur. As everyone who finished here was classified, you could say it was the first finishing straight. Everything was very well organized. I quickly found the bag I'd left there with my shower kit and change of running gear and enjoyed the shower and fresh clothes. I was also glad to put on different running shoes, replace the plasters on my blisters and smear Vaseline on my chafe marks. Fresh out of the shower and then to the catering! Oh man, it's worth doing the race just for this! ⬜ This year, they had really gone to town on the catering! It was top class. Two small glasses of bear later and my electrolyte levels were back to normal!

We ran right through the town and the people were clapping and cheering us on. It was really something to savor! But the elation was shortlived as now we had to run from 1,226 m / 4022.3 feet to 2,022 m / 6633.86 feet above sea level in 3 km /1.86 miles. Gone were the freshness of the shower and the clean clothes! At Refuge Bertone, km 75, I filled up with water and then the course passed through some very hilly terrain through the beautiful alpine scenery of Italy. From Lavachey, km 83, we then went from 1,690 m / 5544.6 feet to 2,537 m / 8323.5 feet above sea level to the Grand Col Ferret at km 90, where we crossed over the border into Switzerland. The next 10 km ranged from steep to slightly downhill to La Fouly. I was looking forward to seeing Walter who was due to be waiting for me there.

I was still feeling great and enjoying the weather and the splendid views. In La Fouly, I couldn't believe my eyes, for not only was Walter there but Frank too. He had to drop out at km 80 due to acute shin splints and was unable to run any further.

They made me some delicious spaghetti on the gas cooker and I ate this with various other tasty treats that they had brought with them.

Then off I went again toward Issert, another 10 km down the mountain. Looking back, these were the most enjoyable 20 km of the whole race. It was slowly getting dark and more climbs lay ahead. From Issert, we had to conquer an incline of 400 m / 1312 feet over 4 km. Here I overtook Anke Drescher, who seemed to have a few problems, although she still managed to finish the race. In Champex d'en Bas, there was the next chance to end the race with a rating. By now it was pitch black, and I suddenly felt quite tired.

I didn't want to lie down though. I showered and put on clean and warmer clothes for the nighttime, as there were another few passes to scale. Then I took made turned out to be my best decision of the whole race. I put on my proper hiking boots and decided to limit myself to walking during the night.

So, onward and upward! I was fired up and motivated by Frank and Walter through the two long nights. The next 5 km to Fermes de Bovine included a climb of about 700 m / 2 297 feet. The terrain was very hard to run on and there was also the odd mountain stream to cross. Due to fatigue and the nature of the trail, this was the most demanding part of the course. At Fermes de Bovine, at km 122, there was hot soup, which must be my favorite night refreshment. It was really cold and the hot soup went down like a treat. Then another downhill section: 7 km to drop from 1,987 m / 6519 ft to 1,279 m /4196.2 ft above sea level in Trentoo, at km 129. In Trento came the worst part of the race: cross-country down over a meadow. I guess I did about 100 m / 328 feet on the seat of my pants only to retrace my steps to the aid station on the way to Trentoo.

This really annoyed me as it was totally unnecessary and dangerous. In Trentoo, Walter was waiting for me and he put me back together again. I was now convinced that I could finish the race. I was a good 4 hours inside the cut-offs and only 26 km from the finish. After Trento, the trail headed uphill again, and involved a climb of about 700 m / 2297 ft over about 5 km, and this really hurt! On the way down to Les Essert, at km 136, we crossed the border into France again.

Then further down the mountain to Vallorcine, at km 139 and an altitude of 1260 m / 4134 ft. Walter was waiting for me there as usual and, as it was now daylight, I changed my running shoes again.

Now we returned to an altitude of 1,670 m / 5479 feet above sea level at km 148 (Sentier des Gardes). I don't know for sure but I think that a mistake has been made with the profile in the last 15 km. Until then it had been really accurate! But the rest…

But what did it matter? Then at some point the course went downhill again toward Chamonix. I was now dead beat. At the entrance to the town, a tingling sensation ran through me the like of which I had never felt before. I started to run and was cheered from all quarters. Nobody in front of me, nobody behind me! Everyone was cheering for me. I arrived around midday and the town was packed. Chest out, stomach in, and enjoy.

I had never had such a feeling of happiness running down a finishing straight! Better than the first marathon or the finish in Biel. Everyone was there, Kuni, Frank and Walter. At the finish, our names were called out, officials hugged and congratulated us – it was just fantastic!

I received my finisher sweatshirt, drank the two most delicious beers of my life and staggered to my apartment.

After a gala buffet in a swanky hotel in Chamonix, the words: "So much torture, so much beautiful scenery!" were going round in my head.

20.3. INTERNATIONAL ISARLAUF, FROM MAY 17 TO 21, 2004

The first International Isarlauf in 2004 was a multi-stage race over 5 days. The stage lengths varied between 56.2 and 74.5 km (35 and 46.3 miles). The race started on May 17, 2004, in Scharnitz, Austria and ended on May 21, in Plattling in Bavaria, Germany.

In preparation, that year I had already run about 1,500 km / 932 miles in training. My training mileage varied between 18.64 and 99.42 miles, and it had increased constantly each month. For the long runs, I used distances between the marathon and 100 km in Grünheide, which I incorporated into my training as preparation.

May 16, 2004
Trip to Scharnitz

Around 8am, the train left for Austria. According to the organizers, we were only to take 44 lb of luggage. When carrying my suitcase, I hoped fervently being broken would be accepted an excuse. I traveled with the Intercity train to Munich-Pasing station and got on a slow train to Scharnitz in Austria. The nearer we got to our destination, the more the scenery transformed into a fantastic mountain landscape, and I felt overwhelmed by the desire to run. It was raining harder and harder, which dampened my spirits somewhat, but I was hopeful it would soon stop.

In Scharnitz, a few more warriors got off the train with me. We stood in the pouring rain on the platform and had to run the 440 yards to the hotel. We got soaked to the skin in just this short distance. I feared the worst for the first stage the following day.

On arriving in the hotel, I was put in a double room with Rainer Wachsmann, a businessman from Münster with a weakness for multi-stage races.

According to the organizers, not everyone might get a bed. We were lucky, for nobody had to sleep on the floor on the first night. Rainer already had multi-day experience, and I bombarded him with questions. It also emerged that he had already run with Markus Fischer, from the group of Cologne ultrarunning regulars, who had also run the Swiss Jura Trail from Geneva to Basel.

Then we went down to get our starting documents. I met my running buddy and organizer of the Isarlauf, Uli Welzel, and we greeted each other warmly. We had first met two years previously and had been in constant contact since then. Uli was very busy as usual, and I estimated that his resting heart beat must have been about 150.

Gradually the runners and supporters arrived. We sat in groups together and discussed the following day's race. Many familiar faces were there, but also many newbies, which reassured me that I would not be the only novice.

About 6:30 pm, we had dinner, and it was quite a feast. I only thought, if it went on like this, I would put on weight during the race! After the meal, came the briefing for the following day. All the details were thoroughly discussed and the weather forecast promised bright sunshine. We were still skeptical about the latter.

May 17
1st Stage from Scharnitz to Vorderriß (56.2 km / 34.92 miles)

The weatherman was right. There was not a cloud in the sky, and it promised to be a dry and sunny day. We enjoyed a fantastic breakfast and still had enough time afterward to chat for a while. The first day's start was at 9 am. Just before that, we met in front of the hotel and went to the start together. The starting pistol was fired by the mayor of Scharnitz and to start, we ran upstream along the Isar.

As the race went from the source to the mouth of the river, we had to first run up to the source. As there are contradictory opinions on the true source of the Isar, it is referred to as the Head of the Isar, which is situated about 12 km / 7.5 miles from Scharnitz. At this point, two small headstreams meet to form the so-called Head of the Isar. On our way there, Kuni Schmitz (like me, the soldier from Cologne wanted to try out a multi-day race for the first time) took it in turns to overtake each other and during the course of the race we tacitly agreed to run the rest of the race together. At the Head of the Isar, there was a landmark and we used this as a backdrop for a nice souvenir photo.

We then returned to Scharnitz. On the way, we had to negotiate an incline of over 300 m / 984 feet. The profile was very up and down. For a while, we were running about 100 m / 328 feet above the Isar and had a wonderful view of a gorge created by the river, here just a stream. Also the other views in the partly still snow-covered mountain landscape were intoxicating. In Scharnitz, we ran behind our hotel and further along the Isar toward Mittenwald. Somewhere in the countryside stood the sign "national border" and almost without realizing, we found ourselves once more on German soil. Then we reached Mittenwald, ran through it and toward Vorderiß. Our route took us through an area of outstanding natural beauty. The countryside was beautiful and slowly coming to life. Unlike in the Rheinland, nature awoke early here and bloomed in a deep, verdant green. It was magnificent. Kuni and I had adopted the same pace (too fast, of course) and we ran the whole course together. Contrary to the profile familiar to us, we still had to climb a few more miles. According to Kuni's new watch, we were then about 565 m / 1 853.67 feet up and about 700 m / 2 296.59 feet down. Sure, it was not really an alpine Marathon but its length

made it no less challenging. The finish was situated at exactly the same place as the accommodation, a cozy mountain cabin. Kuni and I had run a time of 6:17:45 hr and agreed that we had had a fantastic day's running.

At the finish, I was told that I was one of those selected to sleep on the floor, as there were not enough beds available. But as it was just for one night, it was not too hard to handle. That evening we had a wonderful, copious communal dinner outside on the meadow in the sunshine. At the briefing, runners were told who would be starting early or late and the course for the following day was explained. Then we got our things ready for the morning and we hit the sack. Well, I just lay down and was then invited by Uli to drink a beer with him. But after that, it really was time to go to sleep.

This stage was won by Ute Wollenberg in a time of 5:03:48 hr in the women's race and Robert Wimmer and Eberhard Berger in a joint time of 4:33:34 hr in the men's.

May 18
2nd stage from Vorderiß to Wolfratshausen (62.3 km / 38.7 miles)

Today I had to start with the fast guys (for the first and last time). This meant I could take things easy tomorrow as I didn't have to be on the course until 8am. Unexpectedly, I felt really good. Kuni had problems with his stomach, so we did not run this stage together. I set off too quickly once again and had to pay for this later! The weather was great again and the scenery fantastic, through the high mountains and past reservoirs and tiny villages.

Unfortunately, I lost my sense of pace along the way and after about 30 km / 18.6 miles, my legs started to complain. I had to stop to walk more often and stopped to feast as long as possible at the excellently provisioned aid stations that were much better than the previous day. At some point, Kuni ran past me, and I started feeling better. Somewhere after Bad Tölz, some strength returned to my legs.

The high mountains slowly transformed into a hilly landscape. The course now partly took us through shady forests, and I could again run for longer sections. At the last aid station in Waldram, about 4.5 km / 2.8 miles before the finish, Angela Ngamkam ran past (she is a successful Badwater finisher and has been very active on the ultrarunning scene for some years now and boasts a best performance of over 186 km for 24-hours). I ran for a while with her and we decided to finish that stage together.

The miles flew by as we chatted, and we were quite fast. Just behind the city limits sign of Wolfratshausen, we then saw Kuni. Things were apparently not going so well for him, as he was still suffering from stomach problems. Kuni looked around quickly and did not want to be overtaken any more. Finally, he finished about 50 seconds in front of us. The finish was located behind a beautiful wooden bridge in front of the Town Hall in Wolfratshausen. Angi and I finished in 7:23:39 hrs.

The hotel was appropriately called Humplebräu ("Hobble Brewery"), which was entirely appropriate for my running style! The soles of my feet hurt and I was already "looking forward" to tomorrow. After a thorough foot and body massage, it was time to eat, followed by the usual briefing for the following day. So another great running day was over, and I went to bed early.

The stage was won by the Swiss Silvia Pleuler-Frey in 6:11:27 hr in the women's race and by Robert Wimmer in 5:14:09 in the men's.

Rudi Lausmann from TG Heilbronn was disqualified for exceeding the time limit but continued to run outside the classification and had to start an hour before the early group.

May 19
3rd stage of Wolfratshausen to Freising (70.8 km / 44 miles)

This time I started in the early group (and was to remain so). This meant slightly less free time in the morning but this was no problem as I had gotten into the rhythm now. The advantage was that one could run for an hour longer in the cool, as it promised to be another hot day. The race started at the location of the previous day's finish, and the starter's command triggered what was to be the worst running day of my life. With my first step, I felt a sharp pain in my right foot and shin and in my left knee. This stage ran through Munich and was also filmed by a TV camera crew. Despite the pain, I tried to run at least the first 20 km. The 20 then became 30 km and I gradually became optimistic that I could still finish the stage. According to the previous day's briefing, at aid station 3 (km 32), the press would be waiting. As the leaders, Robert and Eberhard, had already overtaken me at km 4 (although they had even started one hour later), I was slightly hopeful that I too could be in the "spotlight." Unfortunately, this was not to be the case, as on this day the sacking of Bayern Munich soccer coach Ottmar Hitzfeld was announced. As for the station, this was more important than an endurance race for crazy people! What a shame. The good thing was that I managed to reach it and had enough time to finish the stage, although it was a real torture for me. I had to walk most of the way and even this was really painful. I had no great hope of being able to continue the race the next day, which made me even more depressed.

Then we crossed the English Garden and after crossing downtown Munich, we again found ourselves in the wonderful Isar wetlands. But by now even Mother Nature couldn't cheer me up. If it weren't for the encouraging words of my fellow runners and the really helpful volunteers, I would probably have dropped out. But I did it, and finished the stage right near the back of the pack in 10:19:57 hr, but still an hour inside the time limit.

As I made my way back to the hotel, I must have looked really dreadful. I got some icepacks, was shown my room and went up without a word. After a quick shower and icing my damaged knees, I still firmly convinced that I wouldn't be able to run the next day. Then I went downstairs for dinner and ate in silence. The other runners tried to cheer me up, but unfortunately without success. I went back to my room before the briefing and continued icing. Rainer Wachsmann dropped by with another tube of ointment and I went to bed very early. When Sigrid Eichner[38] saw me, she said: "Don't give up! You can still do it! It's all in the mind!" Although I didn't really agree with her, I thought: "If she doesn't know, then who does?" After all, she had already run almost all the way round the world. So I didn't go straight to Uli to withdraw from the race, thank goodness!

Bernard Sesterman, the businessman from Leiwen, had to pull out due to a severe tear and inflammation of the periost. I can just imagine how he felt. But if you had seen the state of his foot and shin, you would have known it was the correct decision. The stage winner of the ladies' race was Simone Stegmeier in 7:06:42 hr and Robert Wimmer won the men's in 6:08:10 hr.

I woke up several times in the night, as my foot

The still wild River Isar

hurt with every movement in the bed. Good luck with that!

May 20
4th stage from Freising to Dingolfing (74.5 km / 46.3 miles)

Today would be the "queen stage." After getting up, I again just felt like pulling out and not starting at all. Again, Sigrid told me: "The show must go on!" And I thought to myself: "What the heck? You have nothing to lose!" So I put on my running gear, taped my knee and foot and went down to breakfast. I was still not particularly sure of myself. When Kuni saw me, he gave me the thumbs up to indicate that he was pleased! That made me feel good, and I was at least sure of going to line up at the start. Today, Horst Preisler was also running a stage and he cheered me up a bit. Just as I was finishing off my breakfast roll, Uli came over and looked at me a little plaintively. He asked me whether I wanted to run. I said indignantly: "What kind of question is that?" Uli shook his head, and I was glad that he could imagine the rest!

So, off to the start. After Uli's "Go", I could actually run. I said to myself, if you use the same tactics as yesterday and run the first 20 km, then you can walk the rest again and finish just inside the time limit. It was a miracle. Somehow it worked. At first, the course ran alongside the beautiful Isar and kilometers flew by. The second aid station was at km 22.5 and I had actually managed to run all the way.

Until that point, the course had been quite easy to run and my pain was bearable. But unfortunately after that the terrain was very uneven and I could only walk for most of it. From the 3rd aid station onward, the path improved, and I was able to run for longer sections. In Landshut, I reached the marathon marker, and I had run that far in under 5:10 hr, despite my handicap. I decided from now on to walk for 10 minutes and only run for 5. The rest of the course was now quite boring, as we frequently ran on the dam near the Isar reservoir and for hours we could see the next intermediate finish but it never seemed to get any nearer. I was now sure that I could finish this stage and the whole Isarlauf. I would now run very slowly and save the rest of my energy for the next day. For almost all of the remaining 14 km, there was no protection from the sun and the running surface to Dingolfing was not good. I tried to maintain the above running rhythm and finished in 10:24:52 hr. This time even two hours inside the time limit! I was back in the race. This of course cheered me up immediately, and I had my usual large Kölsch beer!

Unfortunately, Silvia Pleuler-Frey from Switzerland, hitherto on course for overall victory, and Wolfgang Klumpp from Bodnegg, had to drop out. That day, Rudi also had severe problems, and he would not start the next day. Winners of this stage were Simone Stegmeier (women) in 7:52:16 hr and Werner Selch (mens') in 6:26:35 hr.

May 21
5th Stage from Dingolfing to Plattling (62.8 km / 39 miles)

The last stage had arrived. I had had my knee and foot treated and wanted to repeat my tactic of running the first 20 km. Stupidly, I ran the first 10 km with Karl-Heinz Kobus. We chatted a lot and ran fast. When we reached the first aid station, we were running at well under 6 min/km pace, and I decided to go more slowly. I let Karl-Heinz pull away and set my own pace. After the second aid station, I didn't feel so good and had to walk a lot. In the next part of the course, a "jungle trail" had been incorporated, which reminded me of the "Ho Chi Minh path" in Biel. Luckily at least it was daylight

here! I swore loudly using some choice language that luckily nobody could hear!

At the same time, I was worried about my injuries, because I actually love this kind of trail. Today, some lovely countryside was in the cards, and the course was almost as beautiful as in the first stages. After about 30 km, the strength suddenly returned to my legs. I decided to change my tactics and from then on, alternated between running 10 minutes and walking 5 minutes. I ran the running sections in well below 6 km/minute pace and was able to maintain this right to the finish. Meanwhile, I was often overtaken, and now started to overtake one runner after another. It was a great feeling to finally be able to mix it up in the race. I tried the whole time not to think that today was a looping course. We were actually to run past the finish in Plattling, directly to the debouchment of the Isar into the Danube, and then back to the finish in Plattling. At the aid station in Plattling (Vicarage), a friendly mountain biker decided to cheer me on. He shouted to me in a friendly fashion that there were only a few meters to the debouchment. Somehow I really clicked with this guy and hoped to see him again when he was going through a bad time so that I could return the favor! I just said: "that's just what I wanted to hear!" And I ran with this added motivation to the turning point. I was feeling better and better and was sure that I would be able to run a much better time today. On the way to the turning point, the leaders were running towards me. The running order had changed somewhat, for straight after Robert Wimmer was Johann Delp. Johann had already overtaken me at km 30, and was now in fourth place. I already said to him there that today he would run really well, as he looked very fit and was running very fast and relaxed. He didn't really

---

[38] Sigrid Eichner, born 1940, holds the record for the most marathons and ultradistance races completed in the world, and has finished well over 1,000 races of marathon distance and beyond. She still runs sometimes more than 100 marathons per year. Horst Preisler is the equivalent of Sigrid Eichner, but it is not yet clear whether he has already been overtaken by the Hamburg Doctor Christian Hottas in boasting the most completed runs over the marathon distance or longer.

want to believe it, but I was proven right. I shouted after him that he was a beast, which apparently motivated him even more. Johann went on to finish in second place behind Robert in what was only his first ever multi-day race!

Shortly after the turning point, Kuni overtook me. He had started an hour after me, and was having a good race today. Due to my short walking phases I could not hold him off, which did not particularly bother me. I was able to overtake another three runners from my starting group after the turning point and reached the finish in 7:15:04 hr. I was proud and happy to have put these exertions behind me. I stayed at least another hour at the finish to cheer on the other finishers.

Johanna Kress was the women's stage winner in 6:29:19 hr and Robert Wimmer won the men's stage in 5:08:13 hr.

The victory ceremony was held in the Plattling town hall. There was a hot and cold buffet, at which I feasted handsomely. Also, the drinks were on the house and there were the usual speeches by officials and organizers. The best part of the evening was actually the moment when the volunteers stood on the stage and received a richly-deserved one minute standing ovation!

Overall winner of the women's race was Ute Wollenburg in a time of 33:51:20 hr and of the men's, Robert Wimmer with an total time of 27:30:42 hr.
All in all, it was a very nice and fitting victory ceremony, to which every runner was invited and was applauded as they received their certificate on the stage! Then we headed to the Plattling gymnasium, which had been turned into a dormitory for that night.

May 22nd
After a lavish breakfast in the hall, we headed to the railway station and the start of the journey home.

Here the Isar is "tamed"

Summary
A really fantastic cross-country multi-stage race. Uli did a great job, supported by a first-class team of volunteers on the ground. By itself, the work of Jürgen Schoch, course coordinator and course marker was fantastic. They had really gotten everything right. The food and drink provided at the aid stations were hard to beat. The volunteers were all really nice and above all, professional, as many of them were ultrarunners themselves. We would definitely have liked to stay with Uli Schulte. The landscape was, apart from very few sections, an absolute dream. I am still totally enthusiastic and captivated by this running experience. Next year, the race will be from the debouchment to the head of the river, where the highlight will be an alpine ultra as the final stage. So Uli, if you can get the weather gods on your side again next year, we can be certain that this race will again be the highlight of the running calendar! (It was held for the last time in 2007, when it was called the Isarrun).

Scotland – we all know a little about it, even if we have never been there. The stories of William Wallace, Rob Roy, Robert the Bruce and other freedom fighters are well-documented in word and film. And, of course, bagpipes, kilts and whisky are the best known Scottish cultural products worldwide.

Scotland forms the northern third of Great Britain and has belonged to the United Kingdom since 1707. However, Scottish parliament was reinstated in 1997, which deals with Scottish national issues. The capital city is Edinburgh, but Glasgow has 50% more inhabitants than Edinburgh.

The official language is, of course, English, but it is influenced by the national languages Scots and Gaelic. Sometimes one has to pay close attention in order to understand everything that is said.

Scotland is divided into three geographical regions: Southern Uplands, Central Lowlands and Highlands. One part of the Highlands is the West Highlands, which contains mountains, as its name "High" would indicate. Ben Nevis, near Fort William, is the highest mountain in the whole British Isles at 1,344 m / 4409 feet. Peaks over 1,000 m / 3281 feet are not uncommon, and the visual impression is often really alpine. On many peaks the last snows are still glistening even in the middle of June.   The West Highland Way is a path that crosses the Highlands – it is 153 km / 95 miles long with an elevation gain of 4,499 m / 14 760.5 feet. It is on this trail that the West Highland Way Race (WHW) has taken place since 1986. Duncan Watson and Bobby Shields were the first to run the trail in 1985 with a private race, and the following year, they invited friends and acquaintances to give it a try. 1991 was the first official race with timekeeping, and the WHW is now a firm fixture on the Scottish ultramarathon calendar. The course record is 15:44 hr, which shows that the standard is very high.

It is quick and easy to fly to Glasgow Prestwick Airport on Ryanair, although typically it is quite far from the city itself. The best idea is to hire a rental car, as a basic requirement for admission to the race is a two-person support crew that can accompany their runners along the course.

The start is in Milngavie, right on the outskirts of Glasgow, and the finish is in Fort William. In between, the runners only have one aid station set up by the organizers, which is only rudimentary. In Inversnaid, roughly at km 70, the organizers provide water, and the runners must transport the rest by drop bag. If the personal supporters actually went to Inversaid, they would not reach the other side of Loch Lomond in time to take care of their runners later on.

The start is on a Saturday morning at 1 am, and the finish cut-off time is 35 hours later, i.e., midday on Sunday. In between, runners and supporters can expect many hours of ups and downs, both geographically as well as physically and mentally. There are a few checkpoints at which the runners are monitored, on the one hand, if they can carry on running and on the other hand, they are on the way weighed twice as well as at the start and finish. If their weight fluctuates too much, either up or down, they are disqualified. The runners' crews also naturally ensure that they do not eat too little. All kinds of food are used as refreshments. Local crews sometimes have huge boxes of pre-cooked food in the boot. Others have camping stoves on board just to boil water for tea, coffee, or cook soups or quick snacks, or prepare entire ready meals in a pan. The menus were as different as the runners themselves.

And above all, the crews must arm themselves against the wild animals that abound in Scotland at this time of year. I don't mean wild boar, bears or other four-legged creatures, but tiny midges, which are men's natural enemy in these parts. It is advisable to wear a midge head net, and gloves, and to tuck the bottoms of your trouser legs into your socks. Even so, these tiny little creatures still find a way to reach the skin of their victims. The only effective midge protection is a spray that is so aggressive that it comes with a warning that if you spray it on your clothing it can destroy the material. However, there are still actually people who go camping in these conditions in heavily affected areas.

The runners themselves remain largely spared from being eaten alive by the midges. Anything going faster than 7 km/hour is not interesting for them as it is too quick.

There are no course markings by the organizers; the runners must find their way using hiking maps and looking for the official WHW markings. The trail always leads back to civilization, more often almost the only road link along the WHW to be crossed. Of course, the long-distance hikers do not cover the course non-stop.

Locally based runners, as anywhere in the world, have a great advantage. At the WHW, there is a group that meets once a month to run sections of the course together. This obviously greatly facilitates the task of route finding in the race itself. There are also two races over the two halves of the WHW at other times of the year organized by different promoters.

Each year, there are always a few foreigners taking part in the WHW. As well as two Austrians and an American, this year there were also three Germans, although one of them was only "half" German. Thomas Löhndorf has lived and worked for several years in Scotland. Unfortunately, he had to retire from the race after 110 km / 68.35 miles.

Maya and Jens Lukas traveled from Karlsruhe. Maya had already finished the WHW in 2005, then with Jens as one-half of her support crew. They had decided that on their next visit to Scotland, Jens would race and Maya would take her turn in the support crew. Since then, they had married in the autumn of 2007 and on their wedding list were "two support crews for the WHW 2008." Their wish was granted, and they found running friends who were willing to help. The wedding present was therefore, if it can be expressed so negatively, many hours of "suffering" all the way across Scotland.

There were a total of four married couples on the course, some of whom wanted to run together. Not so the Lukas's as they each wanted to run their own race. Maya finished in 39th place overall after 22:41 hr, which was almost 5 hours faster than three years previously, and she finished in the same place out of 97 instead of 48 finishers.

The WHW limits the number of entrants to 150, which is reached in a few days after the opening of registration in August of the preceding year. As such a challenge can only be attempted when in very good shape and health, it is inevitable that ultimately there are slightly fewer runners who actually start the race. This year there were 132, more than ever before. And there was also a record number of finishers, both absolutely and as a percentage.

This was partly due to the weather. By Scottish standards, it was positively mid-summerlike, but in terms of actual temperature, very pleasant for running. The rain held at least for the first 24-hours, apart from light showers that only lasted a few minutes. Now and then, the sun shone and the thermometer rose to 61 °F. At night, it was up to 13 ° C colder, but as the race always took place around midsummer, the night was very short. It was only really dark for 3 hours, and when morning came, the temperatures quickly rose again to comfortable levels.

Jens Lukas, also a well-known 24-hour racer, is three-time Spartathlon winner and other successes include a fourth and second place in the Ultratrail Mont Blanc. He is also a well-known and enthusiastic cross-country racer. The longer and more trail-based, the better. No wonder that his main training ground is the Black Forest, specifically the northern part, but when he needs to do very long runs, he is also known to run the whole Westway (230 km / 142.9 miles) in a long weekend. The WHW is therefore a race right after his own heart, and it seemed

The last kilometers to the finish

to be just made for him. As was his wont, he ran slowly but surely. At checkpoint 3, The Bridge of Orchy, situated at around km 96, he took the lead and did not let it go until the finish. With a comfortable 34-minute advantage, he won the WHW 2008 in 17:06:03 as the first German participant. Now he felt really ready for the UTMB at the end of August and the 24-hour World Championships in October in Seoul. Two goals for the season that could not be more different.

The fastest woman finisher was the American Donna Utakis, who finished in overall 8th place in 19:38:49 hr in Fort William, thus making her the third woman to run the race in under 20 hours.

The finish is not actually at the end of the trail but a few hundred yards further in a leisure center, i.e., in the warm and dry, which is also much more comfortable for the volunteers who are on duty for around 18 hours.

A lot of care went into the organization of the victory ceremony on the Sunday afternoon. Boss Dario Melaragni came up with little anecdotes about many runners. The WHW runners are a strong internet community, the running forum is a source for Dario's stories. Every finisher is called to the front and receives a glass cup, which rumor has it are used as wine glasses by some runners. Although this makes the ceremony last longer, it stops it from being boring!

Scotland is definitely worth a visit. Both for itself and even more so for keen ultra trail runners. It also still has the highest number of 4 qualification points for the UTMB.

For more information and results: visit www.westhighlandwayrace.org

20.5   60 KM MONKS' TRAIL (MONNIKENTOCHT, NETHERLANDS) ON SEPTEMBER 1ST 2007

At 5am, we were to get up and travel from Cologne to Ter Apel, where Dagmar and I wanted to run the 60 km together.

It was only 149 miles away and the journey went well so that we arrived around 8 am. The race was due to start at 9.30 am, so off to the registration desk to do in a quick late registration. The entry fee of $21 was more than reasonable for such a course and the efforts made for it were considerable. There were aid stations every 5 km with water, isotonic drinks and cola as well as bananas, oranges and honey spiced cakes. As the course is a point-to-point that runs from Ter Apel to Bourtagne, a luggage transport service to the finish and a return bus service to Ter Apel were also included in the price. And, as a bonus, we also received a handtowel with the race description! So all in all, a very good service package.

We received the starting documents in the Hotel Boschhuis in Ter Apel, which was also the location of the start. As well as the 60 km course, there was also 29 km hiking and Nordic walking and a 33 km

Registration

running course. We discovered that a total of 10 runners (2 women and 8 men) would be running. We were the only Germans, which meant that all we had to do was finish the race to be the top Germans! And better still, we would finish in the top-10 in an ultrarunning event!

Winschoten, where this year the IAU World and European Championships were also taking place and the Dutch 100 km championships, which were taking place the following week, had probably adversely affected the participation figures, although the average was in any case only about 20 runners.

At 9.30 am sharp, the 33 km and 60 km races started together. Dagmar and I had settled into a comfortable 7 min / km pace and then quite quickly found ourselves near the back of the pack. But we were not deterred, not even when after around 12 km, the last runner ran past us and from then on we ran with only the "broom wagon" for company. On the contrary. It gave us an escort that knew the local area and even spoke very good German. In this way, we learned a lot about the country and people, the event itself and other very interesting running events organized by the club. The course ran through very beautiful, partly already trail-like paths, through forests, along canals, cycle paths and through small Dutch villages. In addition to the long straights along the canals, which for me were decidedly pleasant and enjoyable! Dagmar found these course sections beautiful as she likes to run next to water. It's all a matter of personal taste!

An occasional glance at the GPS showed that the aid stations were not necessarily where they were supposed to be, and/or the kilometer markings of the aid stations were not correct. Our "broom bike" escort came to the rescue once again and explained the situation. A few years previously, the finish had to be relocated thus necessitating a detour. As the total distance remained 60 km, the start of the race was shortened. Only the kilometer markings of the aid stations had not been changed in the relevant documentation! Ok, then unfortunately nothing saved though! Due to the weather and the associated temperatures, the aid stations were more than adequate and we didn't need to wear drink belts.

After about 20 km, we started to overtake the odd runner in the 33 km race who had set off too fast. Unfortunately, this stopped after 25 km, as then the route changed and the 33 km racers ran directly to Bourtagne and we had to complete a small additional loop! Ragardless, we were right on track with our time and we really didn't mind if we crossed the finish line in last place. So we trotted on, enjoyed the scenery and feasted copiously at the aid stations. Overall, there was a real family atmosphere, all highway intersections were made safe with traffic cones (and this was despite for the few people and the notice previously that everyone must adhere to the traffic regulations and ran at their own risk) and through our bike escort, we even had our own travel guide. Unfortunately, that situation changed at about km 45, when we saw a runner ahead of us who had definitely set off too fast. So, we overtook him near the aid station at km 45, at which point he started to run on frantically. We ate quite normally and then ran on again. At the next aid station, at around km 51, he ran up to us again, took his drink on the run and accelerated! Good for you ... we set off again at 7 min / km pace...

About 1 km later we overtook him again and that was the last we saw of him. So, we could pass on the wooden spoon to someone else! Unfortunately, we had to find our own way now and could no longer rely on our knowledgable escort rider. But the Monks Trail is very well signposted so it is hard to get lost. Wooden signs were banged into the ground; further on, colored signs were used and

then also red and white barrier tape. Also in this respect, the organization was exemplary.

The finishing straight was also great. It was in the center of Bourtagne, in a medieval fort complete with moat, several wooden bridges and of course appealing to tourists and worth a visit even without the race. Dagmar and I finished in 7:03 hrs and were therefore completely on-target timewise. My GPS also confirmed the course length of 60 km and at the finish we received the promised handtowel. The only downside was now the remaining 930 yards on foot to the showers on the nearby campsite, from where the bus was also to leave for Ter Apel. Also at the finish we were then given another escort with local knowledge who showed us the way there. Unfortunately our luggage was at the finish and we had to lug it all the way there. So, next time we would remember to travel light!

The showers were clean though and we were even supplied with the 50 cent pieces required to operate them! First class organization here, too. The bus then left at 5.30 pm sharp for Ter Apel and we could go home with another ultra under our belts that year. Both joint seventh in the overall ranking, as another runner had to drop out. OK, so there were only 9 finishers, but we didn't have to tell everyone that!

Information about the race can be found on this website: www.monnikentocht.nl

All in all, a great event that we were sure to visit again. (NB: the race is now run over "only" 50 km / 31.07 miles.)

s a final preparation for the Spartathlon this year, I really wanted to run two stages at the DL 2007. Beforehand, I had initially intended to attend the event as a volunteer, which unfortunately proved totally impossible for reasons of scheduling.

Dagmar did not need much coaxing (actually none at all) and so on Saturday, September 15, we found ourselves on the train to Eisleben. We reached the sports hall lodgings at about 8.30 pm and most runners were already asleep. Ingo was still awake and sitting with a small bottle of beer on his sleeping mat. He gave me a typical hearty greeting: "Hello Wolfgang, old fruit!" As he then immediately offered us a chilled lager, he was forgiven!

After the friendly greeting, we set up our beds and then set off to find something to eat, which we managed to do after a long walk. Reinvigorated, at around 10.30 pm, we hit the sack.

The light went on at 4.15 am and the hall suddenly became a hive of activity. The odd familiar face popped up and looked at us rather incredulously as they didn't know we would be there.

The first thing that struck us was the brightly colored taping sported by the runners. Yellow, blue and red were the favorites and the different patterns were quite stunning!

Unfortunately, many runners had already dropped out, including many who had extensive multi-stage experience. Also, many battle-scarred runners were there who would most likely be pulling out in the next few days. Ingo himself hoped that he could bring home 50% of the runners as finisher sto Lörrach.

It is impressive to think that for 17 days you have to go through the same procedure every day. 4:15

am get up, 5 am breakfast, starting preparations, pack things, pack up sleeping gear, take everything to the taxi, 6 am start of the "slow group," 7 am start of the "fast hares." Then, depending on the runner and the course, there are 6-14 hours of hard running work, then showers, evening meal, possibly a massage, treating injuries, setting up the bed, lights out at 9 pm and everyone asleep!

But it is not any easier for the volunteers, as they have the same schedule, except that they cannot take it easy after the end of each day's race as boss Ingo has more work for them to do.

We, in any case, were happy that we only had two days of these exertions to put up with! The first day, the seventh stage from Eisleben to Sömmerda, a distance of about 71 km / 44 miles, I ran in the later group because I wanted to run quite fast. Dagmar had already been running for an hour.

I ran from the start with Uwe Schietzoldt and, after establishing that we had the same profession and also had a few other things in common, we decided to carry on running together. After the second aid station, we started to overtake some of the slower runners and this continued up to the finish. This made the running more varied and we were also able to exchange a few words with the runners we overtook.

The course was varied and partly also quite hilly. What I found a little disturbing were the sometimes long sections along the roadside. The fast-moving trucks and vans did not exactly alleviate my concerns. But occasionally we also ran over beautiful country lanes and hiking trails, so all in all it was a really beautiful course. Also the good and sunny weather helped, because we had excellent clear views.

After about 50 km, we overtook Dagmar, who was running with 100 MC friend Heiner and the finish was within our sights. But what I found hard was always having to leave the excellent aid stations so quickly. They really offered everything to please the runners' palates. Everything was set out to make it look appetizing! Amazing! But Uwe was relentless.

After 7:46 hours, we reached the finish together in Sömmerda. Unfortunately, I had learned in the meantime that Uwe had dropped out after the 12th stage, so near to the finish! Too bad Uwe, but chin up and try again!

Dagmar arrived about one hour later and we went straight off for a nice beer and a massage. This service too, like the physiotherapy and taping, was absolutely first class and highly praised by all the runners! Furthermore, another scientific study was being conducted, in which the Run Across Germany runners could volunteer to participate. You can read about this on the website of the race: **http://www. deutschlandlauf.com/deutschlandlauf/index.php? lan=en&page=Startseite&content=Anfang**

At 7 pm, we had a nice dinner and then went to bed. The next day, the course was the 80 km / 50 miles from Sömmerda to Ilmenau. Dagmar and I planned to run together and drop out at km 48 so that we could catch our train. Ingo had told us that this would be organized with the transport there. Of course we knew we could rely on this!

This time, we both started in the early group. It was still pitch black and the first part of the course ran for miles along the highway, which was even more frightening because the drivers only spotted us at the last minute and we had to be constantly ready to jump onto the grass verge and actually had to do it on a couple of occasions.

After about an hour, it got lighter and we felt much safer. The good thing about today was that we could indulge ourselves at every aid station. My compliments again to the organizers!

Also today, the landscape was very varied and in places quite hilly. Dagmar and I dropped out as planned at km 48 and were then driven to the hall in Ilmenau. A quick shower, bags packed and then unfortunately we had to go straight to the station so that we did not miss our train.

We were both very taken with this atmosphere and the professional organization. Ingo was remarkably calm, which wasn't like him at all! The course sign-posting by Joachim Barthelmann was also praised by all participants. A race cannot work if the odd hiker finds it amusing to remove the arrows or point them completely the wrong way....

After not racing for over a year, I wanted to make a comeback in Hanau-Rodenbach. I was able to train completely without pain for more than 6 months, and I had set high goals for myself this year! Or rather a primary goal and a secondary goal. The primary goal was to run the Spartathlon and obtain the necessary qualification time for this in the German Championships in Hanau-Rodenbach with a time below 10:30 hr. My secondary goal was to run the 100 km in a time as far below 10 hours as possible.

Thanks to my foreign assignment in Kosovo since 2005, I had the opportunity to train without having to consider my family and other responsibilities (apart from my duties as DUV Team Manager), and could easily do between four and six training sessions a week. It was a little problematic finding places to run in the mission areas, and due to the very low temperatures (sometimes well below 4°F) I carried out nearly all my running workouts on a treadmill in a gym until the end of February. This also included the long runs, which did tend to be very monotonous. But it was better than nothing...however I did really enjoy the interval running sessions on the treadmill, as it made a change from running at the same speed all the time and added a bit of variety to the training. I quickly drew up a training plan by gleaning ideas from the appropriate training forums and websites and putting them all together, which seemed to be sensible and also suited my personal preferences.

In this way, I was able to run well over 1,000 km / 621.4 miles almost injury-free, and it was great to also be able to achieve my goal. The previous evening, the Ultrarunners get-together was held in Cologne (www.wolfgang-olbrich.de/ultrastammtisch-koeln), in which I wanted to participate briefly and then I left from there with Werner Winkhold, a teacher at the European School in Cologne, en route to Hanau-Rodenbach. We arrived around 10.15 pm and prepared our beds. After a swift lager with Björn Lachenmann, legal consultant of the DUV who worked in Switzerland as an electrical engineer, it was off to bed.

About 30 minutes before the alarm clock was due to go off, I was rudely awoken by Björn asking me to get up. Very unwillingly, as befits the morning grouch that I am, I did as he asked and struggled out of bed. Off to the gym, and we wolfed down breakfast after paying a small fee. There I met my best running buddy Frank, who this year also wanted to go on another running adventure with me, this year the Spartathlon. Frank also wanted to run the qualifying time here and was positive he could do it. Frank is also a good example of how once you try one ultradistance race, you find it hard to stop.

Our initial virtual acquaintance on an internet forum had turned into a really good friendship, which clearly transcends just occasional car pooling, as we were now veterans of many a long run together in the mountains and the odd mountain tour.

Shortly before 6 am, new DUV functional fabrics arrived as promised, which we wanted to wear during the race to publicize them. Stefan Hinze, our DUV President, Jürgen Köllner, DUV Executive Secretary, Jürgen Schoch, DUV Statistician and Björn Lachenmann, DUV Legal Consultant, also turned up. Many other acquaintances were also spotted and there was much laughter and talking shop. Jürgen Schoch and Björn had just decided that they wanted to run in the "Bambini run" over 50 km. Björn didn't have the training mileage behind him for the 100 km, and Jürgen just wanted to do a quick, training run, as at the time he was preparing for the Isarrun and his weekly training mileage was already high, and he had a long run planned for the following day. Stefan, Jürgen Köllner, and I definitely wanted to run the longer race though. Jürgen wanted to run with me and Stefan wanted to run a little faster with Björn. I packed up my new running gear and went to the car to get changed and ready to race.

I also wanted to look out for my clubmates from SG Neukirchen-Hülchrath. They wanted to set up their own aid station at which the active runners could reach everything they needed. Just before the door, I came across the club coach. Our trainer Adi Rosenbaum, Michael Göhner and Stefan Blasche took on the role of supporters. Jörg Just, Dr. Stefan Weigelt (not in the photo), Horst Graef, Willy Helfenstein and I would take care of the running side of things. Unfortunately, our "best man," Dr. Bernd Juckel had to drop out at the last minute due to back problems. A good location for the SG Neukirchen-Hülchrath stand was quickly found (aid stations km 6 and 8), which meant that the route passed by the aid stations twice so we could therefore be supported better! Michael worked flat-out on it, and with support from Stefan Blasche, I received extras that I had gotten ready beforehand! Many thanks to them! Adi took on the role of cheering on and checking the number of laps in the stadium. Here too everything went according to plan!

We went to the starting line just before 7 am. Frank Klaka, Jürgen Köllner and I ran the first 3 laps together. We ran even 57/58 minute laps and I felt really good. After 3 laps, Frank took things a little more easily and Jürgen and I ran the next 2 laps by ourselves. From the 5th lap, Jürgen also slowed down and I was still able to maintain my starting pace. Everything went smoothly and I gradually started to hope that I could maintain it to the finish. My only slightly weak phase came between km 40 and 50, but this was just psychological, and I had prepared myself for it in advance. I had already experienced something similar in Kienbaum, when I indulged in negative feelings and almost dropped out. Then I just sat down for 20 – 30 minutes and walked a lot

afterwards, although physically I felt great! I did not want that to happen this time, so I was able to convince myself that there was absolutely no room for these thoughts in Hanau! And what do you know, it worked perfectly!

The 6th and 7th laps also went smoothly and I was still lapping in under 60 minutes! I now had a 14- minute cushion for the magic 10-hour barrier. I now decided to change my previous tactics slightly. Until then I had run past the aid stations, and at the last 3 laps I wanted to walk past them and make sure I drank enough. Due to the cold weather with sleet and rain showers, I drank plenty of hot tea and directly after running out of the stadium, the hot ultra-buffet. So from then on I ran a little over 60 minutes per lap, but I felt more certain that I could pull the whole thing off. My last 3 laps were run in 62, 61 and 64 minutes.

My finishing time was 9:53:28 hr and I almost burst with pride! I had managed to beat my previous best time from Kienbaum by 1:03 hr and finally break the 10-hour barrier! I proudly accepted my finishers cup and took a hot shower.

The race was won by "serial winner" Michael Sommer from EK Schwaikheim, again in a time of under seven hours, im 6:57:19 hr to be precise, in front of Jörg Hool from LTF Marpingen with 7:08:37 hr and Thomas König from SuL Lölnitz in 7:09:12 hr. As for the women, the winner was Birgit Schönherr-Hölscher, PV Triathlon Witten, in a new personal best time of 7:48:33 hr, in front of Marion Braun of SV Germania Eicherscheid in 8:13:22 hr and Carmen Hildebrand of SC Hanau-Rodenbach in 8:33:37 hr.

From a supporter's perspective

As the 48-hour race in Brno, Czech Republic, had been canceled, my partner Dagmar had decided at the last minute to run in the Athens 7-day race instead.

Instead of the general timed races that "only" lasted 6 days (144 hours), Costas Baxevanis, himself one of the top Greek multi-day runners and a Professor at the University of Athens, founded a 7-day race in Athens that was now in its 5th year. The reason was, according to hearsay, a "little rebellion" against the church, which stated that the 7th day was to be a day of rest, which is why all the other extreme multi-day races ended after 144 hours or 6 days. However, national and International ranking lists were only compiled for the 144-hour results and actually only these are relevant for the participating runners. But even though the split time after 6 days can not be included in the ranking lists, runners still wanted to hang on to run the last day!

Unfortunately, Dagmar's training had not been going as planned during her preparation. Something always got in the way, be it work, weather or illness. Many long sessions were planned during Carnival time and at least these were mostly do-a ble. Dagmar's last long session was the 6-hour race in Stein, Netherlands, which she managed to run easily and calmly.

Afterwards, Dagmar was still nervous, and she planned everything at least 200 times. Of course, each time was completely different. So I was glad that the date of the flight to Athens was getting nearer. Unfortunately, this time, I couldn't be there from the start. My daughter Fabienne was still at school and the holidays didn't start until Friday, March 26, and only then could we catch our plane.

So, Dagmar had already left on Monday, March 22, for Athens in order to prepare calmly and set herself up properly in the gym and maybe even do a bit of shopping. A 1,000-mile race had been underway since March 16, which had been led from the start by ultrarunning superstar Wolfgang Schwerk from Solingen, Germany. Wolfgang reeled off a cool 190 km in the first 24-hours!

In addition, after the start of the 7-day-race, other races were scheduled over 24, 48 and 72 hours, but back to Dagmar and her 7-day race experience.

On Wednesday, March 24, at 1 pm, the race started in the 2004 Olympic Park. The course itself is a 1 km circuit, completely asphalted and slightly perforated??? It is also right next to a very busy 6-lanehighway, no spectator access and no view. So there was really nothing that could remotely help to break the monotony of the circuit. But Dagmar was up for it, which I found amazing, never mind the 1,000-mile runners who had to run 1,609.344 laps before their race was finished.

For the 7-day racers, there was no minimum daily limit that had to be completed to stay in the race. But in the 1,000-mile race, runners had to cover 50 miles a day to be able to continue.

Unlike Cornelia Bullig from Erkrath (Germany), who wanted to break some records, Dagmar had no big goals. She just wanted to see what happened. She had wanted to run a 6-day race for ages, but this wasn't planned until 2011. This year she had planned her first attempts over 48-hours in Brno and Cologne. She wanted to break the 300 km barrier in Cologne at the latest. It was only after the cancelation of the race in Brno that Athens became a possibility.

Secretly, Dagmar was aiming to reach the 500 km mark in 144 hours. However, she didn't broadcast this before the race but remained modest. At the end of the day, it was all new territory for her and she had never run that far before. In any case, she had to avoid going off too fast. She planned to run about 130 km the first day, and she stuck to it. 137 km was a prudent start and a sensible way to manage her energy.

Cornelia Bullig was in the lead after day 1 with 170 km, however, she had to retire injured on the second day after running 181 km. Dagmar suddenly found herself leading the women's race, in which the only other competitor was Mireille Cormier from France.

Unfortunately, the external conditions in the organizational area were not satisfactory. The catering was very sparse and totally unsuitable for a vegetarian like Dagmar. There was mostly highly chlorinated tap water, blue Gatorade isotonic drink ("Smurf wee"), coffee and occasionally cola. The hot meals were, to put it mildly, very Spartan. Otherwise there were crisps, a little chocolate and savory snacks. Only on the last two days did the catering improve significantly, probably after the organizers realized that otherwise they would have too much left over.

The organization was also completely lacking in terms of music or other entertainment. The only highlight was the display board with the results that were constantly updated in real time on a large flat screen. That was really very impressive. Also next to the time measurement pad, another control pad was placed on the back straight that made it impossible here to gain an illegal advantage by taking rest periods e.g., tactically favorably after a change of direction.

The running direction was changed at 9 am and 9 pm, which provided some variety for the runners. The runners then on the course ran once around the time measuring pad and high-fived each other. Every runner enjoyed this and at this point, most of them were still in the race.

Another regular procedure was the morning blood pressure check and weigh-in carried out by a medical doctor. As Dagmar's blood pressure was always quite low in the morning, she tried not to see the doctor until she had drunk a coffee and walked or run a couple of laps.

We phoned each other every morning and evening and now and then I received news of Dagmar and the race from Siegfried Bullig. However, I could hardly wait until Friday came when I could pick up Fabi from school and travel to the airport. Finally the day came. At 2.30 pm, the plane took off from Düsseldorf heading for Athens. We landed on time at 6:30 pm local time and took the bus X96 to the 2004 Olympic Park, where everything now lay mostly unused and slowly disintegrating. It was really sad to see it like this. Just think of all the good that could have been done for the sport with this wasted money.
But anyway, back to Dagmar's race.

We reached our destination just before 9 pm and celebrated our reunion. The poor catering for the runners was the number one concern on the course. But what use was that? So, first thing the next morning, I went shopping to buy the missing items. Fabi and I then rejected the "special offer"

Reception on the running course

of being able to buy into the catering as supporters, and we preferred to just organize ourselves.

Dagmar had set off well and maintained a brisk walking pace the whole time. She was putting together the miles well and was slowly but surely increasing her lead over Mireille. She had spoken to many experienced multi-day runners beforehand and planned the tactic of moving 20 hours a day on the course. The course was only to be left to go to the toilet or sleep. Anything else, like eating or drinking, had to be done on the course. To come straight to the point, she actually managed to do this and was always on the course for at least 18 hours. She was so strong-minded!

I then constantly tried to find things for Fabienne to do and to look after Dagmar as well as possible. Dagmar had to manage by herself at nights between midnight and 8 am, as I was then in beds. I could at least manage to be half-way effective.

But this seemed to work ok. When I did short or long trips with Fabi, I had usually prepared everything for this period and at hand on a table at the course.

As well as the sparse basic provisions from the organizers, we also had some candy like gummy bears, licorice, smarties, etc., as well as gerkins, and tomatoes that were used to make the necessary salt more palatable. Then there was also mostly fennel tea, which Dagmar digested best, coffee with a lot of sugar (which she never drinks in "normal life") and in the evening mashed potato or couscous with olives, gerkins and tomatoes. To compensate for the missing protein, this time we experimented with protein powder, which we mixed with water and added cappuccino powder to improve the taste.

Dagmar always tried to do as much as possible on the course. So always a dish with food on the way eating instead of sitting down at a table to do it, etc.

Important to have your own catering table

It was already quite boring. Every 10-11 minutes Dagmar came past. I always asked her what she needed: "I don't need anything!" was always the reply. But if I pressed something into her hand, she always appreciated it. Always when Fabi and I returned from our trips, we usually brought a nice ice cream with us. For Dagmar, that was always a real treat. It is astonishing how such little things in a race like this become so important and how much joy this puts on people's faces.

In the evenings, I also cooked a little for Dagmar. If you can call it cooking, as our only equipment was a kettle. On the menu was either mashed potato or couscous livened up with finely sliced tomato, gerkins or olives with lots of salt to keep mineral levels up.

Dagmar was always very appreciative, which of course made this supporter's heart beat faster.

Wolfgang Schwerk (right) winner of the 1,000 miles

The monotony of lap running was relieved occasionally by the finishing 1,000 mile runners. Leading the pack was Wolfgang Schwerk, who delivered a really classy performance, especially under these conditions. Hiroko Okiyama also ran a very controlled race. I had already noted with surprise in Germany when I read about her daily performances, as normally at the start of a race like this she started at a "breakneck speed" and then usually had to drop out. Now that I was actually there, I could see why she ran so sensibly.

She was constantly slowed down by her supporter Seppo Leinonen as soon as she tried to push the pace, as she usually tended to do. This clever arrangement allowed her to pass Martina Hausmann at some point and finish the race under control in first place. Although Martina fought her off for a long time, Hiroko was able to prevail at the finish due to her higher basic speed.

The race was further enlivened by the simultaneously run races over 24, 48 and 72 hours. With the start of the 24-hour race, the catering also gradually improved. Unfortunately, by then the 1,000-mile race had then already been underway for more than 10 days.

Equally unacceptable was that hot water was only available for two hours a day for showering or having a proper wash. These hours were usually only communicated the day before. For the runners, it is naturally completely stupid to have to get washed at a time when they didn't want to sleep or rest and then go back out onto the course and get sweaty again. This only makes sense if they wanted to sleep anyway and have a shower beforehand in order to go to bed clean. So, for Dagmar, this meant 7 days of just a quick wash.

The 24, 48 and 72 hour races ended at 2-hour intervals. Neither were the showering times planned for these runners so that they could at least have a hot shower after the race. This too shows that the organization left something to be desired.

On Monday, I only saw the victory ceremonies of the 3 races. I thought it was a shame that first the 24-hour runners, then the 48ers then the 72ers were honored. I would have thought that the reverse order would have been more fitting. After all, for example, the 72-hour racers had been running for two days longer. After the victory ceremony for the 24-hour race, it was a bit chaotic as many already left the race or stood around chatting. Here, too, I would have wanted/expected a more sporting behavior from the athletes.

Dagmar noticed none of this and just carried on running. She mostly put up with the shortcomings without complaining and concentrated on the race and the little things that cheered her up.

As well as the small culinary delights, these certainly also included the many chats with and mutual support and encouragement from her fellow runners on the course as well as the encouragement from the sidelines from supporters or runners who had already finished or had had to retire. In particular, the group of Schwerk, Schieke, Schlotter and Zimmermann[39] distinguished themselves through their cheering and occasional chanting at the side of the course, which did not have great entertainment value for Dagmar. The four of them often sat for hours at the side of the course and cheered on those athletes still in the race. They were also always present when a 1,000-miler finished, whether in the middle of the night or day. This was sportsmanship that I rated very highly!

From the 5th day, Dagmar ran head-to-head with Sheng Wu Ming for 5th place overall. The Chinese runner from Taipei wanted to avoid being beaten by a women at all costs, and I watched with joy how Dagmar narrowed the gap between them mile by mile. Wu needed longer breaks, but then usually

Made it! 7 days, 671.405 km

breaks. Dagmar just kept on running/walking as she had been doing and in this way continued to catch to him. As she then started to catch up him even when walking, he was quite frustrated. In fact, Dagmar just had to run the 7th day very loosely but in view of this competitive situation, she didn't want to give up the 5th place now and ran as fast as she could even on the last day.

ran faster when he returned to the course. But at one point, he could run no longer and needed more

At the end, Dagmar finished with a really great result, having covered 671,405 km in 7 days. The 588 km covered in 6 days put her in 7th place on the German rankings.

[39] Wolfgang Schwerk, for many years at the absolute world elite in multi-day racing, is usually supported by Helmut Schieke in his record attempts, who is responsible for looking after him. Helmut himself used to be one of the best German 24-hour runners and has, among others, finished the Trans Australia Footrace. Hans-Jürgen Schlotter has made a name for himself in multi-day racing over recent years, and is now among other things holder of the German age group record over 48 hours on the track. Unfortunately, he, like Walter Zimmerman, Germany's farther running postman from LG Würzburg, had to retire early from the race.

USEFUL LINKS

www.wolfgang-olbrich.de Author's website that includes a lot of information about ultramarathon running and ultrarunning training in general.

www.ultramarathon.org Official website of the German Ultramarathon Foundation with information about ultrarunning, training, sports medicine, forum, international race calendar and statistics.

www.deutscher-leichtathletik-verband.de Official website of the German Athletics Association

www.americanultra.org Official website of the American Ultrarunning Association (AUA)

www.acu100k.com Official website of the Canadian Association of Ultramarathoners (ACU)

www.iau-ultramarathon.org Official website of the International Association of Ultrarunners

www.steppenhahn.de My favorite ultrarunning website

BIBLIOGRAPHY / SOURCES

Baumann, S. (2009). *Psychologie im Sport*, 5. Auflage, Meyer & Meyer Verlag, Aachen.

Barrett, S., et al. (2002). Retrosprective study of outcomes in Hyalgan tretated patients with osteoarthritis of the knee. *Clin Drug Invest, 22*, 87-97.

Burke (2010). Fueling strategies to optimize performance: training high or training low? *Scand J Med Sci Sports, 20*, 48-58.

Butcher (1993). Runner's diarrhea and other intestinal problems of athletes. *Am Fam Physician, 48*, 623.

Cameron-Smith, Burke & Angus, et al. (2003). A short-term, high-fat diet up-regulates lipid metabolism and gene expression in human skeletal muscle. Am J *Clin Nutr, 77*, 313, 8.

Collings, Pierce & Rodriguez-Stanley, et al. (2003). Esophageal reflux in conditioned runners, cyclists, and weightlifters. *Med Sci Sports Exerc, 35*, 730.

Demers, Harrison, Halbert & Santen (1981). Effect of prolonged exercise on plasma prostaglandin levels. *Prostaglandins Med, 6*, 413.

di Prampero, Salvadego & Fusi, et al. (2009). A simple method for assessing the energy cost of running during incremental tests. *J Appl Physiol, 107*, 1068, 75.

Fischer, Pelka & Barociv (2005). Adjuvante Behandlung der Gonarthrose mit schwachen pulsierenden Magnetfeldern. *Z Orthop, 143*, 544-550.

Fischer, Pelka, Baravic (2006). Adjuvant treatment of osteoarthritis of the knee with weak magnetic fields. *Aktuelle Rheumatologie, 31*, 226-233.

Flakoll, Judy & Flinn, et al. (2004). Postexercise protein supplementation improves health and muscle soreness during basic military training in marine recruits. *J Appl Physiol, 96*, 951, 56.

Garland, Moses & Salyer (1991). Long-term follow-up of fracture nonunions treated with PEMFs. *Contemporary orthopaedics 22*, 295-302.

Goldberg et al. (2005). Hyaluronans in the treatment of osteoarthritis of the knee: evidence for disease-modifying activity. *Osteoarthritis and Cartilage, 13*, 216-224.

Gossling, Bernstein & Abbott (1992). Treatment of ununited tibial fractures: a cmparison of surgery and pulsed electro-magnetic fields PEMF). *Orthopedics, 15,* 711-719.

Hamm, Ellrott & Terlinden, et al. (2010). NEM in der fachlichen und öffentlichen Diskussion. *Dtsch Apothek Z, 150,* 3906, 13.

Holmes (1994). Treatment of delayed unions and nonunions of the proximal fifth metatarsal with pulsed electromagnetic fields. *Foot & Ankle International, 15,* 552-556.

Ivy, Goforth & Damon et al.(2002). Early postexercise muscle glycogen recovery is enhanced with a carbohydrate-protein supplement. *J Appl Physiol, 93,* 1337, 44.

Jubb et al. (2001). Structure modifying study of Hyaluronan (500-730kDa, Hyalgan) on osteoarthritis of the knee. *Arthritis Rheum, 44,* S9: 155.

Kam, Pease & Thompson (1994). Exercise-related mesenteric infarction. *Am J Gastroenterol, 89,* 1899.

Lachtermann & Jung (2006). Sport und gastrointestinales System: Einfluss und Wechselwirkungen. *Deutsches Ärzteblatt, 103,* Ausgabe 31-32, A-2116-20.

Lennartz, (1983): Diplomarbeit. "Geschichte des Ultralangstreckenlaufes – unter besonderer Beachtung der Entwicklung in Deutschland".

Lucas & Schroy (1998). 3rd. Reversible ischemic colitis in a high endurance athlete. *Am J Gastroenterol, 93,* 2231.

Mammi, et al. (1993). The electrical stimulation of tibial osteotomies – double blind study. *Clinical Orthopaedics and Related Research,* 288, 246-253.

Marquardt, M. (2009). Natural running, quoted in *focus* 17-2002.

Mayer, F., et al. (2001). Verletzungen und Beschwerden im Laufsport. Deutsches Ärzteblatt , 98A, 1254-1259.

Milroy: *Diverse Publikationen über die Geschichte des Ultralangstreckenlaufes in englische Sprache auf der Internetseite von Andre Milroy.*
(http://www.ultralegends.com/history/general-ultra-articles/andy-milroy-articles/)

Moses (2005). Exercise-associated intestinal ischemia. *Curr Sports Med Rep, 4,* 91.

Morton & Callister (2000). Characteristics and etiology of exercise-related transient abdominal pain. *Med Sci Sports Exerc, 32,* 432.

Moses, Baska, Peura & Deuster (1991). Effect of cimetidine on marathon-associated gastrointestinal symptoms and bleeding. *Dig Dis Sci, 36,* 1390.

Nikolakis, et al. (2002). Pulsed magnetic field therapy for osteoarthritis of the knee – a double-blind sham-controlled trial. *Wiener Klinische Wochenschrift, 114,* 678-684.

Olympiastützpunkt Rheinland: www.koelnerliste.com

Quellenberg & Eissing (2008). Die Ernährungssituation bei Dortmunder Studierenden. *Ernährungs-Umschau, 55,* 202-209.

Recommended Dietary Allowance: empfohlene Zufuhr pro Tag lt. Nährwertkennzeichnungsverordnung (NKV)

Riddoch & Trinick (1988). Gastrointestinal disturbances in marathon runners. *Br J Sports Med, 22,* 71.

Rontoyannis, Skoulis & Pavlou (1989). Energy balance in ultramarathon running. *Am J Clin Nutr, 49,* 976, 79.

Rost & Stitch (1986). the side pain of athletes. *N Z Med J, 99,* 469.

Ryan, Bleiler, Carter & Gisolfi (1989). Gastric emptying during prolonged cycling exercise in the heat. *Med Sci Sports Exerc, 1,* 51, 8.

Saltin & Astrand (1993). Free fatty acids and exercise. *Am J Clin Nutr, 57,* 752S, 58 S.

Sawka, Montain (2000). Fluid and electrolyte supplementation for exercise heat stress. *Am J Clin Nutr, 72,* 564S, 72 S.

Stewart, Ahlquist & McGill, et al.(1984). Gastrointestinal blood loss and anemia in runners. *Ann Intern Med, 100,* 843.

Sherman, Costill & Fink, et al. (1981). Effect of exercise-diet manipulation on muscle glycogen and its subsequent utilization during performance. *Int J Sports Med 2,* 114, 8.

Schultz, W. (1993). *Untersuchungen über die Reparationsmöglichkeiten des chronisch geschädigten Gelenkknorpels am Kniegelenk bei korrigierten Achsfehlstellungen.* Habilitationsschrift der Georg August Universität Göttingen.

Schultz, Hedrich & Göbel (1997). Verhalten von Meniskusgewebe bei operierten Varusgonarthrosen. *Orthopädische Praxis, 33,* 524-528.

Sinclair & Stitch (1951). The side pain of athletes. *N Z Med J,* 50, 607.

Sullivan (1987). Exercise-associated symptoms in triathletes. *Phys Sportsmed, 15,* 105.

Thalmann, Sodeck & Kavouras, et al. (2006). Proton pump inhibition prevents gastrointestinal bleeding in ultramarathon runners: a randomised, double blinded, placebo controlled study. *Br J Sports Med, 40,* 359.

Tarnopolsky, MacDougall & Atkinson (1988). Influence of protein intake and training status on nitrogen balance and lean body mass. *J Appl Physiol, 64,* 187, 93.

Trock, Bollet & Markoll (1994). The effect of pulsed electomagnetic fields in the treatment of osteoarthritis of the knee and cervical spine. Report of randomized, double blind, placebo controlled trial. *Journal of Rheumatology, 21,* 1903-1911.

Worobetz & Gerrard (1985). Gastrointestinal symptoms during exercise in Enduro athletes: prevalence and speculations on the aetiology. *N Z Med J, 98,* 644.

Wandel, et al Effects of glucosamine, chondroitin, or placebo in patients with osteoarthritis of hip or knee: network meta-analysis. *BMJ, 341,* 711.

Wikipedia

Yazaki, Shawdon, Beasley & Evans (1996). The effect of different types of exercise on gastro-oesophageal reflux. *Aust J Sci Med Sport, 28,* 93.

CREDITS

Photography: © North Face, © imago Sportfotodienst, © iStockphoto/Thinkstock, www.sportonline-foto.de, © Damiano Levati, © Stefan Schlett, © Dr. Dietmar Göbel

Portrait photography: Dean Karnazes (p. 36, © North Face), Ryoichi Sekiya (p. 37), Robert Wimmer (p. 39), Yiannis Kouros (p. 40), Rainer Koch (p. 41), Elizabeth "Lizzy" Hawker (p. 43, © North Face)

Cover Photo: © iStockphoto/Thinkstock

Cover Design: Sabine Groten

Book Design: Claudia Lo Cicero

Editing: Sabine Carduck, Manuel Morschel

Proofreading: Michelle Demeter